ROUTLEDGE LIBRARY EDITIONS: TRANSPORT ECONOMICS

Volume 8

THE ECONOMICS OF CONTAINERISATION

THE ECONOMICS OF CONTAINERISATION

K.M. JOHNSON AND H.C. GARNETT

Routledge
Taylor & Francis Group
LONDON AND NEW YORK

First published in 1971 by George Allen & Unwin Ltd.

This edition first published in 2017
by Routledge
2 Park Square, Milton Park, Abingdon, Oxon OX14 4RN

and by Routledge
605 Third Avenue, New York, NY 10017

Routledge is an imprint of the Taylor & Francis Group, an informa business

British Library Cataloguing in Publication Data
A catalogue record for this book is available from the British Library

ISBN: 978-0-415-78484-9 (Set)
ISBN: 978-1-315-20175-7 (Set) (ebk)
ISBN: 978-1-138-62850-2 (Volume 8) (hbk)
ISBN: 978-1-315-21068-1 (Volume 8) (ebk)

Publisher's Note
The publisher has gone to great lengths to ensure the quality of this reprint but points out that some imperfections in the original copies may be apparent.

Disclaimer
The publisher has made every effort to trace copyright holders and would welcome correspondence from those they have been unable to trace.

THE ECONOMICS OF CONTAINERISATION

K. M. JOHNSON

H. C. GARNETT

London

GEORGE ALLEN & UNWIN LTD

RUSKIN HOUSE MUSEUM STREET

FIRST PUBLISHED IN 1971

ISBN 0 04 380009 2

Printed in Great Britain
in 10 point Times Roman
by Alden & Mowbray Ltd, Oxford

PREFACE

Scarcely a day passes without some reference in the press to containerisation. Many reports have been written on the subject and a number of national and international conferences organised to evaluate and explain its impact. The term 'container revolution' is invariably used.

As a number of reports had already been written on containerisation in overseas trade, the research project itself as well as the book laid greater than normal emphasis on the impact of containerisation on inland distribution: four chapters out of nine are exclusively devoted to this subject. Almost all the empirical content of the research was concerned with inland containerisation. A sample survey of wholesalers on Clydeside was undertaken on the assumption that containerisation was likely to have a major impact on intermediate distribution. However, this was found not to be the case: hardly any wholesalers handled containers destined for or sent from overseas countries and few even had direct experience of inland (freightliner) containers. All the main road-haulage users of containers in the Glasgow area were also questioned, for they provide a large proportion of the total freightliner traffic, and their views and activities provide a factual basis for parts of the inland distribution chapters. One of the more interesting pieces of empirical work was a sample survey of the freightliner traffic between the Glasgow terminal (Gushetfaulds) and the rest of Britain. This provided valuable insights into the nature of the traffic, the charging patterns, and the location of consignees and consignors relative to the terminals.

The book is not solely concerned with this technical change in transport from the point of view of the transport operators. One of its persistent themes is that the full development of containerisation (or any other technical change) is partly a function of the willingness and ability of firms to appraise its costs and benefits in a meaningful way. In this respect the book represents an attempt to persuade firms to take a broad view of distributive costs, i.e. apply Total

Distribution Costing (TDC) or Physical Distribution Management (PDM).

Finally, the book is concerned with the role of the state in planning and regulating the distribution and transportation activities of manufacturing firms, ports, and transport agencies, including British Rail and the newly formed National Freight Corporation. Of particular interest are the 1968 Transport Act's reorganisation of nationalised transport and extension of the controls over private road haulage, and the proposed nationalisation of the larger ports.

Our first acknowledgement is to the Scottish Office and the Glasgow Chamber of Commerce who financed our research into containerisation—early in 1970 a report was submitted to them by the Universities of Glasgow and Strathclyde, mainly concerned with the likely impact of containerisation on the Glasgow conurbation. Acknowledgements are also due to our colleagues in the Department of Social and Economic Research who have helped in the organisation of the research and read the many drafts of this book: especially, Professor D. J. Robertson, to whom the authors owe their opportunity to write this and whose tragic death occurred shortly before its publication, Professor L. C. Hunter, Mr G. L. Reid, Dr A. W. J. Thomson and Mrs M. Robb, our technical assistant. Thanks are also due to the University of Strathclyde half of the research team: Professor R. Nicoll, Messrs J. Cullen, R. Alpine, T. Gillan and J. Milligan. We also owe a considerable debt to all those who provided the empirical basis of this book: the wholesale distributors, British Rail, the Freightliner Company, and the road haulage firms. Finally, we are grateful for the invaluable assistance of Miss E. Fairgrieve who had the unenviable task of deciphering our writing and typing the drafts.

K.M.J.
H.C.G.

CONTENTS

CHAPTER 1

GENERAL INTRODUCTION TO CONTAINERISATION AND THE BOOK'S PURPOSE

Containerisation has been acclaimed a revolution in transport, and yet a container is functionally no more than a box. In common with every other box, containers economise in the number of movements required to convey a given quantity of goods and afford these goods greater protection from damage and loss than they would otherwise receive. There are, however, two unique features of this particular box:

a. It has been standardised, making it intermodal: i.e. a container can be carried by almost any mode of transport and easily transhipped between modes.

b. It is large: therefore the amount of transhipment required between modes, for a given quantity of goods, is minimal.

Before describing the historical development of containerisation, it is important to put its impact into perspective. The National Ports Council has estimated that UK containerisable trade for 1973 could amount to 15 per cent of imports and 43 per cent of exports.[1] Although these percentages refer to the weight of imports and exports, not their value, they do indicate that a large proportion of trade will be unaffected by containerisation. On some routes the impact of containerisation may be very much higher: for example, the National Ports Council estimates that 92 per cent of imports from New Zealand and 97 per cent of imports from Hong Kong could travel by container. For inland distribution, not associated with overseas trade, the proportion is much lower: in Chapter 8 it is estimated that no more than 5 per cent of the total UK ton-miles will involve freightliner transport.

[1] National Ports Council, *Port Progress Report* 1969, Table 22: 'containerisable trade' refers to the tonnage of all goods which is physically suitable for containers.

1. *Historical development of containerisation*

Large containers of various kinds have been used in inland and overseas distribution for many years: London Midland and Scottish Railways first used containers in 1926 and unit load systems have been a feature of the Great Britain–Ireland trade since the war. It is perhaps surprising that the 'revolution' has been so long delayed. The potentialities of containerisation were recognised at least as long ago as 1931 when the Royal Commission on Transport reported:

> 'The use of containers is another direction in which we think greater progress might be made. The great advantages of containers, particularly in minimising the risk of damage and in reducing the cost of handling, are so obvious that it is a matter of some surprise to us that they are not more generally used.'[2]

And yet British Rail's freightliner service only started some thirty-five years later. The Rochdale Report on British ports in 1962 considered that:

> 'It is a regrettable fact that British ports, and possibly British shipowners, have been less forward-looking than some overseas interests in developing systems for the carriage of cargo in containers.'[3]

In 1962 there were in fact few containership operators, although two shipping lines had been operating containerised systems of distribution for six years.

In 1956 Sea–Land, which had its origins in road haulage, started its containership service between New York and Puerto Rico, following experimental shipments the previous year between New York and Houston. Port handling costs and times were reduced drastically. Soon after, Matson started its US West Coast–Hawaii service. But for almost a decade other shipping lines ignored or rejected the potentialities of containerisation, even though by 1966 Sea–Land had nineteen container ships and Matson fourteen. An exception was the Australian shipping line, Associated Steamships, which began in 1964 a container service between Melbourne and

[2] *Report of the Royal Commission on Transport*, Cmnd. 3751, page 43, para. 153.

[3] *Report of the Committee of Enquiry into the Major Ports of Great Britain*, Cmnd. 1824, para. 330.

Freemantle with the first specially built container ship 'Kooringa'. The turning point appears to have been in 1965 when Sea–Land announced its intention to enter the transatlantic trade with container ships. The reaction of established lines on that route was immediate: each announced its intention to modernise existing vessels and then build specialist container ships. Ports on the US East Coast and in Europe soon followed with their plans for container berths. Similar developments took place in the Pacific trade when the Japanese government announced in 1966 a massive container ship and berth development programme.

Since 1966 the growth of container services has been explosive. In that year the first edition of the American trade journal *Container News* was published. Its container shipping guide provides evidence of the rate at which containerisation spread. The May 1966 edition reported only 5 shipping lines operating container services from the USA. The January 1967 edition listed 38 lines serving over 100 ports in Europe, Latin America, the Near East, the Far East, Africa, Australasia from the US East and West Coast, and Great Lakes ports. In June 1969 the number of lines had risen to 88, and the number of ports served to almost 200. It should be noted that very few of these lines offer or offered specialist container ship services, i.e. with ships specially designed to carry containers or ships exclusively carrying containers.

It is not easy to explain why the Matson/Sea–Land success was ignored for so long by other shipowners, and why such a large number of lines eventually plunged into containerisation in the mid-1960s. The entrance of Sea–Land into the transatlantic trade is an immediate but not underlying cause. Some have blamed the initial reluctance of shipping lines to innovate upon the American system of shipping subsidies, under which the Federal Government paid as much as half of the capital costs and more than half the operating costs, so that there was relatively little incentive to cut costs by becoming more efficient. It is significant that both Sea–Land and Matson were not subsidised and therefore had to look for cheaper shipping methods to compete with those who were. The subsidy programme came under pressure during the Kennedy Administration from those who saw little strategic reason to encourage the expansion of the American mercantile marine. A major force behind the eventual boom in container transport was the US Army and Navy. At about the same time as Sea–Land entered the North

Atlantic trade, the US army became actively interested in containerisation. It had long operated its CONEX unit load system, but the Vietnam War build-up provided a particular encouragement to improve supply methods. At the beginning of 1966 some 700 containers a month left West Coast ports for South East Asia; by the end of the year the monthly rate had risen to 1,500.[4] This provided a considerable stimulus to shipping lines; in fact a large part of Sea–Land's revenue came, and still comes, from military contracts.

However the most important stimulus was standardisation. Although the International Standards Organisation agreement was signed in Moscow as late as June 1967, the subject of container standardisation had been under discussion since 1961 and for some time the various parties had been aware of the likely standards. They were an 8×8 ft end-section, with lengths of 10, 20, 30 and 40 ft; corner lifting devices were also standardised. A world-wide system of door-to-door transportation could now be established to handle boxes of given dimensions; specialist ships, cranes, lorries and railway wagons could be constructed. Ships need no longer carry their own loading and unloading gear, for ports could now invest in handling equipment suitable for all shipping lines carrying ISO standard containers. It is worth noting that none of the standards conformed to the container sizes used by the two pioneers: the Sea–Land dimensions are $8 \times 8\frac{1}{2} \times 35$ ft, while those of Matson are $8 \times 8\frac{1}{2} \times 24$ ft.

Although it was now easier to conceive door-to-door container distribution systems, the capital cost involved in actually setting one up was enormous. This expense, plus the need to phase out conventional vessels and integrate scheduled services, forced mergers between some shipping lines: ACL (Atlantic Container Line) is an amalgamation of Swedish–America Line, Swedish Transatlantic, Wallenius Lines, Holland–America Line, French Line, and Cunard–Brocklebank; ACT (Associated Container Transportation) is a consortium representing Blue Star Line, Ben Line, Cunard, Ellerman Lines and T. & J. Harrison; OCL (Overseas Containers Limited) which, like ACT, operates between the UK and Australia, is made up of the P and O Group, Furness Withy and Ocean Steamship, and British and Commonwealth. Negotiations invariably took place before the final agreement on standardisation in 1967, but all must

[4] *Container News*, March 1967: article by Brigadier-General A. J. Montgomery.

have been encouraged by the prospect of most transport operators carrying a common box.

The very fact that changes in the shipping environment (standardisation) plus the competitive pressure exerted by the more progressive (the entry of Sea–Land into the North Atlantic trade) were necessary to induce the majority of shipping lines to adopt container methods of transport implies that they were conservative, unenterprising or simply unable to evaluate the potential cost savings. Containerisation is almost as profound a technological change in the carriage of general cargo as the changeover from sail to steam. The shipping lines may well have lacked the machinery to evaluate fully the impact of containerisation on their operations. It is certainly the view of some economists specialising in shipping that economists or modern economic techniques of analysis are insufficiently or inadequately utilised by shipping lines, port authorities and ship designers,[5] which, of course, may be as much the fault of the economists as anyone else. To take the case of ship design, naval architects are able to optimise the design of one part of a ship relative to another in *physical* terms, but they are unable to assess the economic costs and benefits of having, for example, a faster, smaller ship rather than a slower, larger one.

So far little consideration has been given to the development of containerisation in inland transport. Inland container transport is an essential component of door-to-door overseas distribution and also forms a domestic transport system in its own right. There have been many attempts to integrate road and rail transport to take advantage of rail's lower unit costs over long distances and road haulage's lower local delivery costs. American and Continental railways have for some years operated 'piggy-back' systems: the carriage of road trailers on railway flats. The narrower loading gauge precludes this in Britain, although experiments were carried out with road/rail trailers, which had two sets of wheels, one for road and one for rail travel. Instead British Rail developed its freightliner system: high-speed trains, with permanently coupled wagons, carrying ISO standard containers which are lifted off or on to road vehicles at specially designed terminals. This was announced in the Beeching Report[6] in 1963 and the first service began in November 1965 between London

[5] See the introduction to R. O. Goss, *Studies in Maritime Economics*, Cambridge University Press, 1968.

[6] British Railways Board, *The Reshaping of British Railways*, HMSO, 1963.

and Glasgow. Freightliners are also employed in foreign trade, providing inland distribution links for deep-sea container operations as well as British Rail's own short-sea shipping services. Continental services have been aided by the formation of one international railway company, Intercontainer, to co-ordinate rail container services.

2. *The aim and scope of this book*

It is clear that many shipping lines and railway companies have heavily committed themselves to containerisation as a means of lowering their operational costs by introducing capital-intensive methods to the traditionally labour-intensive field of general merchandise. The aim of this book is to examine the viability of that commitment and evaluate the likely impact of containerisation on the transport operators' customers and the community in general. The implications of containerisation for national and regional planning will also be assessed, particularly in the light of the proposed ports nationalisation and the recent reorganisation of nationalised rail and road transport.

One of the main themes of this book is that the potentialities of containerisation for a particular firm are not easily perceived, even if it is easy to list the possible savings involved for firms in general. The savings in damage, loss and packaging are universal, but few are in a position to evaluate the potential costs and benefits of faster door-to-door transport and the larger unit load. This is because the vast majority of firms lack the necessary organisation of management. Few have an executive or a department which integrates all the various components of distribution costs. Most firms are therefore unable to evaluate the potentialities of a new technology in distribution. The purpose of Chapter 2 is to state the functions of distribution, show the inevitable conflicts between the various costs (in the sense that to minimise one component does not necessarily minimise another) and the consequent need to integrate distributive decision-making. It will also indicate the practical difficulties of doing this.

Chapter 3 will introduce the principles of containerisation by analysing its impact on ports and shipping. The theoretically ideal system will be described, followed by an evaluation of British short- and deep-sea berth requirements. Chapter 4 will consider the implications of this system of overseas transport for the distribution policies of shipping lines' customers. The need to evaluate all the costs and benefits will again be emphasized. Some of the problems posed by containerisation will be discussed, as well as a longer-term evaluation of its viability in relation to the alternatives likely to be open to shippers over the life of the existing container ships.

Although many reports have been issued on the subject of containerisation and overseas trade, inland distribution has been largely ignored, even as a component of overseas distribution. This book therefore devotes four chapters to inland container transport. Chapter 5 will establish the broad features of inland container systems and consider in some detail the nature of the inland freight market. Chapter 6 will evaluate the competitive position of freightliners on the basis of the costs of road and rail transport as well as the patterns of charging. Chapter 7, like Chapter 4, will consider the transport operators' customers. It will examine the factors considered by firms in selecting inland transport modes, the present features of the use of freightliners by firms, and the factors which limit the use of container systems. The present and future role of inland container systems will then be assessed in Chapter 8. Future technological changes and developments in routes and systems will be considered, as will the likely government role in influencing the competitive balance. An assessment of how the freightliner system should develop will be made, followed by an estimate of the inland freight market in the 1970s.

The final chapter will draw together the various threads and assess the implications of containerisation for the location of the various distributive facilities: ports, inland clearance depots, freightliner terminals, groupage terminals, wholesale and distribution depots and even manufacturing establishments. This chapter will also attempt to derive the broader meaning of this or any other technical change in transport for transport planning in general, at the national or regional level.

CHAPTER 2

THE CONCEPT OF DISTRIBUTIVE SYSTEMS

A technical change can only be analysed in terms of the economic framework within which it operates. As it is claimed that containerisation will revolutionise the domestic and international distribution of goods, an assessment of its impact requires an analysis of the distributive process. This chapter will define the function of distribution in a general sense and examine its component parts showing how they interact one with the other. The need to take full account of all activities relevant to the distribution of a commodity from a producer to a consumer will be made apparent, as will the practical difficulties involved in doing this.

1. *The function of distribution*

Distribution costs arise because goods are produced and consumed at different places and times. As geographical and industrial specialisation increases the space, in a time and distance sense, between producers and consumers, the amount and nature of distribution required by an economy depends on the degree of specialisation. For this reason, distribution in a real sense absorbed less of the gross national product before the Industrial Revolution than it does now. This is modified by the fact that the converse of the above is true: lower transport costs themselves increase the opportunities for specialisation. One of the main themes of this book is that the progressive lowering of transport costs increases the distance over which producers can exercise effective direct control over the distribution of their goods.

The 'market' can be perceived as a gap between producers and consumers. From the point of view of the producer there are four dimensions to this space or gap:[1]

[1] W. A. McInnes, in R. Cox, W. Alderson and S. J. Shapiro (eds.), *Theory in Marketing*, American Marketing Association, 1964.

a. Spatial separation: the potential parties to an exchange are separated by geographic space, which can only be bridged by *transport*.

b. Temporal separation: there is a time lag between production and consumption, and, as the two are not necessarily phased together, this requires the holding of *inventories*.

c. Perceptional separation: producers are, in varying degrees, ignorant of the needs of consumers, while the latter are ignorant of most of the choices open to them in fulfilling particular needs; with ignorance may go inertia. This can only be overcome by market research and *promotion*.

d. Separation of ownership: *transactions* are required finally to achieve the exchange of values.

In each case the producer can perform the function himself or delegate it, partially or completely, to another firm. For example, the producer may allow a wholesaler to carry out all local deliveries and all sales to small retailers, thus taking over some of functions (*a*) to (*d*).

This is essentially a *functional* view of distribution which contrasts with the *institutional* approach of those who concentrate on explaining interactions between distributive institutions such as production, wholesaling and retailing. This school tends to describe events actually taking place rather than analyse underlying causes.[2] On the functional view, we can accept the historical fact that wholesalers have developed over time, and describe their functions as follows:

a. To minimise the channels of distribution required. If three firms wish to serve 20 customers, each has to maintain 20 channels of distribution; 60 in total. However, if these three firms were to sell all their goods to one intermediary, who in turn traded with the 20 customers, only 23 channels of distribution would be required, with an obvious saving of the community's resources.

b. To minimise the stocks held by the community. Because the rates and phasing of consumption and production rarely coincide, an intermediary is required to hold buffer stocks. If a relatively small number of wholesalers hold stocks, rather than a large number of producers (or consumers), then the total

[2] R. Cox, in W. Alderson and R. Cox (eds.), *Theory in Marketing*, Richard D. Irwin, Inc., 1950. See also M. Hall, *Distributive Trading*, Hutchinsons.

stocks held by the community are less than they might be. At the extreme, if there were only one wholesaler, stocks would tend to be at an absolute minimum. This is because demand as a whole is less subject to random fluctuations than any of its local components, as a larger sample is under consideration.

With one wholesaler both the above functions would be perfectly satisfied, but an extremely elaborate and costly transport system would have to be set up to accommodate the more frequent demands by consumers, unless the consumers themselves were willing to hold larger stocks. Therefore the actual number and location of wholesalers represents a compromise between minimising the channels and stocks and providing the quality of service demanded by customers: i.e. minimising the service interval subject to the cost of doing so.

The functional and institutional approaches have much in common, but the latter is weaker when a dynamic view of distribution is taken. When a change in the technology of distribution takes place, the tendency is for firms to continue to use existing channels, i.e. middlemen, but encourage them to alter their activities so that they can cope with the new technology. For example, if goods tend to be moved on pallets, the wholesaler will buy fork-lift trucks and continue to serve producers as before, although more efficiently. However, in such a situation it would be better for the producer to reappraise his whole system of distribution, including the role of the wholesaler in the system. The functional view stresses that wholesaling is only part of a system, not a system in itself as the institutional approach implies. In the case of a widespread use of pallets, the producer may promotionally encourage customers to take full pallet loads by a system of rebates and institute direct factory-to-customer deliveries for these loads. For smaller customers, distribution may be via a wholesaler. The producer has therefore decided that he maximises his profits by selling and distributing larger units of his product. In this, the wholesaler is merely a large customer providing a channel of distribution for small retailers; i.e. he performs a particular function, but is not necessarily used.

The availability of institutions through which it is possible, if not optimal, to distribute may provide a more powerful constraint upon innovation in distribution than, for example, the lack of cost data. Most producers accept existing channels, and set up a least-cost distribution system subject to operation through them. There are many examples of new intermediate stages being devised, but fewer of changes at the retail level. Five of the few exceptions are petrol, some baby clothing, sewing machines, shoes, and beer; in each case retailing is producer-controlled. The overall tendency for producers to exercise greater control over the whole distributive process will be discussed in the last section of this chapter.

2. *Distributive decision-making by manufacturer*

All managerial activities within a firm are in some way related, especially when the firm is planning its longer-term strategy. However a group of activities, related to the functional 'spaces' outlined above, form a significant functional decision-making set. They are concerned with physical distribution management. Although promotional activities (sales, advertising) are strongly related to the others, this particular functional space is often omitted from this group of activities. Physical distribution costs sometimes make up more than 40 per cent of total sales. A report by A. T. Kearney and Co.[3] provided the following breakdown of these costs obtained from a survey of 270 American corporations:

		% sales
Administration		2·4
Transportation		6·4
of which, inbound	2·1	
outbound	4·3	
Receiving and shipping		1·7
Packaging		2·6
Warehousing		3·7
of which, in-plant	2·1	
field	1·6	
Inventory carrying costs		3·8
of which, interest	2·2	
Taxes, insurance, obsolescence	1·6	
Order processing		1·2
	TOTAL	21·8%

A similer breakdown for a survey of UK firms, published in a NEDO

[3] A. T. Kearney and Co., *Total Distribution*, published by Industrial and Commercial Techniques Ltd.

pamphlet,[4] shows the overall average at 16 per cent; it is less than the US figure largely because of proportionately lower transport and packaging costs.

Few firms give any one executive control over as wide a range of activities as these. The choice of a transport method should include all such cost and demand considerations, and yet this rarely happens. The irrationality underlying most transport decisions provides the basis of much of the recent Transport Act. The licensing of transport managers and the quantity licensing itself is an attempt to force firms to cost alternative methods. If firms prefer road to rail transport because of the greater flexibility or service it provides, then they should be able to present to the licensing authorities the cost savings involved. As the 'Transport of Freight' White Paper states:[5]

> 'The sole basis for an objection (by the National Freight Corporation or British Rail) to the issue of a quantity licence will be that the rail or combined road/rail service offered by the NFC can provide a service which overall is as satisfactory as that of the applicant, taking into account a combination of speed, reliability and cost in relation to the needs of the consignors and the nature of the particular traffics concerned.'

Recent surveys by A. T. Kearney and Co.[6] have shown that both in the USA and Britain very few firms could even identify all the distribution cost components outlined by the consultants, let alone integrate them when making distributive decisions. In choosing a transport mode, firms were found to be excessively concerned with transport costs themselves, although on average they formed only one-third of total physical distribution costs. It should be noted, however, that this appears to conflict somewhat with the recent findings of Deakin and Seward,[7] whose work will be discussed in Chapter 7.

A firm's interest in distributive costs is a function of their importance relative to other costs. Many of the innovators in distribution have been food and drink manufacturers, whose distribution costs can amount to as much as one-third of sales revenue. However there

[4] A National Economic Development Office pamphlet summarising an A. T. Kearney and Co. survey.

[5] *The Transport of Freight*, Cmnd. 3470, para. 57.

[6] See NEDO pamphlet, *op. cit.*

[7] B. M. Deakin and T. Seward, *Productivity in Transport*, Cambridge University Press, 1969.

are many exceptions in firms which see the relevant characteristic of distribution costs being their amenability to control, if a sufficiently broad view of distribution is taken.

The concept of Total Distribution Costing (TDC) has gained currency in recent years. The number costing in this way, although small now, can be expected to grow under the influence of management education, trade associations and informative competitive advertising by transport firms, some of which offer a total distribution costing service. Four components of total distribution costs are usually distinguished:

a. the cost of building and operating warehouses;
b. stockholding costs;
c. the cost of trunking from factory to warehouse;
d. the cost of local deliveries to customers.

These have to be minimised relative to each other, for they are interrelated, subject to a constraint from the demand side concerning the level of customer service required. In other words, the time between the receipt of the order and the delivery of the goods to the customer should be minimised, subject to the cost of doing so. As the two criteria work in opposite directions, an initial decision must be made as to the level of service offered. This in turn depends upon an analysis of the effect on demand of varying the level of service.

Each cost component will be discussed separately and then all will be combined to illustrate a least-cost solution. The equations are presented as well as a graph to make clear the assumptions underlying the shapes and slopes of curves in the graph.

(*a*) *Warehouse costs.* There are two component parts of total warehousing costs: the cost of the warehouse itself and the cost of operating the warehouse.

(i) fixed cost = αWS
where W = number of warehouses
S = warehouse size, which may in reality vary
α = construction cost per unit size (measuring size by throughput).

S is a function of the maximum quantity the warehouse is likely to have to hold at any one time. It is therefore somewhat greater than average daily warehouse throughput. However, to simplify matters, assume S is equal to average warehouse size.

$$S = Q/365W$$

where Q = total annual quantity of goods sold by the firm. Fixed cost now becomes $= \alpha(Q/365)$

(ii) operating cost $= \beta Q$
where β is an inverse, non-linear function of warehouse size (S),

$$\beta = \varepsilon/\sqrt{S}$$

The particular root of S chosen is merely illustrative; the relationship shown indicates that as warehouse size (S) increases, β falls, although less than proportionately, i.e. the larger the warehouse the greater the opportunity for mechanisation and labour specialisation

but, $S = Q/\sqrt{W}.365$

therefore,

total warehouse operating cost $= \varepsilon Q/\sqrt{(Q/W.365)}$

(*b*) *Stockholding costs.* Without unnecessarily complicating the discussion stockholding or inventory costs are assumed to be a function of the level of service required, the total volume of trade, and the number of warehouses. Inventory costs (i.e. investment at any one time in inventory) rise very rapidly as the level of customer service rises, especially as the situation is approached where all items are available for shipment on the day the order is received. As has already been stated, a decision as to the level of service provided must come from an analysis of its effect on demand. Assuming such a decision has been made,

total inventory costs $= \gamma Q W^2$

i.e. the greater the number of warehouses the larger the stocks required (see previous section); the power of W is likely to be greater than one, although the particular power chosen is merely illustrative. This reflects the fact that inventory costs are likely to rise more than proportionately as the number of warehouses increases.

As with the rest of this model, the actual situation is much more complex. Account should be taken of the number of lines held in stock and the time taken to produce the commodity to order.

(*c*) *The cost of trunking from factory to warehouse.* Trunk haulage costs are related to the quantity of goods to be carried, the cost of carriage per unit distance, and the distances the warehouses are from the factory.

$T = \mu Q\bar{d}_t$

where T = total trunk haulage cost

$\bar{d}_t$ = mean distance between factory and depot (or factories and depots)

μ is a parameter relating to the freight rate.

But μ is an inverse function of $\bar{d}$, for the longer the distance the lower the rate per mile as more fixed haulage costs are covered; and $\bar{d}_t$ is an inverse function of W, for the more warehouses there are the less the mean haulage distance to them, therefore, μ is directly proportionate to the number of warehouses $= \phi W$ and

$T = \phi W^{1 \cdot 5} Q$

Again the illustrative power of W indicates that trunk haulage costs increase more than proportionately as the number of warehouses rises. The power is less than the inventory cost one, therefore the curve rises less steeply.

(*d*) *The cost of local deliveries to customers.* Local delivery to customers costs are also a function of the quantity of goods, the distance travelled and the freight rate.

$D = \theta Q\bar{d}_d$

where D = total local delivery cost

$\bar{d}_d$ = mean local delivery distance

θ is a parameter relation to the cost of local transport.

Again, $\bar{d}_d$ is an inverse function of W, $\bar{d}_d = \pi/W$; but in this case θ is largely independent of the distance between customers and warehouses, unless the situation is similar to the trunk haulage one, i.e. direct deliveries of complete loads. Therefore, $D = \theta Q(\pi/W)$

This relationship is complicated by considerations such as the size of customers, the size of loads they tend to take, and delays at their premises and in congested urban areas. For example, the total time to make a delivery rises very rapidly with the number of cases delivered, although the relationship will be much less sensitive if a unit load system is employed.

These cost components can be brought together in the following equation:

$$TDC = \frac{\alpha Q}{365} + \frac{\varepsilon Q}{\sqrt{(Q/365 \,.\, W)}} + \gamma Q W^2 + \phi W Q + \theta Q \frac{\pi}{W}$$

'Unit' or Average total distribution cost (*ATDC*) is obtained by dividing through by Q,

$$ATDC = \frac{\alpha}{365} + \frac{\varepsilon}{\sqrt{(Q/W \,.\, 365)}} + \gamma W^2 + \phi W + \theta \frac{\pi}{W}$$

Such a relationship appears in Figure 2.1.

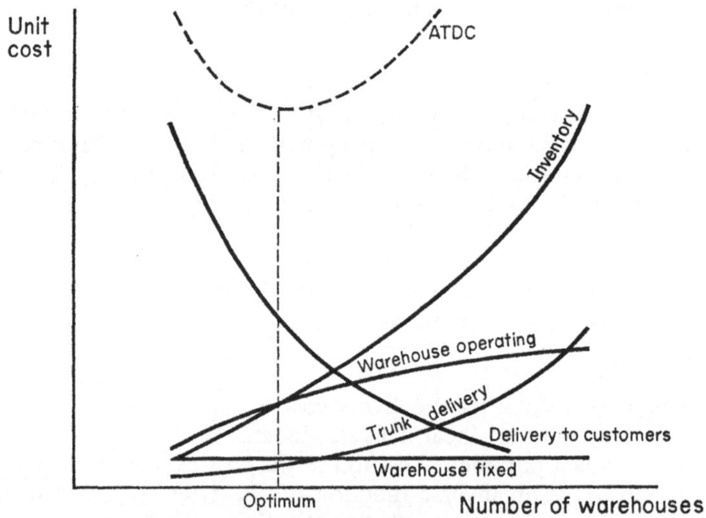

Figure 2.1. Average (total) distribution costs

Figure 2.1 shows some of the relationships as non-linear although they appear as linear in the equations. Very few such relationships are in reality linear, which greatly hampers a practical application of the above analysis by, for example, mathematical programming. In addition, the curves in Figure 2.1 are continuous, when in reality they should be stepped: warehouses come in whole numbers. If all these curves are added together, the *ATDC* curve is obtained. Its minimum point shows the optimum number of warehouses.

The cost analysis above is a gross simplification of reality and is only meant to illustrate the need to consider all the components of distributive costs to arrive at the overall least-cost solution. In this particular case unit costs vary only with the number of warehouses and, of course, firms have many other distributive decisions to make: whether road or rail transport should be used for trunk deliveries, the size of local delivery vehicles, the degree of mechanisation in the warehouse, where they should be located, whether distribution should be via independent wholesalers, the level of service to be given to customers, whether a unit load system be introduced and so on. Even in the form of a static analysis, working from data relating to one time period, the problem is conceptually complex. In fact the analysis should be dynamic, establishing the *sensitivity* of, for example, the optimum number of warehouses to a variation in the level of service, taxes, interest rates, transport costs, or demand.

Although it is easy to establish that all these various distribution variables should be considered together when making any major distributive decision, it is more difficult actually to achieve this. As has already been stated the non-linearities in the relationships make mathematical programming difficult. Computer simulation is only feasible if the problem is a relatively small one, given the size of computers and the cost of computer time. Many in fact rely on following simple rules which give good but sub-optimal solutions.

In recent years, scientific techniques have been devised to handle some elements of the distributive process. Two stand out: depot location and vehicle routing. The techniques developed by Lawrence and Penguilly[8] can handle most of the variables relevant to decisions concerning the number and location of depots required. Their model begins with customers grouped into sub-areas and factories of a given size and, using an iterative technique, sets up warehouses which minimise trunk and local delivery costs, taking account of warehouse rentals and handling costs, hazards (e.g. bridges, estuaries), and the need for overnight stays for drivers. Much less sophisticated depot location techniques can also be applied. For example, the gravity method minimises demand distances, i.e. the distance between a customer and a depot weighted by the importance

[8] R. M. Lawrence and P. J. Penguilly, *Operational Research Quarterly*, March 1969.

of that customer. This can be done mathematically and even mechanically. Holes are bored through a map at the location of each customer and weights, proportionate to the sales to that customer, are attached to a string passing through the hole to a ring representing the warehouse. When this has been done for each customer the ring will come to rest at the location which minimises demand distances. One of the weaknesses of such a centre of gravity method is that it assumes that transport costs are proportionate to the linear demand distances. It has been shown that demand distances are poorly correlated to transport costs, and that such a method may give poor depot locations.[9]

Attempts have been made to use computers to plan daily vehicle routes and loads to minimise vehicle capital and operating costs. The great number of combinations of routes and loads possible from a given depot causes serious computer capacity problems. Some of these problems have been overcome and computer-planned vehicle routing has been practised. Success has been limited, but there is no reason to suppose that the remaining problems will not be overcome, as has, to a certain extent, the most serious one of computer capacity.[10]

3. *Changing systems of distribution*

The extension of total distribution costing and more scientific management in this field implies an increasing control, direct or indirect, of distribution by the producer. The importance of the independent or specialist wholesaler can be expected to decline in many trades. Reasons for this, as shown in the previous section, are partly outside the control of the independent wholesaler, but his reluctance or slowness to respond to modern marketing conditions and distribution methods has not helped his cause. For example, it became evident in the course of the wholesaling survey[11] mentioned in the Preface that most of the independent wholesalers which had relocated had done so mainly because of local authority pressure

[9] M. J. H. Webb, *Operational Research Quarterly*, September 1968.

[10] See G. Clark and J. W. Wright, *Operations Research*, Vol. 12, No. 4, 1964; H. G. M. Pullar and M. H. J. Webb, *Computer Journal*, Vol. 10, No. 10, 1967; K. W. Knight and J. P. Hofer, *Operational Research Quarterly*, September 1968.

[11] A survey of the activities, location and relocation of wholesalers in the Glasgow area, carried out by the authors for the Scottish Office and the Glasgow Chamber of Commerce.

(i.e. compulsory purchase). What is more surprising is that these wholesalers, almost without exception, found their new location preferable to the old one. Transport conditions are such that city-centre wholesaling locations are uneconomic. This has been realised by manufacturers which have set up new depots on the periphery of urban areas, but external pressures are apparently required to convince most locally based independent wholesalers of the economic superiority of such locations.

Linked with the producers' broader view of distribution is the close contact he has achieved with final consumers through standardisation, branding and advertising: the promotional space is diminishing. He wants to ensure efficient distribution to the customers gained by his sales and advertising efforts. The multi-product, independent wholesaler has other interests to consider. This contact with final customers, or the retailers who sell to them, has been aided by technical innovations: the telephone, telex, and faster transport. Transport improvements have not only solved problems of human contact, but they have also effectively speeded up the whole physical distribution process. In the past, specialist wholesalers served local markets, receiving goods in slow, often irregular flows, mainly by rail, canal or sea. Manufacturers concentrated on sales to wholesalers: that part of the transport process was a sufficient concern. The precariousness and unpredictability of the old transport system contrasts with the fast road and containerised rail services currently operative. These radically improved communications have reduced the need for general and even specialist wholesalers who could in the past both offer unique local market knowledge and hold stocks to counter the unpredictability of goods flows as well as fluctuations in production and demand.

Wholesalers will be increasingly required to receive larger unit loads, break the bulk more efficiently, and have good access to customers. These have always been their functions, but the economy of their efforts will be more critically examined by producers which regard wholesaling as part of a system, not a system in itself. Producer-orientated distribution will grow. This does not mean that consumers at the other end of the distributive chain will suffer, but that the producer–consumer contact will be more direct. Nor does it necessarily imply more depots under the direct control of producers. Some nation-wide wholesaler specialists claim that their distributive expertise is so unique that manufacturers will find increasing use for their services. In this respect, a significant recent development is the increasing involvement of road haulage firms in wholesaling. An alternative sometimes practised is for a manufacturer to take over an existing wholesale organisation.

Containerisation is a change, often referred to as a revolution, in distribution. As following chapters will show, it may cause firms to re-examine their export or trunk delivery methods, packaging, or even product design. A realistic appraisal of its benefits for any particular firm requires an evaluation of all the ramifications of containerised distribution on the various distributive functions and, in so doing, on the channels of distribution currently employed. Although containerisation has largely developed from the initiative of transport operators, the achievement of its full potential is largely dependent upon firms so organising themselves as to be able to carry out a total distribution cost analysis.

CHAPTER 3

THE EFFECT OF CONTAINERISATION ON PORTS AND SHIPPING

As outlined in Chapter 1, containerised systems of distribution have been practised for many years by inland and overseas transport operators. However, their recent rapid expansion owes most to the initiative of certain shipping lines. This technological change in transport will therefore be examined first from the point of view of overseas trade to establish and evaluate the principles involved. The basic system of movement will be described before proceeding to an identification of the likely cost savings. This analysis of shipping cost functions will concentrate upon the effect on unit costs of (*a*) reduced port time (derived from faster cargo handling speed), and (*b*) a faster, more reliable and, for these and other reasons, cheaper inland journey. The implications for ports of these changes in shipping methods will be discussed, followed by an evaluation of British short- and deep-sea berth and shipping requirements which is largely derived from secondary sources. Finally the predicted and theoretical optimum will be related to overseas general cargo distribution as it is actually developing.

1. *The system of movement*

Containerisation is the application of mass or systemised production techniques to international, and inland, general goods distribution. There are four elements in *any* system of automation;

a. a standardised product to be handled;
b. faster movement between terminals (terminals in the broadest sense of the word, i.e. points of transhipment as well as the end of the production line or transport system);
c. faster transfer at terminals;
d. a control system.

As outlined in Chapter 1, the first is available in the form of the

ISO container,[1] standardised by length, end-section and corner lifting devices, which replaces the large number and wide variety of consignment sizes and shapes normally handled. Some operators have their own systems designed to carry non-ISO standard containers: a notable example is Sea–Land, which developed its system before the ISO standards were agreed upon. The movement of a standard box through the system is of logistical significance; it also affects shipping line and port charging policies. The costs involved are no longer a function of the kind of goods handled and the number of items, but merely the number of boxes. Therefore commodity rates can be replaced by freight-of-all-kinds rates.

In the case of containerisation the second criterion, faster movement between terminals, is of less relevance, for in the past the main delays have occurred at terminals. Under containerisation, movements have in fact tended to be faster, but what is much more significant about this part of the system is its improved quality in that less damage tends to occur *en route*. It is at the terminals themselves (railway and consolidation depots, ports and the shippers' premises) that the greatest time savings to shippers, shipping lines and inland transport operators are achieved, for standard containers can be loaded and unloaded from ships or trains in 2 to 3 minute cycles. Thus total door-to-door movement is much faster. It is also more predictable: shippers can state with greater confidence when goods will arrive because the standardisation involved has simplified movements and reduced the probability of delays. In this the fourth criterion, a control system, is important for it is necessary to organise a system able to react to alterations in its basic parameters. To this end, considerable investment is being made by those concerned in computerised information flow systems. The fulfilment of these criteria requires considerable capital investment and, as with any other systemised production technique, high throughputs are necessary to achieve a profitable utilisation of capital.

The basic system of overseas container movements is illustrated in Figure 3.1. Its characteristics are as follows:

a. High volume flows between ports.

b. Transhipment to road or rail vehicles carried out at ports by specialist handling equipment: one or two giant overhead cranes per ship, plus vehicles (straddle carriers or side loaders,

[1] See Chapter 1 for brief outline of ISO standards.

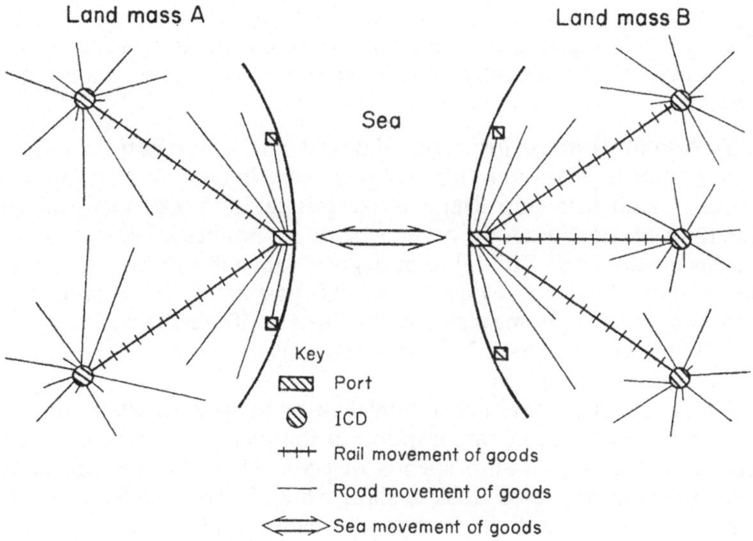

Figure 3.1

for example) to carry the containers about the container park and on to waiting lorries and trains.

c. Long-distance movement by rail to inland clearance depots (I.C.D.S) sited in or close to major conurbations; these also have specialist handling equipment.

d. Customs clearance away from the docks at these I.C.D.S.

e. Transhipment between rail and local delivery vehicles, as well as any necessary consolidation or breaking of bulk, at the I.C.D. where the containers may in any case be opened for customs inspection.

f. Local delivery by road.

g. Shorter journeys, and journeys from less densely industrialised areas, to ports by road.

There are, of course, many variations on the above theme and the more relevant will be discussed in subsequent sections and chapters. However, Figure 3.1 does give a general illustration of the overall system of movement associated with containerisation, the economic characteristics of which will be analysed in the next section.

2. *The shipping-cost savings attributable to containerisation*

The simple shipping-cost model discussed in this section and developed mathematically in the appendix has four main components.

(i) Administration, insurance, interest and amortisation, officers and crew costs. Although this group of costs, in common with others, varies in total with ship size, it is exceptional in that this variation is less than proportional. In other words, economies of scale operate on this group, even if in different degrees for each element. Although the authors have no evidence on the matter, it is possible that insurance unit costs may rise with ship size if very large container vessels are constructed. This has certainly been the case with oil tankers and bulk ore carriers.

(ii) Port costs. These are assumed to be proportionate to time in port, which is a 'heroic' assumption in that charges are only loosely related to the time a ship spends in port. There are two elements here: the time taken to dock a ship, which is proportionate to the size of the ship, and the time taken to load and unload cargo, which depends on the amount of cargo. Both elements also depend on port efficiency: the time taken to perform each function is inversely related to port efficiency.

(iii) Fuel costs. These vary with ship size, speed and voyage duration.

(iv) Inland distribution costs. These costs depend upon quantity of cargo, the location of shippers, and the cost characteristics of inland transport modes.

If operation over a particular period of time is considered, the last three cost items depend in total upon the number of journeys undertaken. However, the total quantity of cargo carried per ship also depends upon the number of journeys; and so when unit costs are considered the number of journeys only remains in the denominator of the first cost item. The annual number of journeys is simply the part of a year when the ship is not laid up for repairs or other reasons divided by the voyage duration, which is distance divided by speed plus time in port (see first part of the Appendix to this chapter). Therefore, the first cost item, 'fixed' costs in the sense that these costs must be borne even if the ship is idle, is directly proportional to route length and inversely proportional to speed. Port and inland unit costs are independent of the number of journeys and therefore voyage distance and speed, but fuel costs do depend on speed, voyage duration, and ship size.

Any shipping operation includes the cost elements listed above, and the significant components of these costs will be discussed to identify the economies attributable to containerisation.

(*a*) *Economies of scale.* Although there are economies of scale, they should not be exaggerated. Some McKinsey report graphs at least contemplate the possibility of container ships with a capacity of 5,000 containers (over 50,000 tons of cargo),[2] but there are no plans for container ships with capacities in excess of 2,000 containers,[3] and many currently operating on deep-sea routes have a capacity of only 300 (here, as in the rest of the book, number of containers refer to 20 × 8 × 8 ft equivalents). In general, economies of scale become more important on longer trade routes: as the Appendix to this chapter and Figure 3.2 show, the first cost element is more sensitive (in a downward direction) to increases in size the longer the trade route. However, the OCL–ACT ships on the Australian run have a

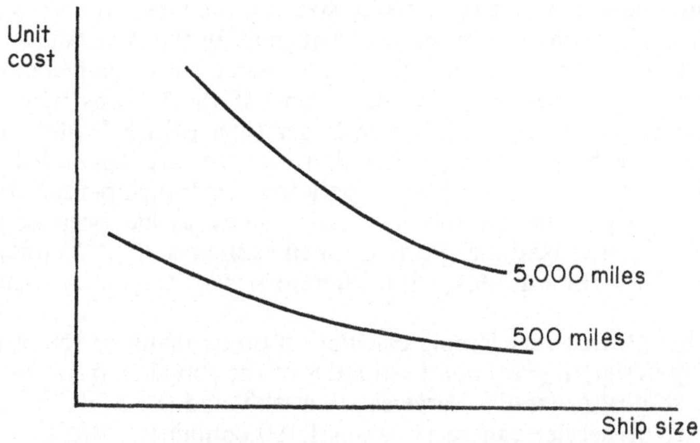

Figure 3.2. The unit-cost/ship-size/route-length relationship

[2] *Containerisation: the key to low-cost transportation*, a report by McKinsey and Co. Inc. for the British Transport Docks Board, 1967. See, for example, Exhibit VI.

[3] Sea–Land plans to launch ships with a capacity of almost 2,000 containers in 1971.

capacity of 1,200 to 1,300 containers, while US Lines plan six 1,200-container ships for the much shorter North Atlantic route and even ACL's mixed container/roll-on–roll-off vessels have a capacity of about 1,000 containers. Such economies of scale as there are have to be weighed against reductions in the service frequency. On demand considerations alone, the size of ship required to serve a given trade route equals the annual quantity of cargo divided by the service frequency, while the number of ships equals round journey time (sea time plus port time, as in the Appendix) divided by the interval between services.

$$R = Q/S$$

where Q = annual quantity of cargo on the trade route
S = service frequency, i.e. how often per year the port is called at.

R should be regarded as a minimum, for the above equation assumes fully loaded ships on every voyage.

$$N = 2\,(\text{journey time})\; S/365$$

where N = number of ships required.

The first equation means that ship size can only be increased at the expense of a reduction in service frequency. In the Australian trade the nature of demand is such that the shipping consortia feel obliged to offer weekly services, this being one of the reasons why their cellular container ships are much larger than British Rail's on the Harwich–Zeebrugge route, where daily services are demanded.

It is an interesting exercise to apply the demand/ship-size/service-frequency equation to particular trade routes, as has been done in Table 3.1, using National Ports Council estimates of 1973 container potential for three routes, with different service frequency assumptions.

Although this very simple calculation omits many of the criteria for ship design, it gives good estimates of the actual ship size on two of the routes. Australian services are weekly and the container ships currently in service can carry about 1,190 containers. British Rail's Eire service will be daily and the ships will only be slightly smaller than the size predicted.

(*b*) *Turnround times.* The main constraint upon the construction of larger conventional general-cargo ships has come from excessive

TABLE 3.1: *Ship size and service frequency*

Route	No. of containers each way*	Service frequency	Ship size (No. of containers, 20 ft equivalents)
UK–Australia	62,000	twice-weekly	600
		weekly	1,190
		fortnightly	2,380
		monthly	4,770
UK–USA	115,000	twice-weekly	1,100
		weekly	2,210
		fortnightly	4,420
		monthly	8,850
Great Britain–Eire	54,000	daily†	210
		twice-daily†	100
		twice-weekly	520

Assuming: full ships; equal weekly quantities; variations in service interval do not affect demand.

* From National Ports Council 1973 Estimates: *Port Progress Report* 1969, Table 22, taking maximum tonnage figure in any one direction and converting into container equivalents, 11 tons = 1 container.

† No weekend service.

cargo handling and therefore turnround times. The growth in size of conventional general-cargo liners, and hence the achievement of economies of scale, has been effectively constrained by inefficient terminal handling methods. It is here that containerisation makes a major contribution towards reducing costs, although it should be noted that large reductions in turnround times are technically possible even with conventional ships and dockside handling equipment. In the New Zealand trade it has been reported[4] that about 60 per cent of total ship time is spent in port and, what is more important, only 15 per cent of that is occupied in working cargo. With such a high proportion of completely non-productive time in port common to all routes, considerable improvements in ship productivity could be achieved, even without containerised handling systems. A case has been reported of three ships doing the work of

[4] Producers' Boards Shipping Utilisation Committee and New Zealand Trade Streamlining Committee: *New Zealand overseas trade; report on shipping, ports, transport and other services*, New Zealand and London, 1964.

four in the inter-war years, the fourth having broken down, through the adoption of a three-shift system.

The general effect of decreasing the turnround time of cargo liners has been studied by R. O. Goss.[5] Considering one ship design throughout, he calculated the effect on the shadow price (the freight rate which makes the net present value, in a discounted cash flow analysis, equal to zero—see Appendix to Chapter 9) of varying voyage length, the proportion of time in port, and the opportunity cost of capital (to which the shadow price is found to be relatively insensitive). His calculations show, for example, that a reduction in port time from 60 per cent to 20 per cent reduces the shadow price by 18 per cent on a 5,000 n.m. (nautical miles) round voyage, and 35 per cent on a 10,000 n.m. round trip. As he admits, his calculations take no account of increases in factor prices resulting from more intensive dockside working; either more overtime or a shift system would increase costs, the former bringing a considerable penalty in fatigue as well as higher payments per hour. In addition the continuous working of a ship causes problems for and imposes costs on inland transport.

Containerisation provides a great *technical* opportunity to increase turnround times. OCL and ACT expect to be able to turnround completely loaded 1,200 to 1,300 container ships in 48 hours, achieving a door-to-door US–Australia time of 34 days instead of the normal 57. An efficiently operated conventional deep-sea general-cargo berth could handle as much as 100,000 tons per annum, but very few are likely to handle more than 50,000 tons.[6] It is claimed that it would be technically feasible for a container berth to handle 2 million tons per annum; British Rail's Harwich terminal is designed eventually to achieve such a throughput. In the near future it is unlikely that such volumes will be handled at deep-sea terminals because trade-route flows are insufficient, when taken with the lower service-frequency requirement (see Table 3.1) to require such a weekly throughput: ship turnround time is much less than one week, therefore such terminals are idle much of the time (see Appendix).

In terms of this section's cost model, faster handling speeds affect the first two cost components. As the annual number of journeys is inversely related to total time in port, greater handling speeds reduce these unit costs by increasing the number of revenue-earning voyages.

[5] R. O. Goss, *Journal of Transport Economics and Policy*, January 1967.

[6] National Ports Council, *Port Progress Report* 1969, page 64.

The Appendix also shows that unit costs fall more rapidly with increases in port efficiency the larger the ship. The relationship between port efficiency and unit costs is such that, for a given ship size, costs fall more rapidly with the initial increases in the handling rate than later ones, i.e. the curve relating unit costs and handling speed is concave to origin, as Figure 3.3 shows. Port costs, defined

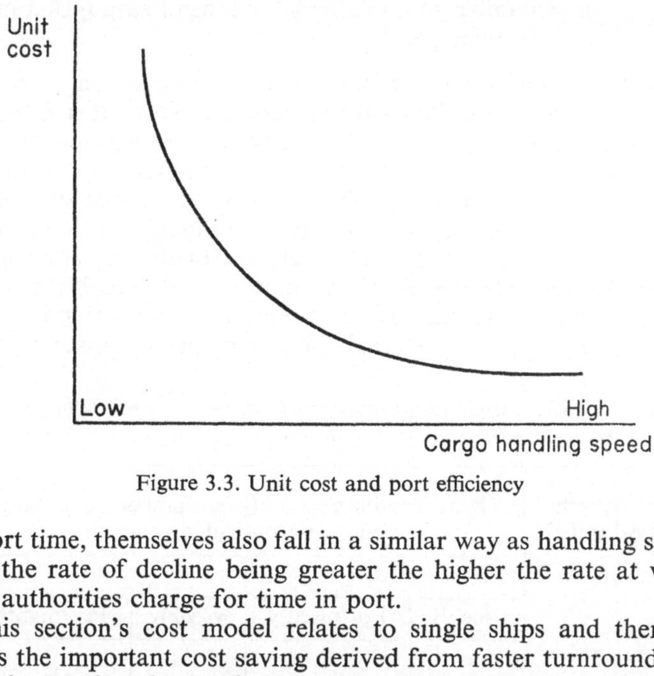

Figure 3.3. Unit cost and port efficiency

as port time, themselves also fall in a similar way as handling speeds rise, the rate of decline being greater the higher the rate at which port authorities charge for time in port.

This section's cost model relates to single ships and therefore omits the important cost saving derived from faster turnround time already mentioned, namely that reduced port time diminishes total voyage time and therefore the number of ships required to carry a given quantity of cargo; therefore, faster turnround time produces a saving on capital costs, as the following example demonstrates:

Assume a berth handling 60,000 containers (approximately equivalent to 600,000 tons) per annum, each way.

The number of ships (N) required is given by the equation,

$N = 2$ (journey time) . $S/365$
where S equals the annual number of calls made at this port.

As journey time has two components, sea and port time, this equation becomes (see Appendix):

$$N = 2(J/24V + R/\mu)(S/365)$$

where J = route length
V = speed
R = ship size or capacity (in tons or containers)
μ = number of containers (or tons of cargo) that can be handled per day.

It is assumed that μ is not a function of R, i.e. handling speeds do not vary with ship size (this will be discussed below). R is, of course, a function of the service interval (see page 36). This means that with weekly services, a 1,200-container ship is required, and with fortnightly services a 2,000-container ship. Each has capacity in excess of the weekly average quantity of cargo, although this is greater in the case of weekly services. It seems reasonable to assume that variations about the mean will be greater with weekly than fortnightly services, although this assumption does not materially affect the figures in Table 3.2. In each case ship speed is assumed to be

TABLE 3.2: *The numbers of container ships required: the effect of varying handling speed, route length and service interval*

Route length (nautical miles)	Cargo handling speed (μ = number of containers loaded and unloaded per day)			
	100		600	
	Weekly	Fortnightly	Weekly	Fortnightly
3,000	6	3	3	2
5,000	7	3	4	2
10,000	10	5	7	4

20 knots. Given that service frequency seems to vary inversely with route length, weekly services on the shortest route should be compared with fortnightly services on the longer ones. The higher value of μ represents a 48-hour turnround of a 1,200-container ship. If μ rises with R (route length), the numbers of ships given in the $\mu = 600$ block will tend to be too low. It is, however, clear that the potential

savings on ship capital costs are considerable, especially with weekly services. In each case the actual value of N has been rounded up to give whole ships: this accounts for the lower differential in the fortnightly service frequency estimates, giving considerable spare capacity in some cases.

(*c*) *Variations in optimum ship size with distance*. The McKinsey report on containerisation claimed that there existed economies of scale on longer routes but that 'the increased proportion of voyage time spent in port progressively erodes the economies of scale inherent in using larger ships'.[7] It further concluded that on short sea routes the unit-cost/size function is U-shaped, and therefore has a minimum point representing optimum ship size, and that this optimum increases with distance. It has already been indicated that economies of scale are greater on longer routes, but for this second conclusion to be true the unit-cost function must have certain characteristics. There is a down-sloping section of the curve: considering the first cost element given above (administration, capital and crew costs), there are obviously economies of scale, for this group of unit costs fall in value as ship size increases. But for there to be an upward-sloping section of this average cost curve, some unit costs must actually rise with ship size. This is unlikely to be so with fuel costs, at least within the size range being considered; there may even be economies of scale here. The implication of the McKinsey report is that port unit costs rise with size, which is certainly true in the case of conventional ships and berths, because of inadequate equipment and general dockside congestion.

The relationship is, however, less sensitive in the case of container ships and berths. It is significant that the container berth simulation studies carried out by the National Ports Council[8] assume a constant ship size when the costs of different handling systems are compared. Ship size would not appear to be a sufficiently important variable to warrant inclusion in their model, although it is suggested that further research take account of it.

Without empirical data, it is difficult to work out whether port unit costs will be higher or lower with larger vessels. Costs may be lower because more crane cycles per hour may be achieved: as each

[7] *op. cit.*, page 19.

[8] See National Ports Council, *Research and Technical Bulletin*, Nos. 2, 3, 4 and 5.

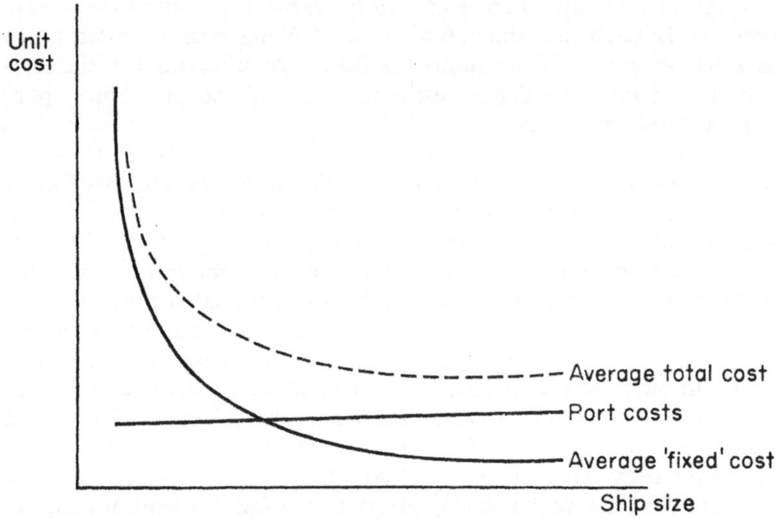

Figure 3.4a. Average total cost and ship size: slowly rising port unit costs

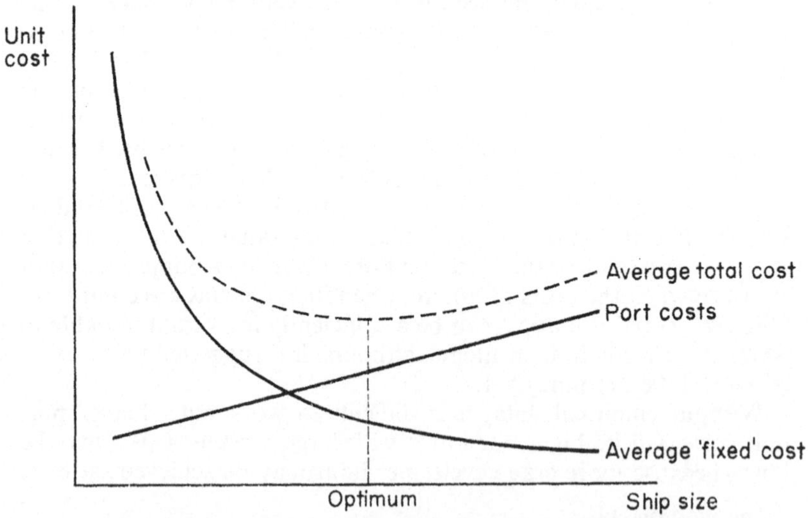

Figure 3.4b. Average total costs and ship size: rapidly rising port unit costs

cell is larger, less crane movement is required to load and unload a given number of containers. In addition, a small number of large ships compared with a large number of small ships carrying the same annual quantity of cargo will give rise to less annual dead time, i.e. less berthing time. On the other hand unit costs could conceivably be higher. Small ships tend to be more tightly scheduled and therefore give rise to better berth utilisation. A more than proportionately cheaper crane could be used for smaller ships because of the shorter outreach required. Although a smaller container park is required when smaller vessels use the terminal, there is no reason to assume that park size increases more than proportionately with ship size. However, cheaper, simpler handling systems are possible in a small park. Finally, general traffic congestion in the immediate vicinity of the berth may raise the inland cost component for larger ships. It is not, therefore, at all clear whether or not larger container ships involve higher port unit costs. However, even if these costs are higher, to have rising port costs does not necessarily imply a U-shaped average-cost/ship-size curve within conceivable limits of ship size, as Figures 3.4(a) and 3.4(b) illustrate. Although port costs are rising in Figure 3.4(a), average total costs fall throughout (they will eventually rise, but with very large ship sizes, which are precluded by the service frequency criteria). This is not the case in Figure 3.4(b), where port costs rise more rapidly and there is a minimum point of the average total cost curve, i.e. an optimum ship size in terms of the variables specified. All this also, of course, depends upon the shape of the average fixed-cost curve: in this case, it is constructed on the assumption of significant shipping economies of scale and has the shape of a rectangular hyperbola (i.e. total fixed costs per annum are the same for all ship sizes). The point to be made is that the shape of the average cost curve depends upon the nature of the costs in a containerised shipping system, and if port costs rise only slightly as ship size increases, then there *may* be no optimum ship size in terms of the variables specified, at least by the McKinsey study.

In reality there must be an optimum ship size, in the sense that shipping lines do decide on ship sizes which must optimise something, and the optimum would appear to grow with distance: British Rail's short-sea container ships are much smaller than OCL's or ACT's deep-sea container vessels (but not much smaller than some container ships trading on the North Atlantic). The exercise carried out earlier in this chapter (see Table 3.1) implies that an important, perhaps critical, constraint comes from the demand size. It is based upon the fact that the nature of Continental trade is such that daily or twice-daily services are required, while those trading with Australia only want weekly services. In Table 3.1, ship sizes were determined by dividing the annual quantity of cargo by the service frequency. In the cases of the Australian and Eire trade, an application of the actual or projected service frequency to the volume of cargo flowing to and from the UK gave a fairly accurate estimate of the sizes of container ships operating or about to operate on those routes. Therefore, ship size is at least partly a function of a demand variable, the service frequency; and, as service frequency is itself a function of route length, then optimum ship size may appear to be a function of distance. This coincides with the McKinsey conclusion, but the logic is somewhat different and it does identify the role of the service frequency and total trade volume in determining ship size. Why service frequency should itself vary with distance is un-

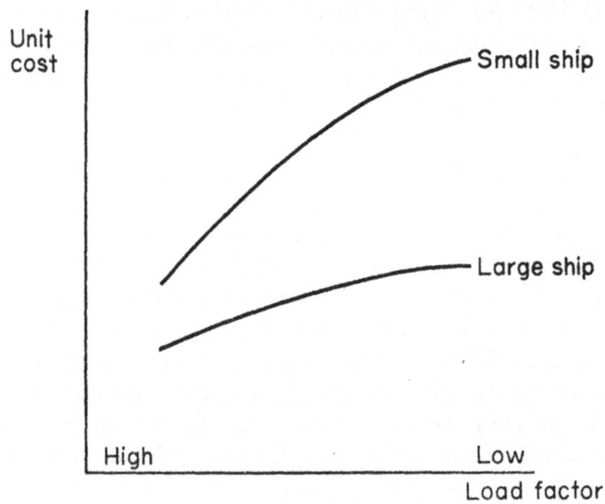

Figure 3.5

clear. It may be due to historical factors or it may be a rationalisation of the underlying costs. In other words, the longer the route, the larger the optimum ship size (on the basis of costs), and therefore the lower the freight rate. Shippers may therefore accept the less frequent services offered by a smaller number of larger ships on long routes. This interdependence of supply (cost) and demand factors is common in economics and it seriously hinders the derivation of functional relationships.

(*d*) *Load factors.* All the various reports on containerisation have mentioned the critical nature of the load factor. For example, low load factors on the North Atlantic were expected by Arthur D. Little[9] to result in very strong competition, implying possible rationalisation (of course, the converse is true: low load factors can be shown to result *from* strong competition). Low load factors increase average costs, but less so in the case of large ships because they have proportionately less tied up in fixed costs, i.e. average administration, capital and crew costs are less for large ships than small ones. However, on longer journeys unit costs are more sensitive to variations in the load factor, for, other things being equal, the longer the journey the fewer the revenue-earning trips (see Figure 3.6). Container-shipping unit costs are particularly sensitive to

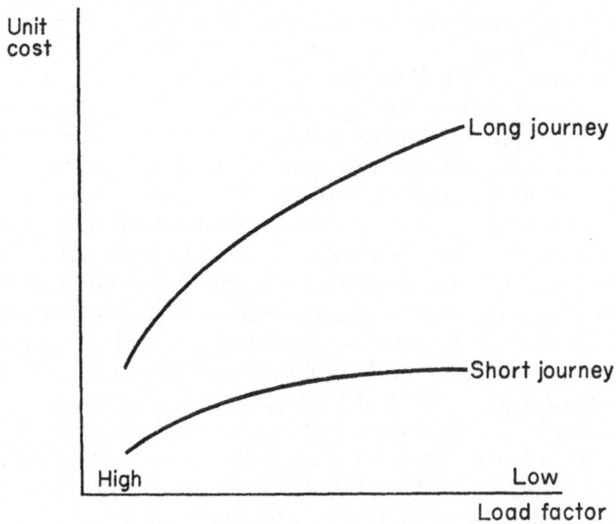

Figure 3.6. The load factor

[9] Report by Arthur D. Little Ltd. for the National Ports Council, *Containerisation on the North Atlantic*, 1967.

reductions in load factors, because they have capital tied up in the containers themselves, which often have to be carried even when empty in order to maintain a balanced flow of shipping space and avoid a build-up of containers at one terminal with a corresponding shortage at another. The Arthur D. Little model showed container-ship unit costs actually exceeding those of conventional ships over long distances if both operate with low load factors.[10]

(*e*) *Inland costs.* Inland costs, the final component of the model, depend upon the distribution of customers as well as rates charged by inland freight operators. There are two relevant aspects to the distribution of customers: the distance each is from the port and the distance they are from each other. The latter is important because the lower the degree of industrial concentration, the less the opportunity for the bulk movement of cargo to ports, which is of particular importance in the case of containerisation. In the UK most industrial development is concentrated into a sufficiently small number of large conurbations to permit the profitable operation of fast unit trains to ports. This possibility of the efficient large-scale movement of traffic and the effective reduction in the cost of inland transport to ports diminishes the need for a large number of ports, one to serve each industrial area. British Rail, for example, can operate their Continental container service through one port. There is, however, one element of inland costs which is higher in a containerised system: less than full container loads have to be grouped and the containers themselves 'stuffed' and 'unstuffed'. The construction of inland clearance depots (I.C.D.s) away from the congested docks will facilitate these processes, but the goods may tend to be handled at I.C.D.s by labour lacking in the docker's skills and the very fact that this is non-dock labour has greatly aggravated dockside industrial relations. The shorter the sea distance the more important the role played by the inland cost element in determining the system to be operated, for it rises as a proportion of average total costs, in some cases to more than half. In the case of conventional and even roll-on/roll-off shipping, the objective of minimising inland costs has resulted in the continued existence of a multitude of British ports. However, the freightliner links between I.C.D.s and ports so diminished inland transport costs that this cost component reduces to a relatively small proportion of total costs and is reduced to a lower rate per mile than

[10] *op. cit.*, page 68.

the sea voyage. Therefore the policy is to replace sea miles with land miles, as British Rail has in fact done. This creates the high-density flows required by any cellular containership system.

(*f*) *Quantification of these savings.* Various attempts have been made to quantify the cost savings attributable to containerisation. As well as identifying the savings in a qualitative or relative sense, the McKinsey report for the British Transport Docks Board estimated the potential savings to the UK of a fully developed container-shipping system. A model was constructed to synthesise, from a series of building blocks, the total cost of transporting containerised cargo. The report's main weakness was a failure to make clear the assumptions upon which the model was based, although it claimed that the accuracy and validity of the model was tested in consultation with major transport organisations in the UK and by a sensitivity analysis which subjected the model to reasonable variation in the key variables.

This criticism cannot be made of the Arthur D. Little report, *Containerisation on the North Atlantic*, which even admitted its own greatest weakness, the omission of inland transport costs.[11] This report's basic cost comparison is illustrated in Figure 3.7 (page 48). From this, the reduction in port-to-port costs of container compared with conventional ships is seen to be based on savings in ship capital (fewer ships because of faster turnround), cheaper ship operation, and much faster loading and discharge, although on the negative side there is the cost of the containers themselves and the cost of stuffing and unstuffing them. However, even in this case it is difficult to make realistic cost comparisons, for in fact like was not compared with like. For example, the large container ship had a capacity of 1 million bale cubic feet (910 containers 20 × 8 × 8 ft), while that of the largest breakbulk ship, also offering weekly services, was only 700,000 bale cubic feet. The latter was smaller because 'the percentage of time at sea would seem to be ridiculously small on such a trade route' if 1 million bale cubic feet were assumed. The report hoped to be able 'to consider breakbulk and container fleets offering identical service in terms of frequency of sailings, space offered and voyage time', but this proved to be impracticable because of the differing 'kinds of service these two types of ships are likely to offer'. Thus breakbulk ships are assumed to call at more ports and travel

[11] *op. cit.*, pages 9–10.

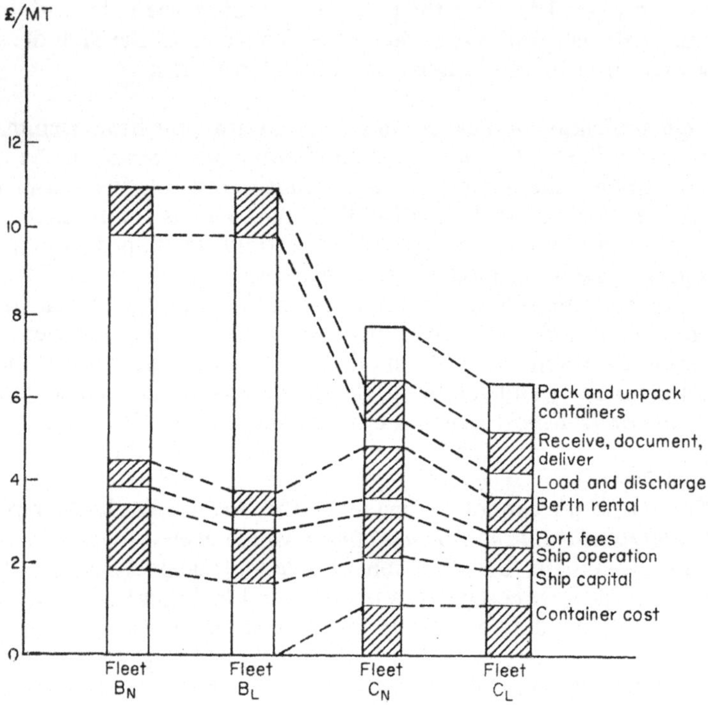

B_N—nominal breakbulk ship: 500,000 bale cubic feet, 17 knots
B_L—large breakbulk ship: 700,000 bale cubic feet, 17 knots
C_N—nominal container ship: 455 containers, 19·5 knots
C_L—large container ship: 910 containers, 19·5 knots

Figure 3.7. Port-to-port costs: base comparison
Source: National Ports Council, *Containerisation on the North Atlantic*

more slowly, the first assumption being reasonable only in terms of the inland distribution problems faced by a breakbulk operation, a consideration specifically omitted by the model. Finally, whereas the McKinsey report erred on the side of excessively large container ships, the largest container ship in the Arthur D. Little report carried only 910 containers and perhaps for this reason it omitted to consider the McKinsey solution 'of one port per trade route'. Although this would have reduced service frequency, excessively on less-dense trade routes, the actual port-to-port costs would have been much lower.

A basic deficiency of both Reports was a failure to build demand components into the models. The savings to shippers in terms of packaging, insurance, greater reliability, etc., are identified, but nowhere is there a clear statement of the savings derived from faster transit (except in terms of interest on goods while in transit, which identifies only part of the savings of faster transit), nor is there an analysis of the effect of varying the service interval. In addition, as has already been discussed, it would appear to be an empirically justifiable fact that the longer the trade route the less frequent the service demanded, but what is not clear is whether the reason for this is psychological, historical or economic. For any shipping investment decision this is critical, for ship size is determined from the demand side, by the quantity of cargo moving per annum and service frequency, as well as from cost considerations. Therefore both reports tend to be limited by their concentration on costs.

The Arthur D. Little report did, however, concern itself with the load factor, which is a derivative of demand as well as supply, as part of the model's sensitivity analysis.[12] It has been shown earlier in this section that the larger the ship the less sensitive it is to reductions in the load factor. On this basis, the report calculated that if a container ship's capacity is doubled it requires only 50 per cent more cargo to yield the same unit cost as before. Calling at many ports increases the load factor, even if at the same time raising port and fuel costs. The report calculated that a 455-container, 17-knot ship, calling at two ports, can afford only about a 20 per cent loss in cargo before its cost per measurement ton rises to that of a four-port service (without any consideration of inland costs), i.e. it is worth while calling at another port if it can provide at least 20 per cent of a ship's total cargo.

To summarise the characteristics of container shipping:

1. The main savings are based upon faster port turnround time, which both reduces the number of ships required to carry a given quantity of cargo and prevents the frustration of economies of scale likely with conventional ships and handling systems. As the economies of scale are themselves greater on longer routes, containerisation is likely to have more impact in deep-sea trade. There is a

[12] *op. cit.*, pages 16–37.

demand constraint, derived from the frequency of service required, upon the full realisation of economies of scale. When comparing conventional and containerised shipping costs, full account should be taken of the reductions in turnround time possible with the former type.

2. With containerised systems, inland distribution is faster, more efficient and, for those and other reasons, cheaper. For short-sea trade, where inland costs are relatively more important, these factors encourage the substitution of land for sea miles. In both short- and deep-sea trade, inland costs are reduced to such an extent that economic operation is possible through a small number of ports, thus creating the high-density flows between ports necessary to achieve adequate utilisation of the specialist capital equipment involved.

3. Low load factors have more serious consequences for container than conventional ships, for the containers have to be carried whether empty or full, raising fixed unit costs. In addition, container ships invariably operate on fixed schedules and therefore cannot, unlike some conventional ships, wait for more cargo or travel to another port if there is spare capacity. Low-load factors, which may prevail in the initial stages of the development of a trade route, encourage multi-port calling, a departure from the theoretically ideal system (in terms of costs).

3. *The implications of containerisation for port development*

In the past, ports have achieved poor turnround times because cargo has tended to be in small, irregularly shaped consignments, handling equipment has been inadequate, and ships and vehicles have arrived with cargo at random. Not only has the whole process been labour-intensive, but the labour itself has been poorly organised, with ships standing idle much of the time. Considerable improvements in dock-side productivity could have, and would have, taken place even without the container revolution. Containerisation has, however, radically altered the role of the ports, making them basically an interface in a total transport system. Their storage and groupage functions have been transferred to I.C.D.s located away from the docks. Expensive, specialised equipment has been installed to achieve the rapid transfer of containers to lorries and trains from ships. Equipment required includes: at least one crane (over £200,000 each), three or four straddle carriers or side loaders to serve each crane (about £35,000 each), additional machines to deliver containers to customers and, to deal with containers arriving in advance of ship sailings, up to 20 acres of container storage space.

There are many variations on this theme, but the capital cost is always considerable; for example, the Greenock container terminal has cost £2·5 million (one berth, two cranes). In addition port authorities contribute to the cost of I.C.D.S. As has already been indicated, berth productivity is very high (up to 2 million tons per annum); this is partly a result of the higher capitalisation and partly because of the transfer of some traditional port functions to I.C.D.S. The high capital cost of container berths requires large throughputs and this in turn implies fewer ports; in some cases the necessary utilisation of capital can only be achieved by one port per country or part of continent serving each trade route. The use of one berth for more than one trade route would achieve a similar capital utilisation but cause occasional congestion resulting in scheduling, storage and handling problems, unless sailings were very infrequent. Fewer ports means longer average inland journeys, but the additional cost is minimised in the case of containerisation by the operation of unit trains from I.C.D.S, located in or near industrial centres, to ports.

In a country with the geographical size and foreign trade volume of Britain the forces requiring one container port per trade route are powerful and are best examined in terms of the shipping-costs components of the previous section. Three situations will be discussed:

a. direct sailings from more than one port at either end of the trade route,

b. a service calling at more than one port in each country or continent, and

c. direct sailings between single ports.

The frequency of service to shippers and quantity of cargo flowing between trade areas are assumed to be the same in each case. Berths are assumed to be fully utilised.

a. Direct sailings from a number of smaller ports result in high capital costs because a large number of smaller ships are required. The greater number of ports increases total port costs, and the larger number of journeys results in high fuel cost, although inland cost will be low.

b. A calling service requires fewer ships than (*a*) but more than (*c*) because journey time is longer. Port and inland costs are the same as (*a*), but fuel costs are lower, unless coastal distances are high relative to those across the sea.

c. In the case of direct sailing from single ports at each end of the trade route, capital, crew, maintenance, and insurance costs are at a minimum, as fewer ships are required. Port costs are lower if there are economies of scale in port operation, which is likely even if only from sharing costs with other port users. In addition, the greater throughput means that the installation of the largest, most productive handling equipment is profitable. Fuel costs are lower than in (*a*) or (*b*) but inland costs are higher because of longer journeys on average and the necessity to establish I.C.D.S. On the other hand, the establishment of I.C.D.S does reduce the adverse effect on costs of longer journeys by, among other things, enabling the consolidation of loads to facilitate the operation of unit trains.

Direct sailings from a number of ports would only be justifiable if each could assemble large quantities of cargo for shipment; in fact when case (*a*) becomes case (*c*). A calling service is preferable to direct sailing from single ports, only if the inland cost component is relatively high. It has already been mentioned on page 49 that the case for a calling service becomes stronger if it leads to a large increase in the load factor. There are other economic considerations external to this total shipping cost model. Cases (*a*) and (*b*) allow competition between ports, which may itself confer economic benefits, and may be thought advantageous in terms of regional development (this will be discussed in the final chapter). The monopoly enjoyed by ports under (*c*) may be exploited to the disadvantage of shippers and shipping lines, and, of more serious consequence from the national point of view, may make Britain's foreign trade particularly prone to strikes. This point can be exaggerated, for a significant characteristic of docks strikes is the ease with which they spread nationally and internationally, as the recent history of containerisation has shown.

Until recently the main concern with the development of ports nationally has been the lack of investment,[13] but now no such

[13] This was one of the main reasons for setting up the Rochdale Committee of enquiry into British ports. See below, Chapter 9.

criticism can be made of port authorities. Each recognises the reduction in ports implied by containerisation, and is determined it should not be the one made redundant. Investment appraisal by each shows that operation of a container terminal would be profitable, but unfortunately each would appear to assume that it will attract traffic which other ports have also claimed as their own in their discounted cash flow analysis. Therefore if the various port authorities' plans, as well as actual developments, are considered there is some evidence of excess capacity, if not now, then in the future. This will be examined in the following two sections.

4. *An estimate of the port and shipping capacity required relative to services and berths planned*

Although the principles of containerisation are similar for deep- and short-sea trade, the two types of trade will be treated separately in this section because (*a*) detailed quantitative estimates have been published for the former but not the latter and (*b*) other current shipping methods present a much more viable alternative in short-sea than in deep-sea trade.

(*a*) *Deep sea.* Between 1965 and 1967 the University of Lancaster's Department of Operational Research, sponsored by the National Ports Council, carried out research into 'UK Deep Sea Trade Routes—The Potential for Container Services based on Physical Cargo Characteristics'. The research method adopted was as follows:

(i) For each trade route the volume of cargo was converted into container equivalents, according to assumed packing policies and volume/weight ratios. A distinction was made between three types of cargo: cargo unsuitable for containers (e.g. most bulk commodities, machinery over 5 tons in weight); moderately suitable cargo (e.g. pulp and waste paper); cargo suitable for containers. In their 'optimistic' estimates the second category was included in both directions on a trade route, but in their 'conservative' estimates this type of cargo was only included to balance flows. On the basis of 1965 trade figures, between 9 and 12 million tons of non-bulk cargo, out of a non-bulk total of about 16 million tons, was estimated as likely to move in containers annually.

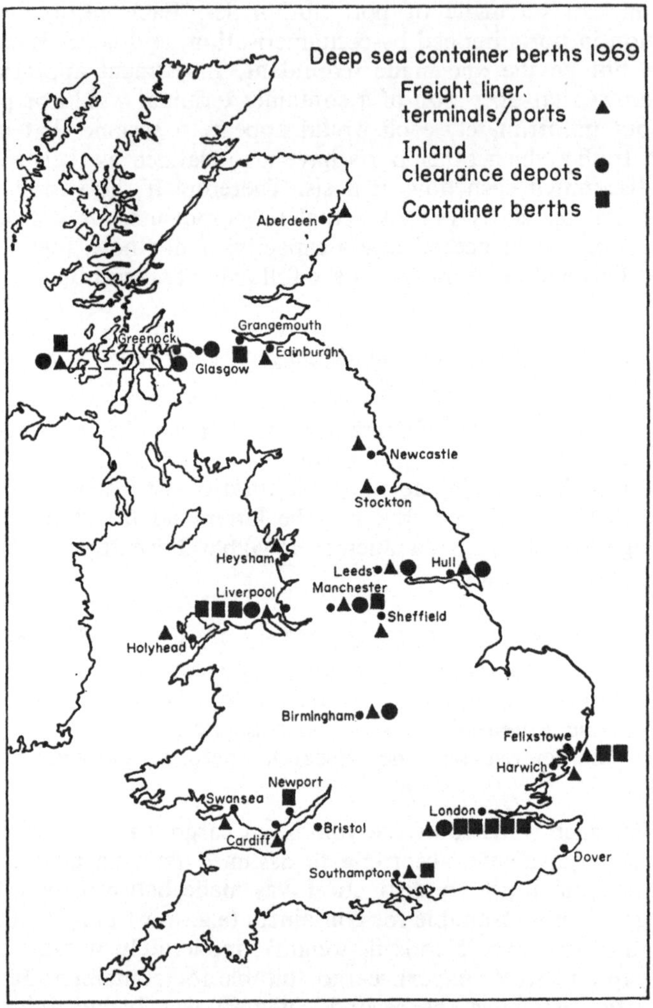

Map 3.1. Deep-sea container berths
Source: National Ports Council, *Port Progress Report 1969*, Map 1

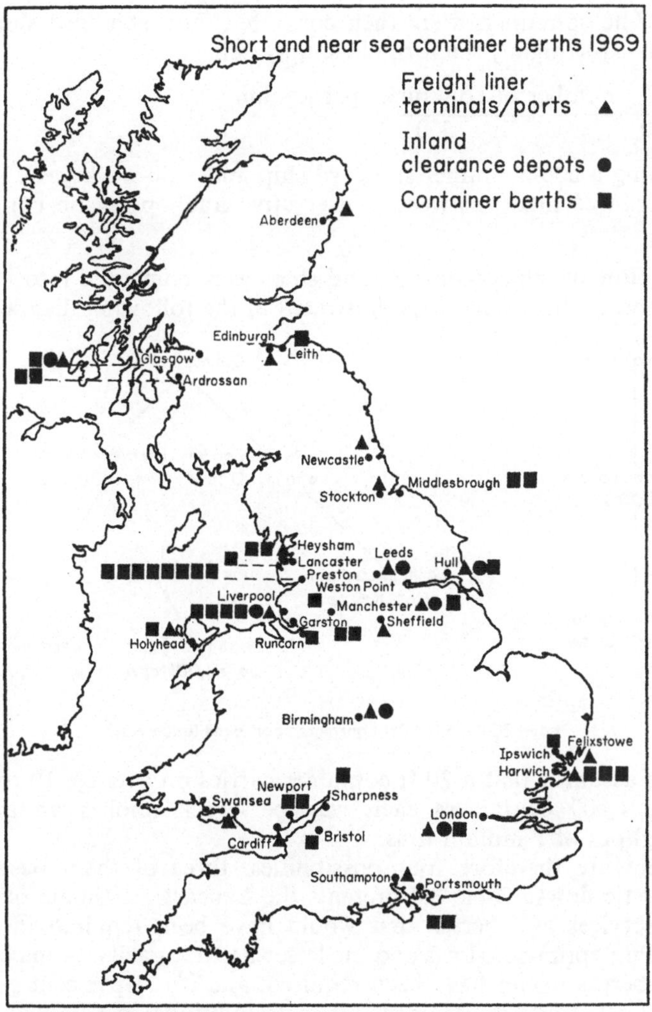

Map 3.2. Short- and near-sea container berths
Source: National Ports Council, *Port Progress Report 1969*.

(ii) The containers were then converted into 'standard ship services per fortnight', the formula simply being

$$\frac{2}{50} \cdot \frac{\text{number of containers per annum}}{500}$$

assuming a 500-container standard ship and a 50-week year. A distinction was made between conservative and optimistic container flows.

(iii) Finally, the containers and ships were converted into berths, considering the possibilities illustrated in the following diagram:

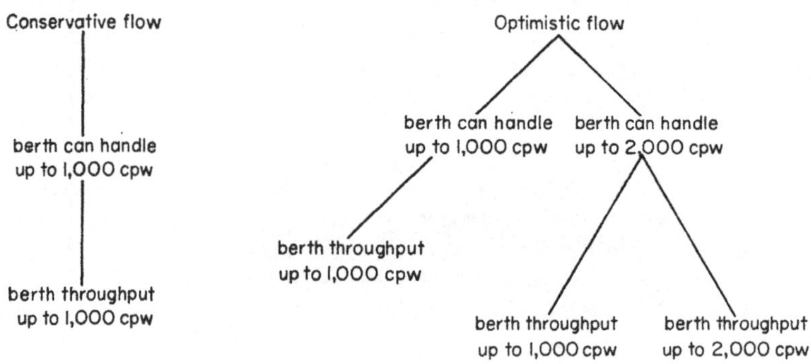

cpw=20ft x 8ft x 8ft containers per week (each way)

If it is assumed that a 20 ft container carries on average 10 tons of cargo, 1,000 containers each way per week implies an annual throughput of 1 million tons.

There are therefore four possibilities, three of them based on optimistic flows. Table 3.3 presents the Lancaster estimate of shipping services and berths that would have been required in 1965, assuming optimistic flows and the lesser berth capacity. A maximum of 17 berths would have been required, and if a 3 per cent growth rate of UK trade is assumed, up to 6 additional berths would be required by 1975. If berth throughputs of 2,000 containers per week (i.e. the routes requiring 2 berths now require 1) and scheduled services (precluding several berths serving one route) are assumed, the 1965 requirement falls to 12. The report estimates that operating with berths capable of handling up to 1,000 containers per week, each will on average handle 720,000 tons per annum. On the assumption that modern conventional berths can handle 150,000 tons per annum (much more than the National Ports Council assessment), this means that a container berth will replace almost 5 conventional berths.

The Lancaster study implicitly assumed an infinitely inelastic demand for shipping services: that the costs reduction brought about by containerisation (which are not necessarily synonymous with price or freight-rate reductions, for other cost savings to shippers are possible and likely) will not themselves increase overseas trade in the commodities likely to travel by container. This is not, however, a serious weakness in the report, which only attempted a rough estimate of berth requirements, for in most cases the cost of sending

TABLE 3.3: *Estimates of shipping and berth capacity required for deep-sea trade—Lancaster's optimistic estimate*

Trade route	No. of ship sailings of 500 container ships per fortnight	Berth requirements (assume they can handle 1,000 containers each way per week)
Major routes		
USA and N. Atlantic	4·4	2
Canada and Great Lakes	4·7	2
Australia	3·8	1
New Zealand	4·2	2
Far East	4·2	2
S. Africa, part S.E. Africa	4·5	2
Minor routes		
USA–other routes	3·2	1
W. Africa	2·1	1
India, Pakistan, Ceylon	3·6	1
E. South America	2·0	1
Central America, Caribbean, and W. South America	2·5	1
E. Africa, rest S.E. Africa	1·7	1

Source: University of Lancaster, Department of Operational Research, *UK Deep Sea Trade Routes*, for National Ports Council (December 1967)

goods overseas forms a relatively small proportion of the total cost and therefore even a halving of these costs would not have a dramatic effect on the total quantity of overseas trade.

Using similar methods, but working independently, Arthur D. Little Ltd. prepared for the National Ports Council estimates of container potential in UK–US North Atlantic trade.[14] On the basis of 1965 trading figures their optimistic estimate (including types of cargo classified as 'prime' and 'suitable', providing a similar basis for an estimate as Lancaster's 'optimistic flows') was that 1,430 containers (20 ft container load equivalent) per week would have flowed westward and 1,240 eastward; this represents no great variation from the Lancaster estimate. The 1970 predictions were 1,800 and 1,580 respectively, and those for 1975 were 2,300 and 1,920. The 1970 predictions indicate a need for 3 or 4 berths, on the assumption (as in the Lancaster study) that each could handle up to 1,000 containers per week each way.

In the *Port Progress Report 1969*, the National Ports Council produced its own estimates of container potential based on its evaluation of the Lancaster and Arthur D. Little studies and the detailed workings of the McKinsey study, to which it was given access.[15] The overall estimate of deep-sea container potential was 12·1 million tons for 1965, equal to Lancaster's upper limit, rising to 14·2 million tons in 1973. Based upon their estimate 'that by 1973 as much as 7 million tons a year of deep-sea cargo may be passing over container berths',[16] and assuming an average container berth throughput of 0·5 million tons per annum, the National Ports Council suggested that 14 deep-sea berths would be required and concluded that, as 15 or 16 berths are planned for that date, there is thus 'as good a match in numbers of berths as is possible on existing data'.[17] This takes no account of the routes these berths are planned, by shipping lines and port authorities, to serve, nor whether they are optimally located relative to the overseas trade areas and the inland markets.

As no details were given concerning the way in which the National Ports Council revised the earlier estimates, this section will continue to be based on the Lancaster and Arthur D. Little predictions, although recourse will be made to the NPC figures in the short-sea part of this section.

[14] *op. cit.*, page 61.
[15] *op. cit.*, Table 15, page 30.
[16] *ibid.*, page 68.
[17] *ibid.*, page 68.

Of the sea trade routes listed by the Lancaster study (see Table 3.3) as suitable for early development, only in the case of UK–Australia does the actual system approach that recommended. The two consortia concerned, OCL and ACT, have decided to operate through a single UK port, Tilbury, but call at a number of Australian ports; for to call at one Australian port would entail uneconomically long inland journeys. Tilbury is served from the more distant parts of Britain by unit trains travelling from I.C.D.S; for example, Scottish trade destined for Australia is brought together at the Gartsherrie I.C.D., to the east of Glasgow. In the near future OCL will have six container ships and ACT three, each with a capacity of about 1,200 containers. They will co-ordinate weekly services through their Tilbury berths. Although capacity would appear to be slightly in excess of container potential predicted by the Lancaster study, it does not imply an unprofitably low load factor. The throughput of each berth must, however, be below that which is technically feasible, at least initially.

In the North American trade it is more difficult to relate predicted and planned capacity, for many ports and shipping lines are vying for this traffic. Tilbury, Southampton, Liverpool, Manchester, Felixstowe, Grangemouth and Greenock all have or are planning at least one container berth in the hope of attracting shipping lines operating on this route. There is not only competition between these ports but also from Continental ports. The McKinsey report did countenance the possibility of British ports feeding Continental ones, such as Rotterdam, where the concentration of large volumes of cargo would encourage frequent sailing by larger container ships to distant continents. Against these economies of scale must be set the cost of the additional voyage from Britain to a European port. Such a system is of doubtful economic viability, and political considerations completely rule it out as a long-term solution, at least until the days of united Europe arrive. And so the reality is competition between British ports. The Arthur D. Little estimates imply a maximum of four UK berths in 1970 for the trade with the US North Atlantic ports; in fact, six are currently in operation. The Little report also compared containerisable cargo with the container spaces likely to be offered in 1970 by eight of the shipping lines operating between the North-West Europe (including the UK) and the US North Atlantic ports and found capacity in excess of potential. This means that container operators will have to push containerisation to its limit and attract substantial amounts of cargo from conventional shipping operators. There is therefore a prospect of strong competition on the North Atlantic between shipping lines, with low load factors for container ships and falling load factors on breakbulk ships. This will work to the advantage of the marginal ports in the short run, for they will be able to attract shipping lines on calling services in their attempt to increase load factors. One of the North Atlantic shipping lines, ACL (a consortium of a number of European lines), intends to call at no less than six European ports and three American; they do not, however, operate cellular container ships, but large mixed container and roll-on/roll-off vessels.

The other major routes in Table 3.1 have yet to be developed, although, as with North American and Australian trade, many containers are, and will continue to be, carried on conventional ships. In December 1968, Sea–Land announced their intention to operate container ships to the Far East, commencing the following December,[18] and then in June 1969 an international group of shipping lines announced that it planned to invest £120 million in some twenty container ships for the Europe–Far East trade.[19] It was expected that each would have a capacity of 1,600 to 1,700 containers (20 ft equivalents) and that services would begin in 1971. A report prepared for the New Zealand government has predicted that containerisation could reduce New Zealand–Western Europe freight rates by up to 20 per cent.[20] In May 1969 four British lines announced that they were planning to invest up to £50 million in container services between Tilbury or Southampton and Wellington and Auckland. The ships would have a capacity of about 1,400 containers, and services, which were expected to start in 1972, would be fortnightly. A particular problem with this route is the serious imbalance of trade and the consequent need to carry empty containers; British imports from New Zealand exceed her exports there. With incomplete information on the plans of shipping lines on these two routes, it is difficult to relate potential to capacity. Currently there is no evidence of excess capacity, except when account is taken of conventional capacity available, for, even on the basis of 1965 trade data, Lancaster predicted that both the Far East and New Zealand trade could support at least weekly 1,000-container ship sailings.

[18] *Ports and Terminals*, May 1969. [19] *Ports and Terminals*, June 1969.
[20] Reported in *Ports and Terminals*, May 1969.

It is even more difficult to predict the future development of shipping to Southern Africa. No plans for container ships or terminals have been published, and yet the Lancaster estimate indicates considerable potential.

(*b*) *Short sea.* Britain's short-sea trade is quantitatively almost as great as deep-sea trade, and according to the National Ports Council a maximum of 9·8 million tons can be regarded as container potential for 1973, compared with 14·2 million for deep-sea trade.[21] Although the economics of containerisation apply with almost equal force to short- and deep-sea trade, the actual system will not develop in the same way. Most of the deep-sea container tonnage will travel in cellular container ships and be handled at ports by the specialist equipment already described. In the case of short-sea container services with cellular ships, the system of movement will be identical, but it is expected that a high proportion of the short-sea container potential will travel on conventional and roll-on/roll-off vessels. The economics of the cellular container-ship operation require very dense flows and therefore imply operation through a small number of ports, as in deep-sea trade. For each trade route British volumes will be insufficient to support more than one container port for cellular container ship services. The reason for this is that a high proportion of National Ports Council's container potential can and will travel at lower real cost (i.e. taking full account of all the costs involved) on roll-on/roll-off conventional and pallet ships.

Roll-on/roll-off is itself a recent development and, prior to a full evaluation of the implications of cellular container ships, many lines invested in these vessels. This system will continue to offer real advantages to shippers compared with cellular services:

a. The service offers a greater degree of control to shippers, and the hauliers themselves.

b. With road haulage there is usually one less terminal to pass through at each end and no necessary transhipment of the cargo between vehicles or modes.

c. Road transport is, *per se*, more flexible.

d. Road vehicles give a greater 'cube' (i.e. larger volume capacity) than containers, for they can stack higher than the ISO standard of 8 ft.

[21] *op. cit.*, page 30.

The ships themselves offer similar capacities and capabilities. TFS's *Europic Ferry* carries 60 containers on the upper deck, and this can be increased by double stacking, plus 70 to 80 trailers below deck; sailing between Felixstowe and Europort, it makes six voyages a week by taking six hours for the sea journey and achieving a six-hour turnround. British Rail's two cellular container ships on the Harwich–Zeebrugge run, *Sea Freightliner I* and *Sea Freightliner II*, carry between 130 and 200 standard ISO containers and make the round trip in 24 hours.

British Rail initiated their services with much lower freight rates than those of its competitors, many of whom accused British Rail of cross-subsidisation; this has continued to be denied by British Rail's Shipping Division. Some, however, retaliated with corresponding price reductions: TFS, for example, charges the same for a 20 ft container on the Felixstowe–Europort run as British Rail do on the Harwich–Zeebrugge route. Wallenius has also announced large price cuts for unit loads travelling on the Harwich–Copenhagen route. The effect of these attempts to compete with British Rail on profitability is not known, but some have gone out of business, merged, or withdrawn services. Early in 1969 one line withdrew its Great Yarmouth–Rotterdam services and sold two ferries recently purpose-built for the route, blaming devaluation and the TFS and British Rail price reductions. Some see in short-sea cellular container services the virtual extinction of international road haulage, even though the issue of TIR carnets by the Road Haulage Association has been rising: from about 6,000 in 1967, to 11,000 in 1968 and 5,000 in the first four months of 1969. Extinction is very unlikely. Roll-on/roll-off operators and associated road-haulage firms will achieve long-run viability by concentrating on their particular advantages over rail-orientated cellular container-ship operators: a more flexible service, better able to take account of the special characteristics of many shipments which roughly fall within the range of goods identified as container potential.

The consequence of this is that short-sea trade can support more ports and shipping lines than deep-sea. Currently some 45 lines offer short-sea container services from about 30 ports, including lift-on/lift-off and roll-on/roll-off, although only British rail and EUR operate cellular container ships. Both port and shipping line rationalisation is to be expected, but less than on deep-sea trade.

The National Ports Council has given a trade area breakdown of

TABLE 3.4: *Trade area* 1973 *container potential* (*thousand tons*)

	Imports	Exports
Eire	590 (32)	420 (45)
Scandinavia	2,865 (15)	1,450 (35)
EEC	1,835 (22)	2,650 (39)

Figures in parentheses represent percentage of total trade.

its 1973 estimate of short-sea container potential:[22] see Table 3.4. Although it is not clear exactly how these figures were derived, and no estimates were given for Northern Irish and non-EEC Continental trade, they indicate considerable potential. The Scandinavian and EEC estimates are larger than any for a deep-sea trade route. British Rail already offers twice-daily sailings to the Continent. Assuming 150 20 ft containers, carrying on average 11 tons per sailing, this represents an annual throughput of almost 2 million tons, which is a very high proportion of the EEC figure, although some will go to non-EEC countries. British Rail now operate daily cellular container-ship services to Dublin and Belfast via Holyhead; this should also capture a very high proportion of the Irish potential, although many of the Irish Sea lines have had long experience of unit loads. The improvements in inland distribution brought about by unit trains will to a large extent overcome the apparent isolation of some regions from British Rail's two ports. For example, door-to-door time from Glasgow or Edinburgh to Milan is about three days, and cities as distant as Brussels or Cologne can be reached in two days.

The Scandinavian potential seems massive but the usual containerisation principles do not apply with the same force in this case, since the terrain is such that unit trains are unlikely to operate there. Thus although there is no reason why British inland distribution should not be by rail, roll-on/roll-off or palletisation is more likely to dominate. In fact, one of the main Scandinavian shipping lines, Fred Olsen Lines, is a supporter of palletisation against containerisa tion (this will be discussed in the next chapter).

[22] *op. cit.*, page 30.

5. *Conclusion*

Overseas containerisation's cost savings are attributable to faster port turnround times and cheaper long-distance inland transport by unit trains. The former not only increases the opportunities for ships to achieve economies of scale, but also reduces the number of ships required. Economies of scale are less powerful on short-sea routes, where the inland cost component is of more relevance, and are for all routes constrained by service-frequency requirements. The shorter the service interval demanded by shippers, the smaller the ship required to carry a given annual quantity of cargo. As more frequent services appear to be required on shorter routes, short-sea cellular container ships tend to be smaller.

To attain the faster port turnround times, expensive specialist terminals are needed, the full utilisation of which requires large annual cargo throughputs. This implies a small number of ports, in some cases one port per trade route. In short-sea trade, more ports will survive for the cost differential between cellular container-ship operations and roll-on/roll-off is in many cases small, the more personal service offered by road haulage often making the total distribution cost less.

An examination of the deep-sea routes shows that only in the case of the Australian trade is there evidence that the actual development is likely to coincide with theoretical predictions: one British port, the rationalisation of many shipping lines into two consortia, and ships with annual cargo capacities in excess of any previous vessels. There is some evidence of excess capacity, in ships and terminals, on the North Atlantic. This can be expected to result in strong competition between shipping lines operating with low load factors, which is a particularly powerful penalty for container ships as containers have to be carried and handled even when empty unless high container stockholding costs are to be incurred in each country. It is difficult to relate capacity to potential on other deep-sea routes, for few lines have published detailed plans; New Zealand and Far East services should, however, begin in the early 1970s.

The only operators of cellular container ships on short-sea routes are British Rail and EUR. With the capacity and frequency of service planned, British Rail alone should capture a high proportion of Continental and Irish container potential, but some containers will continue to travel on breakbulk and roll-on/roll-off ships.

APPENDIX TO CHAPTER 3

(*a*) *Shipping Cost Components*

Crew $= \alpha R^w$
Officers, administration $= \beta R^x$
Interest, amortisation, maintenance, insurance $= \varepsilon R^y$
Port costs $= \gamma n(R/\theta + C/\mu)$

This reflects the fact that the cost to shipping lines has two components, the dues payable to the port authority and the time spent in port, and that the former is a function of the latter.

Fuel costs $= n\pi(\sigma R V^3 t)$
Inland costs $= nCa\bar{d}$

where

$n = (365 - z)/(J/24V + (R/\theta + C/\mu)$ = annual number of voyages
$t = J/24V$ = voyage duration (at sea)
R = ship size
C = quantity of cargo carried per ship
θ, μ are proportionate to port efficiency:
θ referring to docking time,
μ to cargo handling time
V = ship speed (knots)
a = average cost per mile of inland distribution
$\bar{d}$ = mean distance of customers from port
π = price of fuel
J = route length (nautical miles)
z = laid-up time (days)
$w, x, y, \alpha, \beta, \varepsilon, \gamma, \sigma$ are parameters

Assume $x = y = w = 0{\cdot}5$

Total annual shipping costs =

$$(\alpha + \beta + \varepsilon)\sqrt{R} + \gamma n(R/\theta + C/\mu) + n\pi(\sigma R V^3 t) + nCa\bar{d}$$

the particular power of V appears in many shipping text books. Total quantity $= nC$ assuming no competition between cargo and bunker space.*

* In his *Sea Transport and Shipping Economics*, published by Bremen's Institute for Shipping Research in 1958, A. S. Svendsen constructed a shipping cost model

Assume $C = lR$, where l is the proportion of the ship taken up with cargo and is itself a function of the load factor.

Average cost =

$$\frac{(\alpha+\beta+\varepsilon)}{nl\sqrt{R}}+\frac{\gamma(R/\theta+lR/\mu)}{lR}+\frac{\pi\sigma V^2J}{24l}+a\bar{d} \quad . \quad . \quad (1)$$

To simplify analysis assume $\left(\frac{R}{\theta}+\frac{lR}{\mu}\right)=\frac{lR}{\phi}$ where ϕ represents port efficiency (e.g. number of containers loaded and unloaded per day). Equation (1) becomes:

$$AC=\frac{(\alpha+\beta+\varepsilon)(J\phi+lR24V)}{24V\phi(365-z)l\sqrt{R}}+\frac{\gamma}{\phi}+\frac{\pi\sigma V^2J}{24l}+a\bar{d} \quad . \quad (2)$$

Rearranging the first term:

$$AC=\frac{(\alpha+\beta+\varepsilon)\sqrt{R}}{(365-z)}\left(\frac{J}{24VlR}+\frac{1}{\phi}\right)+\frac{\gamma}{\phi}+\frac{\pi\sigma V^2J}{24l}+a\bar{d}. \quad (2a)$$

(*b*) *Economies of scale*

Finding the partial derivative average cost with respect to size:

$$\frac{\delta AC}{\delta R}=\frac{(\alpha+\beta+\varepsilon)}{2(365-z)\sqrt{R}}\left(\frac{1}{\phi}-\frac{J}{24VlR}\right) \quad . \quad . \quad (3)$$

As ϕ (cargo handling rate) is likely to be in excess of 500 in a modern port, the first term in the parentheses is much less than one. The second term in the parentheses will almost certainly, ignoring the sign, be larger for the only situation in which this will not be so is when J (route length) is very low and R (ship size or capacity) is high. This is unlikely to be the case for, as is discussed in the text of this chapter, J and R tend to move in the same direction. Therefore equation (3) is negative, i.e. unit (average) costs fall as size

to which the one presented in this Appendix owes much. This one specifies more clearly the various components of port costs and, unlike Svendsen, assumes no 'competition' between cargo and bunker space, i.e. cargo capacity is not lost on longer journeys because of the large amount of fuel that has to be carried.

increases, but less than proportionately. The greater the voyage distance (J) or port efficiency (ϕ) the more sensitive the relationship; the greater the load factor (l; lR in the second term inside the parentheses equalling the quantity of cargo) the less steep the curve.

(c) *The effect of less than fully utilising the terminal*

The second term in equation (1), port costs, should contain a fixed cost element, for some costs have to be borne whether or not ships are being docked or cargo unloaded and therefore some charges will be largely independent of ship size or the quantity of cargo. This term becomes $F+\gamma(R/\theta+lR/\mu)$ and the second term in equation (2) becomes $F/lR+\gamma/\phi$, where F is fixed port costs. If the quantity of cargo ($lR = C$) falls, port unit costs rise and shipping lines which less than fully utilise terminals they own or rent are therefore liable to higher port charges per unit cargo (unless for some reason the port is prepared to subsidise them).

(d) *The effect of improved port efficiency (turnround times)*

Finding the partial derivative of unit cost with respect to port efficiency (ϕ), from equation (2):

$$\frac{\delta AC}{\delta\phi} = -\frac{(\alpha+\beta+\varepsilon)}{(365-z)\phi^2} - \frac{\gamma}{\phi^2} \quad . \quad . \quad . \quad (4)$$

From equation (2a) it is evident that AC falls with increases in ϕ, and from equation (4) it is obvious that the curve slopes more steeply downward for higher values of R (ship size) and γ (the rate at which ports charge for time in port). The curve is concave to origin, and therefore costs fall more rapidly as lower handling rates are increased than as higher ones are approached.

(e) *Optimum ship size*

Because R appears in two separate terms of equation (2a), the AC/R curve has a minimum point, ignoring the effect of other variables:

$$\frac{\delta^2 AC}{\delta R} > 0, \text{ and for } \frac{\delta AC}{\delta R} = 0, \; R_{\text{opt.}} = \frac{J\phi}{l24V}$$

Therefore optimum ship size is large the longer the trade route or the greater port efficiency, and smaller the greater the load factor or speed. However, little significance should be attached to the existence of an optimum on the basis of this analysis, for it is attributable to R being in the port time component of n, the annual number of voyages. Had C (quantity of cargo) remained in this part of the equation and were C independent of ship size (i.e. demand determined), this part of average costs would have fallen continuously as ship size increased.

(*f*) *The effect of varying the load factor*

From equation (2a) it is evident a fall in the load factor (l) increases unit costs, but the relationship is of varying sensitivity for changes in distance and size. Assuming a fixed costs component of port costs (see (*b*) above),

$$\frac{\delta AC}{\delta l} = -\frac{1}{l^2}\left[\frac{(\alpha+\beta+\varepsilon)J}{24V(365-z)\sqrt{R}} + \frac{F}{R} + \frac{\pi\sigma V^2 J}{24}\right]$$

The curve slopes downward more steeply for greater values of J, or F, and less steeply for larger values of R.

CHAPTER 4

IMPLICATIONS OF OVERSEAS CONTAINERISATION FOR IMPORTERS AND EXPORTERS

Chapter 3 discussed the economic characteristics of containerisation and considered its effect upon shipping lines, ports and volumes of trade. This chapter will consider the impact of containerisation on shippers and their customers, drawing upon Chapter 2's demonstration of the need to evaluate all the costs involved. Some of the problems containerisation poses for these firms will then be discussed: the fear of shipping and port monopolies, labour relations difficulties at all the terminals in the system, and insurance, legal and documentation problems. Finally the chapter will attempt to achieve a long-term perspective of the viability of containerisation by introducing further constraints upon its development in the form of competition from other transport methods: pallet systems, LASH, and airfreight.

1. *Total distribution cost and containerisation*

Very few exporters concern themselves with the final delivery of their goods to overseas customers; most sell f.o.b., ex-works or c.i.f. to port. As the National Economic Development Office's publication *Through Transport to Europe*[1] emphasises, this reduces their competitiveness overseas. If he is ignorant of his own price in an overseas market, an exporter cannot carry out effective market research and fully evaluate the competitiveness of his product. In a small sample survey, the committee which prepared the report found only two out of eleven firms using the 'Delivered Price Concept': i.e. quoting prices to overseas customers which include the costs of transporting the goods all the way to their premises. Associated with this is the 'Through Transport Concept', which requires that firms ensure the direct flow of goods from their own premises to those of their

[1] NEDO (National Economic Development Office, Economic Development Committee for the Movement of Exports), *Through Transport to Europe*, HMSO, 1966.

importing customer with a minimum of intermediate handling or interruption. One of the consequences of the unwillingness or inability of exporters to take an interest in the whole system of movement is their failure to meet delivery dates. According to another NEDO publication based upon a study by the Metra Consulting Group[2]

a. only 50 per cent of British exports to Europe leave the exporter's premises on time, and
b. more than two-thirds do not give their customers a definite date by which the consignment will be despatched, shipped or delivered.

If these attitudes and practices prevail on other routes, and there is no evidence that they do not, a full evaluation of the savings possible through containerisation is impossible for most firms. On the other hand, containerisation itself provides an unequalled opportunity, even a compulsion, for firms to change their attitudes. As rarely before, the shipping lines have concerned themselves with the whole door-to-door distribution system; some even own the road delivery vehicles, others own railways or have financial interests in I.C.D.S. They can therefore quote to shippers door-to-door rates, state exactly when the ship will sail and arrive at the foreign port, and even estimate the time the container (or consignment if it is a less-than-container load) will arrive at the overseas customer's premises. Movement is much faster and therefore each consignment is exposed to the risk of a delay for less time. In addition, the standardisation of the container itself and the component parts of the system as a whole, plus the computer control exercised over it, increase in a general way the probability of achieving the predicted arrival time. Therefore shippers can quote delivered prices to customers, offer them better service, and be confident that their promises of delivery times will be fulfilled.

In principle, the savings are common to all shippers, even if in differing degrees. This not only aids an appreciation of containerisation, but also eases the sales campaigns of the container shipping lines. The savings apply to cellular and non-cellular container-ship services, but with greater force to fully integrated systems where, above all, the time saving is greatest. A major source of savings lies

[2] NEDO (Economic Development Committee for the Movement of Exports), *Delivering the Goods*, HMSO, 1968.

in the extra protection afforded by the container itself: from sea-water, weather, theft, breakage and contamination. A skilfully packed ('stuffed' in container jargon) container provides almost perfect protection from such damage. However, recent experience has shown that containers are not always adequately stowed; some insurance companies have had an increased incidence of claims. Types of commodities which fill containers to volume capacity at less than or equal to its weight limit (e.g. whisky, cornflakes) present no problem, but dense goods such as electric motors or machine tools which reach the maximum weight when the container is much less than full cause considerable stowage difficulties. Savings can be considerable for exporters of the former type of goods. For example, a firm sending radiators to Australia normally had to package with wooden crates; only paper bags were needed inside containers, a saving of materials and of ten days' labour per containerload. Firms tend to package only for that part of the journey with which they are immediately concerned and it is a short journey if sales are f.o.b. or ex-works. Often goods have to be repacked to withstand more rigorous transport conditions overseas. Such problems are overcome when containers are used, as long as they are adequately stowed. Stowage skills are at a premium, especially as such a high proportion of export consignments are less-than-container loads and therefore have to be grouped at inland clearance and other depots.

Faster door-to-door movements provide another source of savings. The savings in interest on goods in transit is very valuable in the case of high-value goods such as whisky. It can also be shown that the shorter the time between the receipt of an order and its fulfilment the lower the level of stocks that has to be held to achieve a given service. If direct overseas distribution is sufficiently rapid, it may be possible for firms to distribute direct to overseas customers rather than use foreign agents or their own overseas depots. This is more likely to be of relevance on short-sea trade, where container ship services can achieve 48-hour door-to-door deliveries over a wide radius from most parts of Britain. It should be noted, however, that some firms regard faster transit as a positive disadvantage; they welcome the free (to them) warehousing provided by a slow journey. This is mainly applicable to agricultural goods which are produced or harvested some time before their overseas markets require them.

Both faster transit and better protection from damage reduce insurance costs. The faster the door-to-door transport time, the less time the consignment is at risk. However lower insurance costs are, as already indicated, dependent upon improved stowage skills.

A firm calculating the total distribution costs can appraise all these benefits and choose the system offering the least real cost, not just the lowest freight rates. However the most profitable use of containers may require some reorganisation or investment by the firm itself. The great majority of premises cannot adequately handle containers. The height of loading bays is often different to that of the trailers carrying containers, so that fork-lift trucks cannot enter the container, making loading and unloading a slow process. Insufficient loading bays and poorly planned access may cause congestion resulting in long lorry queues. As most overseas customers order less than full container loads, it may be in the interests of some firms to give rebates to encourage the ordering of full loads, or else it may prove necessary to set up overseas depots to break the bulk. One exporter of machine tools to the US has persuaded customers to order machines in multiples of four, the number which fills a 20 ft container. Whether or not such changes in distributive methods are worth while can only be evaluated through a TDC analysis.

Two examples will be given of the reorganisation required and the savings which can be achieved. Since August 1968, Ford Motor Co. has been sending knocked-down Escorts from Merseyside to Genk, Belgium, in company container trains.[3] This was preceded by a long period of planning involving a number of departments at Ford (Central Traffic, Materials Handling, Traffic and Transportation, and Engineering), British Rail, Belgian Railways, and H.M. Customs and Excise. The train leaves Halewood early each morning and, travelling via Harwich and Zeebrugge, arrives in Genk 24 hours later. Total time for moving the parts, including loading and unloading, has been reduced to 4 days compared with 10 to 13 for the previous method. Another car firm, Volkswagen, has also reaped the benefits of containerisation.[4] Originally spare parts were sent from Wolfsburg to US dealers in wooden crates, which were difficult to construct and dismantle; even the disposal of the wood was costly. The introduction of containers involved some initial expenses. All parts have to be packed in cardboard boxes, requiring factory space and additional personnel. Heavier cranes and fork-lift trucks had to be purchased to handle the containers at each end of the

[3] See *Freight Management*, December 1968.

[4] See *Container News*, June 1969.

journey. However the savings, on a TDC basis, are considerable. No wooden boxes are required, and no labour to nail, identify and fit strappings to them. The prepacking of parts not only eased the stuffing and unstuffing of containers but also eliminates the need to repack parts overseas before sending them to US dealers. Containers can be loaded on to trailers in a few minutes compared with hours in the case of the small wooden boxes. At the US end no skilled labour is required to open containers, nor is there a crate-disposal problem. Shipping damage has been reduced to zero. About 90 per cent of all Volkswagen parts are now shipped to the US in this way.

It is therefore clear that containerisation can offer considerable savings to exporters (and importers), especially if they are prepared to maintain an interest in the complete door-to-door movement of their consignments. This is itself dependent upon charging delivered prices and a continuing interest on the part of the exporter in all the ramifications of this door-to-door distributive process. In some cases the greatest savings can be achieved only through some reorganisation of the shipper's normal plant or activities; only firms taking a broad view of distributive costs and functions are in a position to evaluate the profitability of such reorganisation. However, many shippers have reservations as regards the future development and long-term viability of containerisation. They are unwilling to commit themselves to a transport method which not only poses current problems but may, in the near future, be superseded by other transport systems. The nature of any highly capitalised technological development is such that it has to succeed completely, in other words, failure is more costly. Overseas and inland transport operators have invested heavily in container systems of distribution and if they carry low load factors then massive deficits can be expected. Therefore on general welfare grounds it is of paramount importance that the organisers of a highly capital-intensive transport system, with each part dependent on the other, correctly assess its long-term viability. The next two sections will discuss the problems and fears of firms as regards containerisation and the competition containerisation is likely to face from other transport modes.

2. *Problems and fears of firms as regards containerisation*

Most shippers accept that containerisation should bring savings in the costs of overseas distribution. Some are worried by certain technical difficulties inherent in the operation of the fully integrated system, while many fear that the savings may not be passed on to them because of their weak bargaining power against the monopolies or cartels that may develop. Without exception, those concerned with overseas trade are troubled by the labour-relations implications of so capital-intensive a transport method as containerisation. Some regard the dockside conflict of interests as irreconcilable, implying that industrial peace can only be achieved at the price of a virtual loss of all containerisation's benefits. This section will consider these problems and fears, while the following section will discuss the alternative transport methods open to shippers now or in the near future.

(*a*) *Legal, documentation and insurance problems.* These are related and apply to all forms of international trade. None is insoluble, given sufficient co-operation between shippers, transport operators and governments. The Economic Development Committee for the Movement of Exports has reported on the excessive number of documents required in international trade.[5] In an illustrative list of documents raised in connection with the shipment of a container load on a short-sea liner, its report identifies thirty documents concerned with export procedures and twenty with import procedures. These covered the whole process from the placing of an order by an importer to his actual receipt of the goods. It appeared anomalous to the Committee that certain documents were only required by some countries and for some forms of transport. In addition, an excessive number of copies of the various forms were often required. A major complaint is that so many of the communications and transactions require pieces of paper, and, further, that so many of the transactions involve physical human activity. The scope of computerised information flow systems, storing data on computer files, is considerable. In 1967 the National Ports Council commissioned EASAMS to study the information requirements of port management and examine systems of data transfer. The researchers discovered a large amount of duplication and recopying of documents and suggested that each port operate a computer linked by Telex and telephone systems to the various port users.[6] With containerisation the need for improved information systems is more than usually powerful. Door-to-door

[5] NEDO, *Through Transport to Europe*, Appendix XVI.
[6] National Ports Council, *Port Progress Report 1969*, page 67.

transit times are so fast that goods often arrive at ports before the documents required by customs officials.

As far as the shipper is concerned, the fewer the documents the better. The particular problem with containerisation is that a high proportion of containers carry consignments from a number of consignors, and even if one shipper completely fills the container the packages may be destined for more than one consignee. However the grouped container load presents most documentation problems, whether the groupage is carried out by a transport operator or a forwarding agent. Some refer to less-than-container load containerisation as a postal system, with the groupage depot (perhaps an I.C.D.) as the post-box and the consignment as the letter. On despatching the consignment to the groupage depot the shipper requires a single document to perform all the necessary functions. It has to be a receipt for the goods, showing the name of the shipper and consignee, the nature and value of the goods, the method of packing, and the destination. In addition it must have the status of an instrument of title, enabling letters of credit to be issued and the subsequent sale and resale of the goods. For such a document to be accepted by the banks as a document of title, it must be equivalent to a 'Received Bill of Lading' and for this to be so the operator must be an agent of the container-service operator. If the latter operated the depot and all the various transport processes the problem could be solved more easily; in fact, the container-shipping consortia, which have their own depot systems, have made considerable progress in reducing documentation. In the case of shippers sending full container loads, the preparation of a manifest would be required; this would perform the various functions listed above as well as serve customs purposes.

Insurance complications arise from the fact that it is possible that many different carriers handle the goods on their journey from consignor to consignee, so that if damage is discovered by the consignee, it is often difficult to determine who has the primary responsibility. The problem is aggravated in the case of containerisation because the container's contents cannot be checked at various stages of the journey; this would defeat the whole object of through transportation. Where liability cannot be determined, the insurers bear the loss, without recourse to those responsible. In such cases containerisation is less attractive to insurers than conventional transport. Some propose that a new legal entity, the 'Container

Operator', be defined by a new international convention. Shippers and their customers would make claims against the container operator, who would have to insure himself against potential liability and would in turn have recourse against the various carriers. As with proposals for a single document for shippers, the ideal situation would be where the container-shipping line organised the whole through-transport process and owned the collection and consolidation depots.

Moves in this direction have been made by the Australian trade consortia, OCL and ACT. Insurance was included in their original proposal for a 'package' door-to-door freight-of-all-kinds rate. To obtain premiums from a single shipping line rather than thousands of shippers certainly reduces the contacts insurers must maintain, but it does not necessarily reduce insurance costs. If the insurance component of the package were an average of all premiums payable by many individual shippers, there would be less incentive for individual shippers to ensure that the goods arrived intact. With individually arranged insurance, each shipper receives the benefit of better packaging and stowage in the form of lower insurance rates. In the case of 'package' insurance, careful shippers subsidise the others. For this reason, OCL/ACT proposals for a combined bill of lading/certificate of insurance failed to obtain the necessary support, although the consortia announced that they intended to pursue the objective of matching through transport with through liability.

(*b*) *Dangers inherent in the market structure*. Fears of a British Rail monopoly developing in Continental trade have already been mentioned. Although British Rail plans to capture a high proportion of this and the Irish trade, and is succeeding in doing so, a large proportion will remain with other carriers: no shipper will be forced, by the lack of an effective alternative, to use British Rail. More than a year after the inauguration of the Harwich–Zeebrugge service, a large number of ports and shipping lines still offer lift-on/lift-off and roll-on/roll-off container services.

For goods identified as container potential, on some deep-sea trade routes there is, or soon will be, no viable alternative to container ships (including ACL type of mixed container and roll-on/roll-off vessels in the definition of container ships). In the short run the remaining conventional general-purpose ships will provide some competition, but as it is unlikely that many more will be built, they will become less important and give way to the specialist vessel. A high proportion of the conventional ships are owned by the various lines which make up the container consortia: ACL plan that their 10 container ships will replace 32 conventional ships that they currently operate. Containers can be carried on conventional ships (currently a high proportion are), enjoying many of the savings a cellular container-ship service offers; but a large cost differential remains. In some cases overland journeys provide, or will provide, competition. Some of the North American railway companies advocate the use of 'land bridges' from Europe to Japan and these will compete with direct container ship sailing to the Far East. Again, this is only of marginal significance and, in any case, at least one container ship journey is involved in any such land bridge.[7]

The scale of capital investment required to equip and operate container services has forced mergers between shipping lines. As long as there is more than one on any route, there is apparent competition. But the incentive for shipping consortia to co-operate is strong, and informal co-operation may gradually lead to an effective monopoly. Australian–UK container trade has gone furthest in this direction: there are only two consortia, and they have co-operated in scheduling services and planning and financing I.C.D.S. If the monopolistic shipping line operates through a number of agents, then there may be some competition from the shipper's point of view. However the essence of through transport is that one operator controls the whole door-to-door transit; hence, in the case of containerisation, the consortia own terminals, inland depots and agency services. A feature of all door-to-door transportation systems is a tendency to squeeze out shipping and forwarding agencies. The I.C.D.S are required by the customs to be open to all users and, although this may seem to encourage forwarding agents, its only practical effect may be that carriers use the depots for containers travelling on different routes from those covered by the shipping interests owning the depot.

Containerisation will result in considerable cost savings which should mean freight-rate reductions; this will not necessarily happen if shipping monopolies are allowed to develop. They have not yet developed on any British trade routes; some routes suffer from excessive rather than too little competition. Shippers' choice has, however, been greatly restricted in Australian trade, and this choice

[7] See *The Times*, May 11, 1967: Australia was reported as being unhappy about the prospect of monopolies developing in her overseas shipping.

will be still further reduced as conventional ships are phased out. For countries such as Australia the monopoly problem is a particularly serious one, for it is very likely that a high proportion of *all* her dry-goods general cargo will be handled by two shipping consortia. These dangers can only be averted by government pressure, and the best way that this can be applied is through the shipping conferences. The US Federal Maritime Commission has taken its anti-monopoly functions particularly seriously in its relation with conferences; some claim that its demand for 'open' conferences has caused the opposite problem, excess capacity, the very problem conferences are organised to eliminate. On the Australian route itself, the Northbound Conference freight rates depend upon a formula worked out jointly by the shipping lines, the shippers' organisations and the Government. The shipping lines' accounts are openly scrutinised before the rates adjustments are agreed upon. The Australian government itself has a direct financial interest in one of the UK–Australian consortia and it has publicly announced that it is trying to induce European and Japanese shipping lines to compete with its own and British ones. Practices such as these could provide a sufficient deterrent to shipping monopolies, although, in the long run, competition will come from other transport modes and concepts, as will be discussed in the next section.

The conferences themselves may prove a restrictive influence on the reduction of freight rates: there have been, and will continue to be, conflicts between members with container ships, who want to cut rates, and those with only conventional vessels, who do not. It has already been shown that there is evidence of excess capacity on the North Atlantic; the downward pressure on prices this exerts threatens the very existence of the conferences there. A dispute has already taken place between Container Marine Lines and the North Atlantic Conference. The former obtained the support of the US Federal Maritime Commission in its attempt to quote through container rates covering the British portion of the journey. The FMC support is surprising, for it has no jurisdiction over the US internal journey, let alone the British portion. In fact, several conferences have approached the FMC to obtain its approval for the changes in US Shipping Law necessary to enable shipping lines to quote through rates.[8] Proposals for a North Atlantic Container Conference have been put to the FMC.[9]

[8] See *Container News*, May 1969. [9] See *The Economist*, August 23, 1969.

(*c*) *Labour relations in the ports.* The economic characteristics of containerisation, especially its capital requirements, are such that fewer ports will be required to handle general cargo, in some cases one port for each trade route. Some shippers fear this more than shipping monopolies, although the rationalisation of ports and shipping lines is related. Those in the more remote regions claim they will be discriminated against, unless the container service operator charges the same rate for all parts of the country, as OCL and ACT do. However, it is when the port monopoly problem is taken with the labour relations implications of containerisation that the problem achieves its true significance. With one port handling all Britain's trade with, for example, Australia, the consequences of strikes, to which the port industry is particularly prone, can be particularly disastrous.

Container berths are capital intensive, giving potentially large savings in labour costs to the owner of the berth. The National Ports Council has made the following estimates, on the basis of actual performance, of berth productivity for different handling systems:[10]

Containers:	20 men can load and unload 6,000 tons in a 10-hour shift
Pallets:	50 men can load and unload 1,800 tons in an 8-hour shift
Conventional:	90 men can load and unload 1,200 tons in an 8-hour shift.

The container figure is equivalent to the OCL/ACT claim that their 1,200–1,300 container ships can be turned round in 48 hours. Unfortunately for the container service operators, their particular rationalisation problem has become linked with a more general one emanating from the Ministry of Labour's acceptance in 1966 of the Devlin Committee's proposal that the docks be completely decasualised and regular work for all men be instituted. Although all sides agree in principle with these proposals, they are difficult to carry out in practice. Liverpool and London docks have been decasualised for about two years, but labour relations problems remain. The docker's main concern has always been job security and he therefore fears the redundancies implicit in port reorganisation and modernisation plans.

[10] *op. cit.*, page 79.

Containerisation, with its capital intensity, provides a particular threat. An additional aggravation is the transfer of some port functions from the docks to inland depots. OCL's first cellular container ship service was to have started from Tilbury, but owing to a major docks dispute there (only partially concerned with containers) the *Encounter Bay* sailed from Rotterdam. When it returned, it again had to be diverted, this time from Southampton to Antwerp (Rotterdam would have been the destination, but *ACT 2* had already been diverted there).[11] The tragedy of the situation is illustrated by the fact that the dockers who refused to unload the OCL/ACT container ships, loaded the same containers destined for Australia on to other ships which carried them to Rotterdam for transhipment on to the same OCL/ACT vessels. ACT claimed that this cost them £5 million a year in extra ships, which had to be retained because of the ban, plus transhipment costs of over £100,000 per voyage.[12] Freight rates have had to be increased to cover this.

The diversion of the *Encounter Bay* on its return voyage was specifically because of the inland consolidation depot problem. Tilbury dockers refused in principle to handle containers from the Orsett depot (five miles from the Tilbury dock complex) which had not been stuffed or unstuffed by registered dock workers. It had already been agreed that registered dock workers were to have preference over others applying for work there. This is reminiscent of the long American dock-strike of late 1968, which was particularly concerned with the threat to job security of groupage taking place outside the docks. The essence of the settlement reached between the International Longshoremen's Association (ILA), the port operators and the shipping lines is that the dockers maintain the right to unload and reload any less-than-container loads arriving from or destined for any point within a radius of 50 miles of a North Atlantic port, if stuffing or unstuffing at that point is not carried out by ILA members. If this is the solution to the current strikes at British container ports, then estimates of container potential must be revised, for a high proportion of cargo will always have to be grouped. The double-handling involved not only raises through costs, but it may deter some shippers from having their consignments consolidated

[11] The Tilbury terminal eventually became operational in June, 1970.

[12] See *The Times*, August 5, 1969. These figures give an estimate of the cost of operating feeder services to Rotterdam, or another Continental port, from where goods would make the deep-sea journeys.

into full container loads; the more often the goods are handled, the greater the risk of damage and loss.

The 1960 and 1966 American West Coast pacts are taken by some as evidence that port productivity deals can be successfully negotiated without undue ill-effects to either party.[13] Under the first 'Modernisation and Mechanisation Agreement' port employers were encouraged to develop new methods of operation, accelerate existing processes of cargo handling, and reduce cargo handling costs. In return they undertook to preserve the existing registered labour force, guarantee 35 hours of pay, and share with them any savings accruing from modernisation. The employers agreed to pay $29 million into a fund to buy out work restrictions. From 1960 to 1965 cargo handled per man hour rose 30 per cent and although some 2,000 men left the registered labour force voluntarily or through natural wastage, many more were added to it. The reason for this was a 32 per cent increase in the total tonnage of cargo. As labour cost per ton fell from $6·26 to $6·16, the deal was a good one from the employers' point of view. A new agreement was negotiated in 1966. The hourly rates were to rise over a period of 5 years, and the retirement age was reduced from 65 to 63, when longshoremen with 25 years of service would receive $13,000. The pension itself was to rise over a 10-year period, with a general review in 1971. All dock work was guaranteed to longshoremen alone. Employers were promised no work stoppage for 5 years, greater flexibility in the use of men, a reduction in gang sizes (there was no longer a provision that two men out of every specified gang size must be skilled). The agreement was accepted in a referendum held by the union, but the pattern of voting by ports is highly significant. Of the major ports, only San Francisco accepted the agreement (by a majority large enough to create the overall majority). It had the largest proportion of its labour force approaching retirement age; the appeal of the agreement to the older dockers is obvious. There is no guarantee that such a 'mechanisation fund' will exist when the younger men face retirement. The age distribution of the labour force is such that retirements will reach a peak during the next five years and it is likely that the younger labour force will only reluctantly accept a deal in 1971 which so defers the benefits of modernisation.

The success of these productivity pacts appears to depend upon two favourable factors: the rapid rise in trade through the ports,

[13] M. D. Kossores, *Monthly Labour Review*, October 1966.

and the age distribution of the labour force. Although the former may itself be a function of the productivity deal, it is unlikely that all ports will negotiate in as favourable circumstances. American ports are currently particularly fortunate in that the Vietnam war has inflated container trade volumes. As the war de-escalates, they will find much more difficulty in maintaining industrial peace.

In the British case it is fortunate that the two ports with the worst labour-relations records, Liverpool and London, may also face the prospect of rising trade. Both have been favoured with a concentration of container and other cargo-handling facilities (see Maps 3.1 and 3.2, pages 54 and 55): Liverpool's Seaforth development is costing £33 millions, while over £20 millions has already been spent at Tilbury. The age distribution of dockers in most British ports favours a deal such as the American West Coast Pact: 30 per cent of port employees are over fifty-five years, compared with 20 per cent for the national labour force. The National Ports Council has estimated[14] the size of the dock labour force in 1972 under the following assumptions:

a. retirement at sixty-five;
b. the proportion of the labour force dying before sixty-five remains constant;
c. the proportion leaving for disciplinary reasons is halved;
d. the same proportion of the labour force is 'ineffective';
e. the proportion leaving for reasons other than (*a*), (*b*) or (*c*) is halved;
f. no further recruitment for five years.

Under these conditions, it was expected that the labour force would fall from about 55,000 in 1968 to a minimum of 35,000 in 1972. The figures varied for different ports: 22,791 to about 18,750 for London, and 11,944 to 6,850 for Liverpool. Therefore London has much the greater severance problem. This natural decrease in the labour force, taken with the concentration of port development, and therefore trade, at Liverpool and London may make productivity agreements easier to negotiate. Such an agreement has been reached in London's Millwall docks where the unions have accepted that there will be no increase in the labour force while cargo volumes rise the expected

[14] *op. cit.*, pages 78–9.

50 per cent, as long as there are no redundancies.[15] But the figures of berth productivity given above imply a more drastic reduction in port labour requirements than natural wastage will bring, and therefore a serious and continuing conflict of interest at all ports with, or planning, container berths. The problem is still more serious at the ports that cannot reasonably expect a major expansion of trade. There are only two factors favouring industrial peace: the work in container berths is agreeable for the men concerned, even if technically more exacting, and the work level is steady and predictable, because all services are scheduled.

It should be noted that although the Tilbury affair may at first sight appear to be a dispute about containerisation and the drastically reduced labour force required to man such berths, it is in reality only part of a more general confrontation concerning pay and conditions in the whole of London's docks. The unions and men want agreements made with all employers, not just with the container consortia. The most susceptible port operation is being used as a lever to obtain a more general review. Therefore the Tilbury affair should necessarily be used as evidence that containerisation causes industrial unrest. It certainly appears to, even in the railways, but it is invariably the expression of a deeper unrest and conflict of interests.[16]

It is interesting to contrast the London and Liverpool situations with that on the Clyde, with its very good industrial relations record since the war and smooth initiation of container services. The Clyde dock labour force is much smaller (about 2,000), but more important is that there is essentially one employer: the Clyde Port Authority employs almost two-thirds of the labour force. This contrasts strongly with the multiplicity of employers in London. Another factor of importance is that there are two unions which in no way compete with each other: one organises the Port of Glasgow, the other Greenock, the site of the container terminal, located some 20 miles from Glasgow. The working conditions in the Clyde docks are superior to those prevailing in many of the London docks and, as a high proportion of the workforce already receive rates of pay comparable to those demanded for container-terminal operatives, there is less chance of intra-union tensions developing. The Clyde situation is perhaps a unique one unlikely to be repeated elsewhere, but it

[15] This refers to the Fred Olsen agreement signed in July 1969.

[16] March 20, 1970: the men of the No. 1 Group voted to accept the employers' pay offer and return to work.

does serve to highlight the problems faced by other ports, and it should, in conclusion, be noted that although the dockers have worked the terminal since the day it opened in the spring of 1968, they have never ratified the agreement with the employers.

3. *Containerisation in competition with other transport modes*

For some years the specially built container ships will face competition from conventional vessels, many of which will carry containers themselves to achieve some of the savings attributable to containerisation. In fact, of some 180 part and full container ships currently operating, about 130 are converted conventional ships.[17] As conventional ships are phased out, competition from other transport modes and concepts will become increasingly important. This will to some extent be based upon the ability of other vessels to carry containers, one of the characteristics of which is the ease of intermodal transfer.

(*a*) *Pallet ships.* This is the one type of vessel which specifically excludes containers. The proponents of palletisation point out that most cargo is shipped in consignments of 1 to 3 tons, or multiples of this, while very few consignments are big enough even for a 20 ft container. 75 per cent of the exports from the West Midlands passing through Liverpool are transported in consignments of less than 10 tons (the approximate weight carried by a 20 ft container).[18] A unit load system should therefore ideally be based on units of 1 to 3 tons. This would cause the least inconvenience to shippers, many of whom use pallets for intra- and inter-factory movement. In addition, palletisation would eliminate much of the cost of grouping so many consignments into full container loads. It is claimed that containerisation is only viable on very high-density routes, and, as has already been seen, this requires considerable port rationalisation and reorganisation; in contrast, pallet ships can operate profitably on lower-density routes with minor port investment. Even the ships themselves require modification rather than replacement. Pallets present some additional advantages in themselves. They are open for damage inspection during the journey, which eases some of the

[17] National Ports Council, *Research and Technical Bulletin*, No. 5, 1969, p. 213.
[18] METRA study for the West Midlands Economic Planning Council, *Movements of Exports to Liverpool*, 1966.

insurance problems concerned with allocating responsibility, as well as presenting an opportunity to reduce the damage itself. Customs clearance is simpler; inspection of the contents of a container can be very time-consuming. Finally, pallets can be quickly cleared from ports: immediately after being unloaded from the ship they can be loaded on to a lorry for delivery to the consignee. There is therefore little doubt that palletisation realises valuable economies, especially on lower-density routes. The impact has been greatest in sections of the UK–Scandinavian trade, where the success of palletisation may permanently exclude cellular container ships.

Another indirect threat to containerisation comes from the standardisation of pallets. Many Continental countries have a standard pallet of about 32 × 42 inches, and there is pressure upon the International Standards Organisation to declare this an international standard. Container loading and unloading times can be greatly reduced by first putting the goods on pallets, but pallets of these particular dimensions do not fit well inside ISO containers; they give up to 30 per cent space wastage. The 44-inch wide pallet favoured in the US, Britain and Japan gives almost 90 per cent stowage.

(*b*) *LASH*. A more revolutionary transport concept is lighter-aboard-ship (LASH). In December 1969 the first such vessel, operated under charter by the Central Gulf Steamship Company, sailed from New Orleans and moored in the Medway. This 43,000-ton, 20-knot vessel cost about £6 millions to build. It carries 73 lighters, each with a capacity of 400 tons, which are lowered overboard by a 500-ton crane while the ship is moored in the estuary concerned. This particular vessel carried 27 barges, each loaded with 370 tons of paper, for the UK and additional cargo for the Continent. The monthly service will become fortnightly when a second vessel makes its maiden voyage in the middle of 1970. The only specially planned LASH ports are in the USA. A 40-acre terminal is being constructed in San Francisco for the use of Pacific Far East Lines. There are two berths, a container storage area, container cranes, and a lighter loading station consisting of a system of canals to carry away the lighters for discharge and loading. The LASH vessel will only dock at ports providing a high proportion of the total load; in other cases, barges will provide the link to ports. It is important for the 'minor' ports to be in sheltered estuaries, such as the Medway; rough water would make the transhipment of barges impossible.

These and other planned LASH vessels have a very flexible capability; they will be able to carry bulk goods, ISO (and other) containers, pallets, and roll-on/roll-off trailers. This very flexibility itself gives LASH vessels a considerable advantage over container ships, although the large number of possible combinations of ports and cargoes will cause serious planning problems for the operators. Apart from the base port, or ports, no specialist terminal handling equipment is required and therefore LASH barges can serve virtually any port. This multiple calling reduces inland distribution costs. LASH lighters will be welcomed by heavily congested ports with no spare land to construct modern container or bulk terminals. For example, in 1970, Prudential Lines intend to operate an American–Mediterranean service calling at, or releasing barges for, some seven Mediterranean ports, many of which currently complain of inadequate facilities and congestion.

These vessels may tend to avoid some of the labour-relations difficulties raised by cellular container ships, for the barges will be stuffed and unstuffed at the dockside, not at distant inland depots. Although LASH ships will themselves be able to carry containers, and therefore achieve some of the savings associated with them, they will carry them with higher unit costs than the ideal cellular container-ship system: door-to-door times will be greater because of the multiple calling and the capital cost component of the unit costs will be higher. However LASH is particularly suitable for services between ports which are linked to their hinterlands by extensive inland waterway systems, for example, New Orleans and Rotterdam; an additional advantage in the case of an American service is that inland waterways are subsidised by the Federal Government. LASH may also be particularly suitable to serve underdeveloped areas with poor port facilities.

(*c*) *Air transport.* Approximately 10 per cent of the value of UK exports travel by air, although the percentage is much higher for some commodities: hides, skins and fur skins 51 per cent, clothing 37 per cent, and scientific instruments 36 per cent.[19] Goods carried by air tend to have one, or both, of two characteristics: perishability (in the widest sense, fashion clothing as well as flowers) and very high value. Even goods which do not normally have these characteristics invariably adopt them temporarily when air transport is

[19] NEDO (EDC for the Movement of Exports), *Exports by Air*, HMSO, 1967.

used: for example, steel sheets urgently required on a building site some distance away. Of the 222,830 tons of airfreight carried by UK airlines in 1967 (excluding vehicle ferries and mail) about 40 per cent was carried on European, 34 per cent on domestic, and 26 per cent on inter-continental routes; the last figure rises to 80 per cent if ton-miles are considered.[20] Freight traffic is growing rapidly: between 1960 and 1965 inter-continental and domestic traffic grew annually on average about 17 per cent, European by 15 per cent. Although this annual growth rate is rising, it is generally expected to fall from a real annual average of 19 per cent in the 1965–70 period to 13 per cent in the 1975–80 period.[21] This growth of airfreight implies competition for container ships at the margin over the life of those in, or soon to enter, service.

Airfreight's advertised advantages are similar to those of surface containerisation. Both offer faster door-to-door transit time, which reduces inventory and insurance costs, and each claims savings in packaging and documentation. The differences between the two are of degree rather than kind, although airfreight rates are much higher. As airfreight door-to-door times are much faster, a potential user must weigh inventory and storage savings against the higher freight rate he must pay. It is significant that the problems that both air and sea transport have in common are that terminals are the weakest links in their total distribution systems. In both cases, containerisation or unitisation offers the opportunity to reduce these delays. In the case of airfreight, to increase the airspeed of aircraft will prove far less productive than a good ground-handling system (plus incentives to shippers and agents to send larger consignments). This can achieve the same improved turnround times as container ships are experiencing.

As with conventional general-cargo shipping, airfreight's terminal problems are rooted in the large number of small consignments each aircraft must carry. Only 1 per cent of BOAC's consignments weigh more than 1,000 kg (about 2,200 lb), although these make up one-third of the total weight carried.[22] This effectively rules out the widespread use of the size of containers carried by ships and railways; in addition the containers themselves waste much of the air-

[20] *Report of the Committee of Enquiry into Civil Air Transport* (Edwards Committee), Appendix 26.

[21] *ibid.*, Appendix 27.

[22] Survey carried out for the Edwards Committee.

craft's valuable payload, in weight and volume. Until recently airlines have been unable to offer adequate financial incentives to encourage the use of pallets, containers and igloos (lightweight containers shaped to fit aircraft), a problem shipping lines are also facing in their relations with Conferences. However, at a recent meeting of the International Air Transport Association (IATA) realistic rebates were agreed upon: for example, a flat rate will be charged for consignments on pallets or igloos travelling across the North Atlantic, with a tonnage rate only applying if a certain weight limit is exceeded.

The limited availability of adequate aircraft has also hindered the development of efficient, door-to-door, unitised systems. Very little cargo is carried in specially designed cargo aircraft, and little more in aircraft exclusively carrying freight (i.e. freighter versions of passenger aircraft). In 1967 almost 75 per cent was carried on passenger services. Airlines have in the past tended to regard freight as a secondary activity, merely to improve poor passenger load factors. About 9 per cent of BEA and 13 per cent of BOAC total revenue came from freight (excluding mail) in 1967–8, but BEA freight ton-miles are rising faster than passenger-miles flown.[23] The growth rate over the past two years is about the same in BOAC's case. More freighter aircraft are now available; for example, the Argosy and freighter versions of the Boeing 707, VC10, DC8 and Vanguard. These aircraft have much greater capacity than those of some years ago, the economies of scale involved reducing rates per capacity ton-mile. The DC4 can carry only 7½ tons, while the DC8F or the Boeing 707–320C can carry up to 50 tons. The Lockheed L-500 is expected to have a payload capacity for a New York–London service of about 150 tons; it could carry fifteen 20 × 8 × 8 ft containers. However the Edwards Committee expected that the proportion of airfreight carried on scheduled inter-continental all-cargo services would actually fall in the 1970s, because of the large increase in freight capacity available on jumbo-jet passenger services.

The carriage of so much cargo on non-specialised aircraft makes dramatic reductions in door-to-door times and costs more difficult to achieve even if the holds of passenger aircraft are specially designed to hold and handle unit loads. Few terminals have adequate freight ground-handling systems; all will face serious problems in handling the passengers and freight carried by the jumbo jets.

[23] See 1967–68 Annual Reports of BOAC and BEA (HMSO).

However the 'topping up' of spare passenger capacity with freight may provide lower overall costs for airlines and lower freight charges (although exactly how to allocate costs to determine profitability does present problems for airlines). If the quantity of freight travelling by air is partially a function of passenger load factors, it is even more than normally difficult to estimate the threat of air to sea transport. The Edwards Committee estimates imply that it will not be a serious threat. However they were basing their estimates on existing practices on the part of shippers and it is very likely that many more could achieve savings from the use of air transport if they were so organised as to be able to evaluate the profitability of alternative distributive systems. If the airlines could promise a shipper that his goods would be at an international airport within twenty-four hours of the shipper receiving an overseas order, that shipper could reduce overseas distributive costs greatly through a complete dependence on air transport. Overseas salesmen could be served direct from the home factory. This is happening in the US, where some electronics firms distribute exclusively by air. Another difficulty in estimating airfreight's potential and competitive power against surface container systems lies in evaluating, quantitatively, the benefits to shippers of faster door-to-door transit. In UK–Continental trade, exporters (and importers) seem conscious of the time savings which modern shipping methods yield. In this particular case, the competition may come from surface containerisation to airfreight rather than the other way round, such has been the improvement in through transport times. If time is so important a factor, airlines may have to concentrate on traffic destined for European customers located outside the forty-eight-hour delivery time radius of rail-sea or road-sea distribution. Fast unit trains provide even stronger competition to domestic airfreight services.

4. *Conclusion*

The advantage to shippers of containerisation are clear: cheaper insurance and packaging derived from the protection afforded by the container, faster transit, and lower freight rates. These can only be fully evaluated by an analysis of all the costs and benefits involved. To this end, it will invariably be to the shipper's long-term advantage to quote delivered prices and concern himself with the whole through-transport process. It will often be the case that some reorganisation of the shipper's plant or marketing strategy is required to take full advantage of containerisation.

Containerisation poses, or aggravates, many problems for shippers. Excessive paperwork is a complaint common to all forms of international transport; all would benefit from a reduction in the number of documents required for international transactions. Two particular problems with containers are the speed with which they move through the system, often faster than the necessary documents, and the fact that such a high proportion of loads are not from one consignor to one consignee. These documentation problems are minimised when the shipping line controls the whole through-transport process and offers one document and a 'package' rate to shippers. There is, however, a conflict here over insurance. If the insurance component of the package rate is the same for all shippers, and there are many shippers, then none has an incentive to reduce his own incidence of damage. This has resulted in the omission of insurance from the package rate.

Many shippers feel that some of the cost savings inherent in containerised transport systems will not be passed on to them because of the formation of monopolies. The high capital costs of container ships, terminals and depots has encouraged the formation of a small number of consortia on some routes. The fear of low-load factors on this expensive equipment may force further mergers, or at least close informal agreements, between shipping lines to keep rates up. This has not yet happened and it can best be avoided by government pressure, supported by the shippers themselves, exerted through the Shipping Conferences.

Another monopoly problem is that of the ports. With only one port handling all, or a large part of, a country's trade along each route, there can be little competition between ports. In such a situation, shippers feel particularly prone to strikes. Labour-relations problems have in fact greatly hindered the initial development of full, door-to-door, cellular container-ship services in this and other countries. Dockers see in containerisation a serious threat to their job security, both because of the capital intensity of terminals and the transfer of their stowage function to inland depots. There are, however, grounds for some optimism: productivity deals have been successfully negotiated; many are voluntarily leaving the docks, and others will be encouraged by the financial inducements offered under voluntary severance schemes; containerisation will eliminate the unsteady and unpredictable work level which is at the root of many dockers' grievances.

In the long run the monopoly threat can best be overcome by competition from new transport concepts or technical changes in existing modes. For some years conventional ships will be the mainstay of many routes and continue to operate services on others. Shippers with commodities wholly unsuitable for containers will still have conventional capacity available. In short-sea trade, competition to British Rail's cellular container-ship services will continue to come from conventional (especially where containers are used) and roll-on/roll-off shipping. Palletisation, which causes least disturbance to existing distributive practices, as well as having positive advantages of its own, will compete with and possibly exclude containerisation on lower density routes. These types of routes may also prove particularly appealing to LASH vessels, which can handle almost any type of cargo and require no elaborate port facilities. LASH is also particularly suitable where there is an extensive inland waterway system at either end of a trade route. In inter-continental trade, airfreight's challenge will become increasingly effective as larger aircraft come into service and more cargo is consolidated into large unit loads. For shorter journeys it is more likely that surface containerisation will reduce airfreight's growth than the other way round.

CHAPTER 5
THE INLAND CONTAINER TRANSPORT SYSTEM

1. *Introduction*

Following the analysis of container transport on overseas services, this and subsequent chapters will consider the operation and competitive position of container transport in inland trade. There are two reasons for this order of treatment: firstly, inland systems were developed after those for sea transport and can be seen as a subsidiary feeder element of the sea transport operation; and secondly, because the inland system is a more marginal operation in Britain, and one faced with direct competition. This is not meant to belittle the importance of inland container transport; indeed the field in which it is competing is much more important, for, whereas 197 million tons were imported and exported from Great Britain in 1967, inland transport handled 1,787 million tons of freight.

The discussion of the operation and use of containers in inland transport has been divided into four sections over Chapters 5 to 8. In this chapter the system of operation of containers in door-to-door transport will be closely examined to establish the characteristics and constraints of the system. Before this is done, however, the scale and nature of the freight market in which container transport is competing will be examined, with a brief review of the published studies of the system. Chapter 6 will then build on this operational framework estimates of cost of operation of the system and consider these in relation to estimates of road haulage costs, thus deriving a concept of the balance of competitive forces between the two modes of transport. Chapter 7 will consider the other cost features of transport use, and assess the balance of these 'indirect costs'[1] to conclude with an assessment of the total competitive position be-

[1] In the following discussion, direct costs of transport are the rates quoted for the haulage operation while indirect costs are the additional costs of transporting the goods—for example packaging, warehousing, etc.

tween road haulage and the inland container-transport system. Finally in Chapter 8 the reality of this competitive balance will be evaluated in the light of operating experience and an estimate made of the potential traffic on the system.

It is necessary, before proceeding with the discussion of this chapter, to sketch the broad features of the transport system and thus clarify some basic, but not widely appreciated, points. Despite the fact that inland transport is an extensive market, container transport can handle only a fraction of the total freight because the system makes use of rail for trunk haul. The transfer capabilities of the container, already seen in the context of shipping services, make possible a door-to-door unit load service using both rail haul for low-cost trunk haulage between large population centres and road haul for collection and delivery.

In this system, road transport operates as a feeder service to and from the rail terminal but it will not use the container for its own direct long-haul operation. Rail uses the container to make the transfer of loads for collection and delivery more efficient and thus improve its door-to-door operation. Road haulage, on the other hand, can already operate from door-to-door, and also has the advantage of a flexible loading configuration, as opposed to one set by the standard dimensions of a container. For many loads of low density the small cubic size of the container does not allow an economic load to be hauled. Consequently inland road transport has not used, and will not use, containers for a door-to-door road haulage operation. Note, however, that this does not exclude road haulage from making a very important contribution to container transport in the collection and delivery of loaded containers to and from rail and sea terminals; nor does it exclude the possibility of the haulier using the railways for the trunk haul of a container load.

The rail container operation, the British Rail freightliner system, uses permanently-coupled, fast-running trains operating scheduled services on the longer-distance trunk routes of the country, with one, or at most two, terminals at each end of the respective routes. In general the system operates as follows: after loading the container at the customer's door the container is carried by road vehicle to a specially equipped terminal where it is transferred to the appropriate train for trunk haul to the destination terminal. Here the delivery process is effected in the reverse order of events. Therefore, in the main part of this chapter where the operation of the freightliner system is considered, the operating features and constraints of the following elements of the system will be discussed, leading to an overall evaluation of its characteristics:

a. the container,
b. the train,
c. the route network,
d. the terminal,
e. the collection and delivery operation,
f. the groupage of less than container consignments.

2. *The inland freight market*

In 1967, 1,787 million tons of goods were transported on inland journeys in Great Britain, or, in potential revenue terms, 73·2 thousand million ton-miles. The absolute total and relative shares of the transport of freight were as shown in Table 5.1. By tonnage, road accounted for 84 per cent of the total traffic, but only 59 per cent of the ton–miles traffic, while for rail traffic these figures were 11 per cent and 19 per cent respectively. These differences in shares are accounted for by the different average length of haul of a freight ton by the two modes of transport (see Table 5.1). Of the remaining four modes, coastal shipping dominated the group, accounting for 21 per cent of all ton-mileage—a share greater than that of rail.[2] Because containers enter into the competition between road and rail, attention will be focused on these two transport forms.

Since 1954, inland freight traffic has increased by 30 per cent with a pattern of growth which has largely responded to the variations in economic prospects. Figure 5.1 illustrates the growth of total inland freight traffic (in ton-miles), and also shows the change of traffic on the two main inland transport modes—road and rail—over the period 1954–67. Note first the three troughs in total freight growth —1957–8, 1962–3, 1966–7—each of which corresponds with a period of economic stringency and lower industrial activity. For road and rail freight two contrary trends are apparent: road transport doubled

[2] Note that the relative importance of coastal shipping in the statistics was altered in the 1967 figures by the estimation of ton-mile figures from the statute miles travelled by sea, instead of from the equivalent inland mileage. In 1966 rail, with a share of ton-mileage of 22 per cent, was of greater importance than coastal shipping—16 per cent.

TABLE 5.1: *Inland freight transport in 1967*

	Tons (millions)	Ton-miles (millions)	Average length of haul of a freight ton
Road	1,500 (84%)	43,000 (59%)	29
Rail	201 (11%)	13,600 (19%)	68
Coastal shipping	52 (3%)	15,500 (21%)	298
Pipelines	27 (2%)	1,000 (1%)	37
Inland waterways	7 (—)	100 (—)	14
Air	0 (—)	10 (—)	0
TOTAL	1,787	73,200	41

Source: *Annual Abstract of Statistics*, 1968, Table 229.

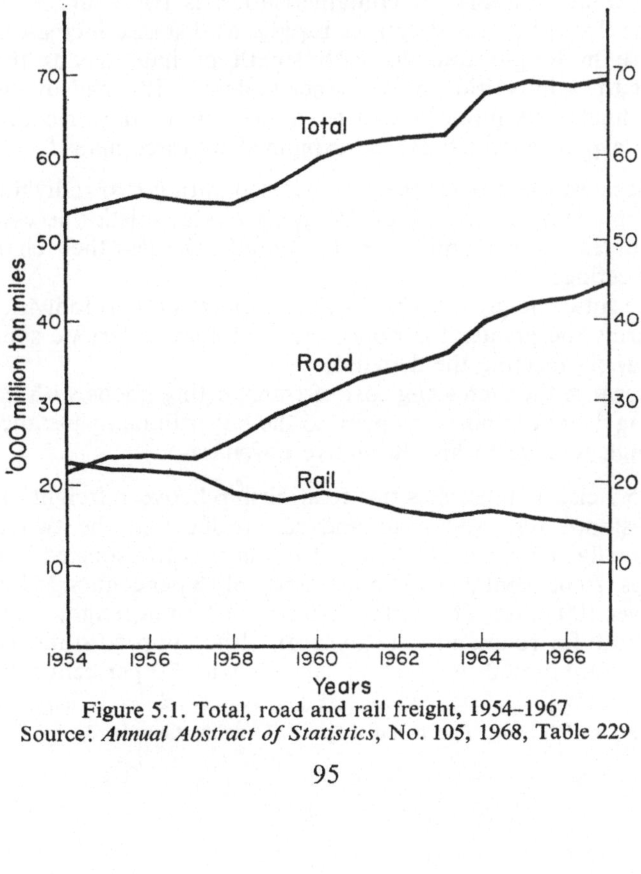

Figure 5.1. Total, road and rail freight, 1954–1967
Source: *Annual Abstract of Statistics*, No. 105, 1968, Table 229

its 1954 ton-mileage volume from 21·1 thousand million ton-miles to 43·0 thousand million ton-miles; while rail lost a third of its 1954 traffic, falling from 21·1 thousand million ton-miles to 13·6 thousand million ton-miles. In part these two divergent patterns of growth are explained by the growth of the industries that road and rail transport served; for example, the decline in coal and steel industry traffic for rail, and the growth of light industry and distribution favouring road transport; in part by an actual shift from rail to road transport over the period.

Containerisation has been regarded as a means to recapture some of rail's declining market. The container market is however limited by length of haul and commodity. Only certain kinds of goods travelling over relatively long distances can be expected to go by rail. The first severe limitation upon the portion of total inland freight traffic suitable for containerisation is based upon the fact that the flow of goods decreases rapidly as distance increases.[3] The decrease in freight tonnage with length of haul means that the weaker the competition of container systems with road on shorter-length hauls, the more limited the market potential of containers. This is a pattern which can be explained by three main factors:

1. because the greater the distance separating two individuals or firms with the demand and supply characteristics necessary to contract a sale and transfer of goods, the less their chance of meeting;
2. because the greater the distance separating two individuals or firms the greater the opportunity of some alternate source of supply meeting the demand;
3. because the increasing cost of transporting goods with increasing distance makes the price to the buyer in many instances too high relative to his alternative purchases.

Table 5.2 clearly illustrates this relationship between freight tonnage and distance for total road and rail traffic and the two modes individually: 67 per cent of freight tonnage is transported less than 25 miles, 25 per cent 25 to 99 miles, and only 8 per cent or 144 million tons over 100 miles. This distance decay pattern of freight movement holds both for road and rail transport, although road traffic is more highly concentrated on short distances—with 70 per cent travelling

[3] For the most comprehensive discussion of the nature of the relationship and examples, see W. Isard, *Location and Space Economy*, Chapter 3.

TABLE 5.2: *The movement of freight over distance—1966*

	Total Road and rail (%)	Road (%)	Rail (%)
25 miles	67	70	45
25–99 miles	25	23	35
100 miles	8	7	20
TOTAL TONS (millions)	1,664	1,450	214

Source: *The Transport of Freight*, page 25.

less than 25 miles—and only 7 per cent over 100 miles; while rail transport is more heavily concentrated on distances over 25 miles with 55 per cent of traffic on these hauls and 20 per cent on hauls over 100 miles.

It will be seen below that the British Rail report, *The Reshaping of British Railways*, and other studies consider that the freightliner system will effectively compete with road transport over distances greater than 100 miles. If this is accepted as the lower limit of the 'long'-distance haulage, and thus as the main limit of the freight market for container transport, the potential market is limited to 8 per cent of total freight tonnage carried on inland routes in Britain—relatively a small share of all inland transport activity but in absolute terms a total of at least 150 million tons in 1968.

Apart from this abstract view of the length of haul presented above, it is important to consider the actual routes of more than 100 miles which have large flows of goods capable of creating the demand necessary for a rail container service. Generally the large-volume routes are those linking the main population centres, and the distribution of these centres in Britain is therefore of crucial importance for the inland container market. Over a third of the population of Great Britain is concentrated in the triangular area defined by the three conurbations of London, Merseyside and West Yorkshire. Within this area the maximum length of route is under 200 miles—for example, London–Leeds 190 miles, and London–Liverpool 197 miles; while many routes between main population centres are about 100 miles—for example, London–Birmingham 110. Outside this area major population centres are isolated and three main centres stand out:

1. South Wales,
2. the North-East,
3. the Scottish Central Belt.

Of these, only the two northern ones have long-distance routes to London and shorter routes to other centres in the population core of Britain.

TABLE 5.3: *Traffic on routes over 100 miles between major population centres* by 50-mile groupings of routes*

Length of route: (miles)	Number of routes	Tonnage (estimated 1968) (thousands)	Tons per route (thousands)
100–149	18	24,000	1,300
150–199	17	12,400	730
200–249	17	6,000	350
250–299	16	2,400	150
300–349	6	500	80
350–399	10	1,300	130
400–449	2	100	50
450–499	3	250	83
over 500	3	50	17
TOTAL	92	47,000	510

Figures in the table are estimates of traffic flow in 1968 from the 1964 road and rail traffic (see footnote 4).

* Major population centres are defined as those with over 400,000 persons.

Table 5.3 indicates the distribution, by 50-mile groupings, of the length of routes over 100 miles which link major population centres—defined here as those with over 400,000 persons. The table also shows the estimated tonnage[4] carried on these respective route

[4] Tonnages on the various routes were estimated by first totalling the flows between urban areas from the appropriate units of the 78-zone subdivision of Britain in the 1966 British Rail survey of road and rail freight, and then extrapolating to 1968 by the growth of all freight traffic between 1964 and 1968.

groupings in 1968, and the average tonnage carried per route. Of prime importance is the comparison of this specialized market (an approximation to that market in which the inland container system will be competitive) with that of the total freight traffic over distances greater than 100 miles. The total tonnage of traffic on the high-volume routes is estimated to be only 47 million tons in 1968, or approximately a third of the total freight transported more than 100 miles in Britain.

Furthermore, routes of 100 to 150 miles comprise 19 per cent of the total number of routes but carry 51 per cent of the traffic moving between major population centres, while those under 200 miles carry more than 75 per cent of the traffic over 100 miles. Routes over 300 miles comprise 26 per cent of the number of routes but only carry 5 per cent of the traffic. As one would expect from the fall of traffic with distance, the tonnage per route declines through the route length groups from 1·3 million tons for 100 to 150 mile routes to 17 thousand tons for routes over 500 miles long. There is only one main break in this pattern in the two groups in the 300 mile range. The 300 to 350 mile group is relatively small on all counts, while the 350 to 400 mile group is relatively large.

The implication for the freight market facing inland container systems is obvious: the bulk of traffic between major centres is concentrated on the 'medium'-distance routes in the 100 to 200 mile range. Unless the freightliner service can compete effectively in this field then its market share will be low indeed.

Some commodity groups will make little use of containers because of their suitability to bulk transport. Coal and petroleum products are two clear examples. Special containers are available, but the use made of container transport by such commodities is limited. By examining the length of haul of commodity groups, those which mainly could use container transport can be defined from the groups which have a large relative or absolute tonnage transported over long distances. First, by seven very broad commodity groupings it is possible to determine which groups make up the greater part of long-distance freight. For both road and rail transport some groups have a relatively high proportion of traffic moving over distances greater than 100 miles (see Table 5.4) while others have a high concentration of traffic on shorter hauls. Both Chemicals and Other Manufacturers' Materials and Unspecified Goods fall into the former category of long-haul traffic with Other Manufacturers'

TABLE 5.4: *Estimated distribution of road and rail freight traffic in Great Britain, 1966 by mode, commodity, and length of haul*

	Road				Rail			
	Tons (millions)	Under 25 miles (%)	25–100 miles (%)	Over 100 miles (%)	Tons (millions)	Under 25 miles (%)	25–100 miles (%)	Over 100 miles (%)
Coal and coke	140	80	17½	2½	130	55	40	10
Petroleum products	70	55	40	5	10	5	70	25
Iron and steel, including ore and scrap	60	55	30	15	40	40	40	20
Foodstuffs	320	60	32½	7½	6	10	55	35
Building minerals and materials	460	80	18½	2½	15	25	30	45
Chemicals	40	55	30	15	6	20	30	50
Other manufacturers' materials and unspecified goods	360	60	30	10	7	15	30	55
TOTAL	1,450	70	23	7	214	45	35	20

Note: Percentages below 10 are rounded to the nearest 2½.
Source: *The Transport of Freight*, page 25.

Materials by far the most important traffic. For Foodstuffs, and Iron and Steel, including ore and scrap, this concentration on hauls over 100 miles is less pronounced, yet still significant. Foodstuffs and Other Manufacturers' Materials make up nearly half of the total traffic over 100 miles, and both were mainly road traffic in 1966. Over distances greater than 100 miles, road traffic carried approximately twelve times the rail tonnage of these commodities. Therefore, the general group Foodstuffs and Other Manufacturers' Materials constitute the main proportion of the 100-mile-plus market, and are currently road traffic.

A second, more detailed examination of commodity types and their haulage distance patterns is possible from the 1962 Road Goods Survey of the Ministry of Transport. Of the 32 commodity groups defined in the Survey, 19 had a relatively large proportion of their movements in hauls greater than 100 miles and these groups accounted for a third of total road freight, or 412·5 million tons. The commodity groups are listed in Table 5.5, and it is clear that the groups are either high-value-per-unit-weight ones, generally manufactures with production economies centralising production, such as processed foods, iron and steel products and electrical machinery; or, less frequently, commodities with localised production patterns, such as lime and fruit and vegetables.

The container, with its large capacity, presents to the container operator the same problem of groupage that trunk hauliers face, and this factor thus divides the market into two main sections: the first the 'direct market' in which full container loads can be carried from door-to-door, and the second the 'indirect market' where customers' consignments must be grouped into container loads if they are to be carried by container transport. The smallest container in inland transport is approximately 500 cubic feet in size and can be loaded up to 8–10 tons, although the average load is approximately 4 tons.

Consignments, on the other hand, are dominated by small size units, as Table 5.6 shows. Over 50 per cent of consignments in a Ministry of Transport survey[5] weighed under 112 lb and only 20 per cent over a ton. By weight criteria alone, only approximately 11 per cent of consignments could be directly containerised. Consequently, of the 8 per cent of freight traffic over distances greater than 100

[5] *Transport for Industry; Summary Report*, Ministry of Transport, 1968. See more detailed comments on this report in Chapter 7 below.

TABLE 5.5: *Commodities with an above average concentration of traffic over 100 miles—1962*

	Tons (millions)
Fresh fruits, vegetables, nuts and flowers	34·4
Meat and poultry	12·3
Fish	3·8
Flour	7·7
Other foods, tobacco	73·1
Oil seeds, nuts and kernels; animal and vegetable oils and fats	2·1
Wood, timber and cork	24·8
Crude and manufactured fertilizers	10·0
Textile fibres and waste	7·5
Other crude materials	17·6
Chemicals and plastic materials	25·8
Lime	6·4
Cement	15·5
Iron and steel finished and semi-finished products	39·9
Non-ferrous metals	9·8
Metal manufactures	20·9
Electrical and non-electrical machinery; transport equipment	44·1
Miscellaneous manufactures	53·9
Furniture removals	2·9
TOTAL	412·5

Source: *Survey of Road Goods Transport*, 1962

miles, only a maximum of 11 per cent of consignments could be door-to-door traffic.

Therefore the inland freight market in which container transport is competing is not as extensive as one might expect. Only approximately 150 million tons or 8 per cent of total freight moves over 100 miles but, with adjustment of this broadly defined market to include those routes with high freight volumes, only a third of this, or approximately 50 million tons, is potential freightliner traffic. Furthermore, at least 75 per cent of this traffic is carried on the medium-distance routes of 100 to 200 miles. The high-value-per-unit-

TABLE 5.6: *Consignment size by weight groups*

Weight	Per cent	Number of consignments in survey
under 22 lb	28	18,130
22–112 lb	23	14,900
112–560 lb	16	10,570
560–1120 lb	6	3,530
1120–2240 lb	7	4,410
1–5 tons	11	6,870
5–7½ tons	2	1,470
7½–10 tons	3	1,920
over 10 tons	4	2,550
TOTAL	100	64,350

Source: *Transport for Industry*, page 32.

weight commodity groups which are capable of bearing long-distance transport costs were, at least up to the development of containers, mainly carried by road transport. Finally, the direct door-to-door market for consignments is limited to only 11 per cent of consignments, and although this comprises approximately 75 per cent of total freight tonnage, one must expect groupage services to be important to the system.

3. *Previous studies of the freightliner system*

While several comprehensive studies have been made during the relatively short history of containerisation in the shipping industry, surveys of the inland container transport field have been confined to market research and investigation of the systems by the railways themselves. Consequently studies of the inland container system bear the implicit assumptions with which the railways work. *The Reshaping of British Railways*, published in 1963, sets the pattern of thinking and this is, in part, developed in more detail in two subsequent reports, published over a year later, *A Study of the Relative*

True Costs of Rail and Road Freight Transport over Trunk Routes (the *True Costs Study*) and *The Development of the Major Railway Trunk Routes* (the *Trunk Routes Report*). Apart from these publications the only other studies are those appearing in general articles reviewing the reports or other aspects of railway operation.

Prior to the publication of the *Reshaping Report*, compiled under the direction of Dr Beeching, the various regions of British Railways had operated and tested several new unit load systems for carrying general merchandise more efficiently.[6] This experience, as well as that of thirty years of carrying their own small wooden containers, was utilised in the *Reshaping Report*, and while the principle of the unit load system was never in doubt a choice had to be made between a container lift-on/lift-off system and a roll-on/roll-off version. The Report favoured a container system which was to be compatible with the ISO container standards then in draft.

In the system two types of route were envisaged: the first, the direct route linking major centres with high volumes of trade; the second, the composite route linking centres with levels of trade not sufficient to justify a full service. To serve this network, approximately 55 depots, or terminals, of three sizes were proposed, the largest handling over 2 million tons of freight per year, an intermediate size handling 0·5 to 2 million tons per year, as well as several small depots handling less than 0·5 million tons per year. It was estimated that by 1973 the system would handle 39–42 million tons of freight, assuming that operation commenced in 1964. Of this traffic, 16 million tons had to be captured from road haulage, 10–12 million tons were existing rail freight, and 3–4 million tons were to come from the parcels traffic of the GPO and the British Railways Sundries Division. As well as this, the potential of traffic from inland destinations to the container ports was realised but not included in the estimate. These estimates were, in the words of the Report, 'judged to be conservative',[7] and the expectation in the *Trunk Routes Report*, that the tonnage could be increased by 50 per cent with the introduction of road pricing, indicates the extent of this thinking in British Railways.

[6] For a more detailed critique of the Report which raised many of the issues discussed here before the system was developed, see A. J. Harrison, 'Investment in Liner Trains', *Bulletin of the Oxford University Institute of Economics and Statistics*, Vol. 26, August 1964, pp. 205–12.

[7] *The Reshaping of British Railways*, p. 142.

In the light of the discussion of the freight market above, it is interesting to examine the features of this predicted tonnage by length of haul. Fifty-two per cent was to be transported over distances of 150 miles or less, 24 per cent on hauls of 151 to 200 miles and the remaining 24 per cent on hauls of over 200 miles. It is estimated here that these figures represent a penetration of the market[8] to the extent shown in Table 5.7, 45 per cent on 100 to 150 mile routes, 60 per cent on 151 to 200 mile routes and 65 per cent on routes of 201 to 300 miles.

TABLE 5.7: *Estimate of market penetration by freightliner services assumed in* Reshaping Report

Route length groups (miles)	Market* tonnage— est. 1973 (million tons)	Tonnage predicted in *Reshaping Report* (million tons)	Percentage of total tonnage predicted	Approx. market penetration (per cent)
70–99	†	7·0	18	†
100–149	30	13·2	34	45
150–199	16	9·5	24	60
200–299	10	6·6	17	65
over 300	3	2·7	7	90
TOTAL	69	39·0	100	

* Market as defined in Table 5.3—that is the traffic on routes over 100 miles between centres of more than 400,000 people.

† Market tonnage and market penetration figure not available.

Map No. 11 in the *Reshaping Report* depicted the network of routes which, it was claimed, would be developed 'to ensure the maximum ton-mileage is moved with the minimum number of trains'.[9] Yet, in the next sentence this is partially contradicted by the statement that 'The greatest part of the mileage will be run on

[8] The 'market' considered here is that defined in Table 5.3 and is all long-distance traffic between centres of 400,000 people and more. The *Reshaping Report* also included some routes between smaller centres and these estimates are therefore inflated. Nevertheless they do indicate the extent of market penetration expected.

[9] The *Reshaping Report*, *op. cit.*, p. 144.

the more extensively operated main lines in the country serving the areas where population and industry are dense',[10] meaning presumably that some trains will carry low volumes and in this way defeat the maximising process called for. The proposals for a series of small terminals handling less than 0·5 million tons and a series of minor routes further illustrates the nature of this contradiction. It would appear that an economic maximising function of maximum traffic and minimum costs per unit had become confused with the traditional maximum tonnage-at-all-costs criteria of the railways.

The operation of the collection and delivery services and control of the road vehicles was to be left to the existing 'A' and 'C' licence operators, and British Railways was to undertake a minimum of this work, as few of their vehicles were capable of carrying containers and also probably because the operation was considered expensive and required considerable organisation and capital. In a simple comparative costing of the road and rail transport operation, in which few of the assumptions were made explicit, the Report considered that 'except for the 10-ton container moved 100 miles, Liner Train costs compared favourably with [i.e. were cheaper than] capacity ton costs for the largest road vehicles at present permitted'.[11] For example, a haul of 100 miles with 75 per cent utilisation of rail capacity and 80 per cent utilisation of road vehicles and with 16-ton rail and road units was considered to have a cost advantage of 2s 9d a ton. On hauls of 200 miles this rail advantage increased to 16s 6d, and at 300 miles to 29s. At that time the largest lorry allowed by the Construction and Use Regulations was one capable of carrying 16 tons, compared to the maximum capacity of 32 tons in 1969.

Finally, the Report envisaged an amazingly fast rate of growth of liner train traffic and it set a tonnage at which the revenue from the system would break even with costs and a surplus be achieved. In the first full year of operation, then expected to be 1965 and actually 1966, tonnage carried was predicted to be 4 million tons; in the second year this was expected to treble to 12 million tons; and finally the capture of the predicted market was to be effected by the fourth year of operation with 30 million tons. Receipts were expected to cover costs in the second year of operation.

The *Reshaping Report* set the pattern of railway thinking and has been a very powerful influence in all transport fields. The adoption

[10] *ibid.*, p. 144. [11] *ibid.*, p. 147.

of 100 miles as the lower limit for the quantity licensing provisions of the 1968 Transport Act is based on this cost reassessment of the break-even point between road and rail transport. Before this the minimum break-even point was conventionally accepted to be approximately 200 miles on favourable routes.

In 1964 the British Railways Board published the *Trunk Routes Report*. Essentially this Report looked ahead to 1984 and assessed the opportunities for reducing the cost of the major trunk routes by reduction of the number of routes as well as total track mileage, and by improved signalling. This Report accepted that the main advantage of Liner Trains lay in longer-distance traffic on routes between major centres, and explicitly stated that rail could not capture all traffic as some was not physically suited to containerisation—essentially the principles of the *Reshaping Report*, but with the explicit realisation that even on long-distance routes some traffic was unsuited to containerisation. Market potential figures were similar to Beeching estimates, with 26 million tons of freight in 1964 doubling with traffic growth to 57 million tons in 1984. Furthermore, the Report accepted the conclusions of the contemporary *True Costs Study* by advocating an increase in road tax charges on road hauliers and stating that if these were implemented the potential 1984 market should be 80 million tons—a 50 per cent increase.

While the *Trunk Routes Report* did anticipate the same volume of traffic on the future network, it envisaged this being carried on a greater number of routes between fewer terminals. Eleven terminals proposed in the *Reshaping Report* were not included in the origin and destination tables of freight movement, and approximately 250 potential routes were identified—compared with 150 in the *Reshaping Report*. The terminals dropped were in small centres which were extremely unlikely to generate sufficient traffic for the capacity of five full—or part—trains per week.

The basis for the British Rail view of the comparative costs of road and rail transport was more fully developed in the submission of the Board to the Geddes Committee on Road Licensing. The study investigated the full costs of the road and rail systems including those for use of track, a cost incurred by hauliers but one which British Rail has always held was not fully borne by the hauliers themselves. The study elucidated many points which were only briefly mentioned or were implicitly assumed in the *Reshaping Report*. The findings concerning the length of haul on which rail costs equalled those of road were similar to those of the *Reshaping Report* and were assessed as at least as low as 100 miles and probably nearer 70 miles, even for competition between rail containers and a 16-ton road vehicle operating on motorway routes; whereas a 16-ton lorry on motorway routes offered cheaper transport up to nearly 300 miles compared with the conventional rail transport. This meant that the railways saw the container operation conferring on them a competitive cost advantage on routes over 100 miles, thus opening to them a field in which large tonnages were involved.

The study is difficult to evaluate fully but some of the assumptions, explicit and implicit, seem unrealistic. It was assumed, for example, that for road 'collection and delivery (using the trunk vehicle) is performed under the same conditions and for the same terminal distance as in the case of transit by rail'.[12] From this assumption the equality of collection and delivery costs of a load by both rail and road was derived. In the discussion below, in Chapter 6, the validity of this assumption and its importance will be considered. It would also appear that while the railways made an accurate costing of the direct costs of the operation to them, the overhead costs of the system were underestimated in a similar manner to other work.[13] It is always difficult, if not impossible, to anticipate future technological change. However, although the nature of such changes is unknown, it is better to base predictive studies upon the assumption that some technical change will occur in certain areas. The British Rail study unfortunately makes the implicit assumption that there will be no future technological change.

All the studies left many questions unanswered as well as suffering from the general faults of assuming road technology constant (implicitly), and biasing conclusions and assumptions in favour of rail operation. Unfortunately no other comprehensive studies have been published and one must therefore attempt to evaluate the system as it operates and then relate this to its competitive position.

4. *Physical characteristics of the freightliner system*

(*a*) *The container*. As in overseas transport the container is the key

[12] See, 'The True Costs of Road and Rail Trunk Haulage', *Modern Railways*, August 1966.

[13] See a forthcoming publication by A. W. J. Thomson on nationalised transport.

unit in the inland system for it allows, for the first time, the efficient transfer of a maximum-size road-haulage load between rail and road vehicles. The function of the container is the same as that in overseas trade—it standardises the shape of a load for movement through a transport system of more than one vehicle. It makes the transfer of a load at transport interfaces quick and efficient through the use of capital-intensive handling equipment and standardised techniques.

What, then, are the features of the structure and use of the container in inland transport? First, the range of containers and the handling equipment for them are compatible with the ISO standards, with some special containers for certain inland trades. The container lengths define three main sizes, 10 ft, 20 ft and 30 ft, with some old 27 ft containers which were designed for a now-superseded set of road Construction and Use Regulations (see Table 5.8). Within these sizes there are two series of containers:

1. The covered containers, nine types in all, with an 8 × 8 ft end section and top corner lift arrangements. All of these have end doors with the exception of one special type, the 'M', with a curtain side. All except the 'C' type, a 27 ft one, conform to ISO standard dimensions;
2. The open container with no roof, detachable sides and only 3 ft 7 inch in height does not comply with ISO standards. Open containers require bottom lift by the crane grab system and this complicates the crane design. They are designed, however, for certain products; for example, one type is specially constructed with hardwood, as opposed to plywood floors for carrying steel.

It is notable that although the distribution of consignment sizes is markedly skewed towards the low weights as shown in Table 5.6, the container sizes used are skewed towards the large sizes (see Table 5.9). Fifty-one per cent of containers and 65 per cent of container volume on routes out of Glasgow are in 30 ft containers which are capable of being loaded to 20 tons and on average carry approximately 12 tons; whereas only 30 per cent of consignments over 4 tons would adequately fill a 30 ft container. Note that on average the container is loaded to approximately 4 tons per 10 ft length.

This pattern of use is extremely interesting. It was debated in the trade journals before the inception of services on the sea routes that the 20 ft unit would be the most commonly used container size and

TABLE 5.8: *Types of British Rail containers and their rated capacities*

	Size	Type	Rated load capacity
Series I	10 ft	'A'	7 tons 10 cwt.
Covered containers	10 ft	'C'	8 tons 15 cwt.
8 ft × 8 ft end-section	20 ft	'B'	15 tons
(approximate)	20 ft	'L'	17 tons 17 cwt.
	27 ft	'C'	20 tons
	30 ft	'D'	20 tons
	30 ft	'M'	20 tons
	30 ft	'N'	22 tons 19 cwt.
	20 ft	'P'*	16 tons 10 cwt.
Series II	20 ft	'H'	15 tons
Open containers	27 ft	'J'	20 tons
8 ft × 3 ft end-section	30 ft	'K'	20 tons
(approximate)			

* 'P' is a special insulated container for refrigerated freight.

TABLE 5.9: *The use of container sizes on the Glasgow routes*

	Percentage of containers	Percentage of container volume
10 ft	9	4
20 ft	37	31
30 ft	51	65

Source: *Freightliner Survey.*[14]

that 30 ft and 40 ft units would be too large because shippers would find the 20 ft container easier to fill, given the existing pattern of size of consignments. The point is still being debated but this observation of the demand for containers indicates that firms favour, where possible, the economies offered by the larger size unit, and these will be evaluated below, in Chapter 6.

[14] Based on a survey of traffic through the Glasgow (Gushetfaulds) terminal, September 1968.

For users this introduces the first indivisibility in the system. If a firm cannot fill a container itself, then it cannot hire the service, and the decision as to which mode to use is in the hands of a groupage agency to which the firm must go. This is a feature of the system which should not preclude traffic, but it does shift the decision for the method of trunk movement from the consignor to the groupage agency.

(*b*) *Trains.* To the railway freight operation the freightliner train is a revolutionary concept, with its permanent coupling, high-speed running, and scheduled services. Because trains are permanently coupled and generally operate on a single high-volume route between only two terminals, the marshalling of individual wagons has been obviated and the door-to-door service speeded up. Instead, trains are marshalled at the terminals by using the flexibility built into the system whereby a lorry load, but not its running gear, can be transferred from a road vehicle to the appropriate train. In some instances transfer is from one train to another where there is not a direct freightliner route between the appropriate terminals and a 'linked' route is provided. As a result of the direct routing of trains and high speeds the system can offer next-day delivery between any two centres served by a direct route.

The train introduces the second indivisibility in the freightliner system—the capacity of a service in average day-to-day use. For a service to be established it must promise sufficient traffic to cover the costs of the service, that is to break even. Since the standard train carries ninety 10 ft modules, or any combination of the 10 ft, 20 ft and 30 ft container lengths within this limit, the tonnage volume of this average loading capacity is approximately 350 tons on a one-way service,[15] assuming the average loading of containers to be approximately 4 tons per 10 ft module. In terms of weekly flow, the standard train on a five-days-a-week service has a capacity of 87,500 tons per year in one direction and 175,000 tons per year in both directions on the route. Fragmentary evidence[16] suggests that the operation breaks

[15] Note that average loading capacity is a trainload of containers which are carrying an average of 4 tons per 10-ft length. This is distinct from the maximum possible loading of a train container where each container could be loaded to 8 tons per 10-ft length.

[16] Report in the *Financial Times*, May 25, 1969, stated that only four routes in the network were covering costs then, and it was noted in the data available to the writers that there were only four routes with over 70 per cent loadings.

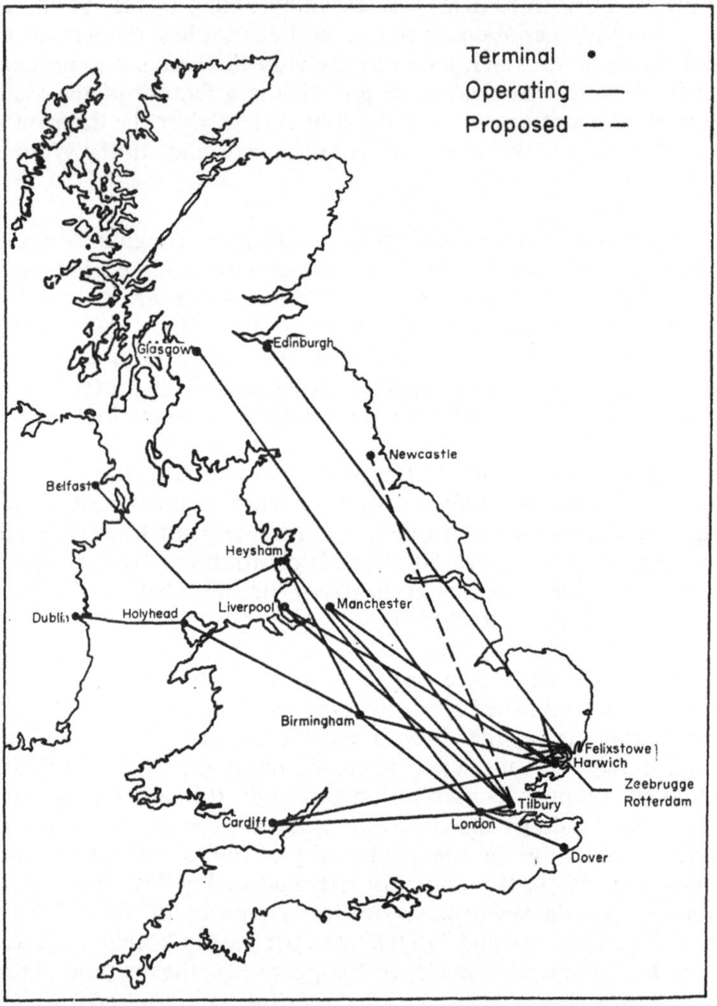

Map 5.1. Freightliner feeder service to ports, March 1969

even at about 70 per cent capacity—that is, with balanced flows and 70 per cent full in each direction; or full one way and only 40 per cent full on return. To accept this as an assumption appears realistic

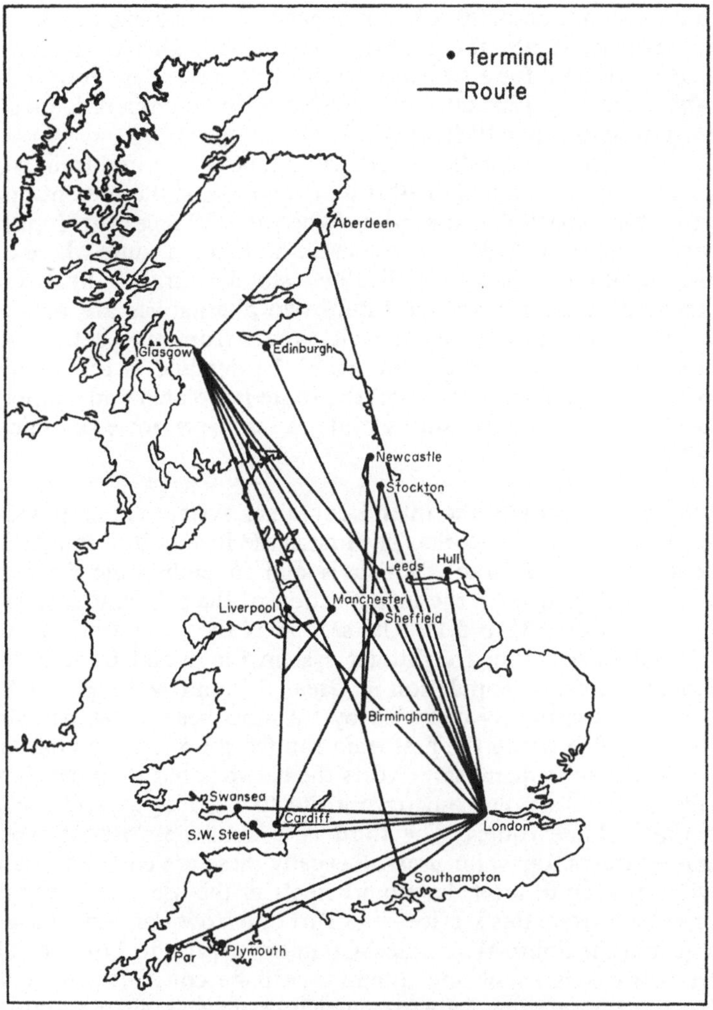

Map 5.2. The freightliner network, March 1969

in the light of break-even capacities on shipping services where it has been variously estimated at about 50 per cent. However, on inland routes with direct competition from road haulage and the system operating on routes of a length which only marginally favour rail, then an assumption of 70 per cent capacity to break even appears to be a realistic, if not favourable, one for rail. Hence, a minimal tonnage threshold for a two-way service with a standard train would be approximately 120,000 tons per year with containers loaded on average to 4 tons per 10 ft length.

On a service where extra transport volume is required train capacity can be increased to 120 10 ft units and this is the present upper limit of the capacity of a service. When this is exceeded duplicate services must be provided. On the other hand, on a route where only a fraction of the capacity supplied by a standard train is likely to be in demand in the foreseeable future two alternatives are possible: either two below break-even capacity routes from one centre can be combined into one viable route or, if the demand is too small to provide a break-even service and the route is isolated and cannot be associated with a similar status route, a service is not economically feasible.

(*c*) *Routes*. Essentially the inland container system is composed of three distinct route networks. The first is the British Rail freightliner system for external trade, which is still in embryonic form but rapidly developing with the inauguration of the full container shipping services (see Map 5.1). The second is the comparatively well developed British Rail freightliner system for inland trade linking the main centres of population in Great Britain (see Map 5.2). The inland routes currently operated by BR have been developed since November 1965, when the first train ran from London to Glasgow, and over the subsequent three years the network has been developed on the basis of a policy giving priority to the longest and highest potential volume routes. The third is a small network of special container trains for major users. Basically these are company trains. Services are run to meet the requirements of the users and only two examples illustrate this service—the Tartan Arrow London–Glasgow service and the South Wales Steel Company service to London. This latter network is small and attention will be concentrated on the former two freightliner networks which operate as distinct units.

When the inland trade section is fully developed it will continue to be the main part of the network conveying up to 40 million tons of freight annually in the mid-seventies compared with perhaps 5 million tons on the external trade services to the ports.[17] The two

[17] Estimates here are based on those of the *Reshaping Report*.

networks are separate both for services and for the use of terminal facilities. This is because the external trade flows pass through customs checks in the I.C.D.s and are in bond in transit to and from the ports, and also because the routes operate from population centres to ports—a different pattern from that of the inland freightliner.

Several features of the routes are important for an understanding of the nature of the freightliner service. One feature which is apparent in Maps 5.1 and 5.2 and has been mentioned above is that many of the routes are units in themselves and operate for end-to-end journeys with no intermediate stops. Numerous examples can be cited: London–Glasgow, London–Edinburgh, Aberdeen–Glasgow, and Cardiff–Manchester. However, where freight volumes are not sufficient to justify a complete service between one centre and another, two services from a centre can be combined and the train split at one destination and terminated at the other. The Glasgow services to Leeds and Sheffield are operated in this manner. Second, the routes link only major centres of population because of the necessity to assure train loads on a service frequency of five days a week. Third, transfer between routes is possible at selected terminals for selected 'linked' routes. This type of service is used to advantage where a centre cannot generate sufficient traffic for a number of its own linkages with centres other than a dominant one, which is generally London. In such instances traffic to the other terminals is routed through a larger centre. For example, in the case of Aberdeen traffic to centres other than London, containers are transferred at Glasgow (Gushetfaulds) for Birmingham, Manchester, Liverpool, Sheffield, Leeds and Cardiff. In a similar manner, a Glasgow–Cardiff service cannot be justified as a direct service but is offered as a linked service via Manchester or Liverpool.

Some overall parameters of the freightliner inland network are worthy of note. In February 1969[18] there were seventeen inland trade terminals operating, and these shared between them thirty-two two-way services. Because of the end-to-end pattern of journeys in the network the terminals are clearly defined nodes with services radiating from and focusing on them with a minimum of through movement, even at transfer terminals. In the Glasgow terminal, which handles the Aberdeen transfer traffic to centres other than

[18] The system was complete to the end of Stage II of the three-stage development programme at the end of 1969. Only one terminal was added to the system in 1969 as well as several new routes.

London, only 3 per cent is transfer traffic. London dominates the network with four freightliner terminals to handle the services on fourteen routes. One is at York Way on the north side of the city, one at Willesden to the west, one at Stratford to the east and one at King's Cross. Other terminals handle between one and six routes on a five-times-a-week two-way service frequency, and, London apart, Glasgow, Birmingham and Manchester have the highest number of services (see Table 5.10). The population of the cities and conurbations with terminals is approximately 500,000 or more, and those centres with populations below this size have special traffics which favour larger goods flows than would be predicted from population size alone—for example, fish traffic from Hull and fish and meat traffic from Aberdeen.

The characteristics of the route network are best measured by the standardised indices of graph theory as summarised by Kansky.[19]

TABLE 5.10: *Freightliner terminals and services—February 1969*

Population centre	Services operated*	Estimate of population in centre (thousands)
London	19	8,200
Glasgow	8	1,800
Birmingham	5	2,300
Liverpool	4	1,400
Cardiff	4	650
Manchester	4	2,500
Newcastle	4	1,000
Sheffield	3	800
Stockton	3	900
Leeds	2	850
Southampton	2	450
Aberdeen	2	450
Hull	2	400
Edinburgh	2	500
Swansea	1	170
Par	1	1
Plymouth	1	250

* Excluding those to the ports for external trade.

[19] See K. J. Kansky, *Structure of Transportation Networks*, especially pp. 11–31.

Many, it will be observed, are formal statements of accepted average measures.

The first is a simple measure of the number of routes per freightliner centre and in graph theory is a measure of the connectivity of the graph, attention being focused on the nodes of the network. This is identified as the beta index (β).

$\beta = e/v$, where e = number of edges in the graph—or routes in this instance
and v = number of vertices—or centres.

For the inland network $\beta = 3{\cdot}94$, or approximately four routes per population centre served.

A more comprehensive measure of the connectivity of the network is the alpha index (α) defined as:

$$\alpha = \frac{e-v+p}{\frac{v-(v-1)-(v-1)}{2}} \times 100\%,$$

where e and v are as defined above
and p = the number of isolated sub-graphs.

The possible values rangefrom 0 per cent to 100 per cent with a 0 per cent value indicating no connectivity in the graph and 100 per cent perfect connectivity with each node connected to every other node. For the inland freightliner network the value is low—10 per cent—indicating that less than 10 per cent of all the possible routes between centres have been taken up.

Other measures assess averages. The eta (η) is simply the average length of route and is defined as:

$\eta = M/e$, where M = total mileage of network and e is as defined above.

For the inland freightliner system this is 239 miles, much longer than the average length of haul of a ton of rail freight which is 70 miles, or of road freight, 30 miles. The theta index (θ) is a statement of the average throughput of a terminal and defined as:

$\theta = T/v$, where T = total goods flows on the network and v is as defined above.

For the inland freightliner system in early 1969 this was 29,000 tons, a relatively low value compared with the throughput of a conventional rail freight terminal in 1967 of approximately 30,000 tons. Finally, the iota index (ι) gives a measure of the density of traffic flow on the network and is the average distance per ton or alternatively if the reciprocal is taken the average freight carried per mile.

$\iota = M/w$ – the average distance per ton
or M/T – the average freight carried per mile,
where M = the total mileage
w = the observed number of vertices weighted by function
T = total traffic flow.

The average distance travelled per ton, for a four-week period in February 1969, was 0·013 miles and the average tons of freight per mile was 78 tons.

TABLE 5.11: *Routes operating and planned, and predicted tonnages in 1984, by 50-mile length groups*

Route length	Number of routes planned in *Reshaping Report**	Number of routes planned in *Trunk Routes Report*†	Number of routes operating	Tonnages predicted in 1984‡ (million tons)
0–49	—	—	—	—
50–99	2	3	1	0·5
100–149	35	63	3	15
150–199	42	68	9	20
200–249	29	45	8	10
250–299	25	35	8	5
300–349	10	16	2	1
350–399	9	13	6	3
400–449	6	6	1	0·5
450–499	4	4	2	1
500–549	—	2	—	—
TOTAL	162	255	40	56

* Estimated from Map No. 11, *Reshaping Report*.
† Estimated from *Trunk Routes Report* Appendices.
‡ *Trunk Routes Report*.

These summary measures of the network in early 1969 describe one with a limited number of linkages and low load factors. The α and θ indices most clearly highlight the position.

On the plans of the *Trunk Routes Report* the network is only partially completed—in 1969, 17 of the terminals were operating and 64 of approximately 250 routes. By the end of 1969, Stage II was completed and on the original plan only Stage III remains. Table 5.11 summarises, in 50-mile length groups, the distribution of route lengths for both existing (1969) and planned ones. The most interesting point in this table is the higher proportion of planned long-distance routes that have been developed. For example, 10 per cent of the routes under 200 miles listed in the *Trunk Routes Report* were developed by early 1969, whereas 31 per cent of those over 200 miles were operating.

If all planned routes were developed the average length of route would fall from 240 miles to approximately 210 miles. Also the routes already established were predicted, in the *Trunk Routes Report*, to have an average of 640,000 tons of freight per route in 1984, while those planned but not yet developed have an average potential of only 150,000 tons of freight in 1984. So not only are those planned but undeveloped routes concentrated on shorter distances but also they are expected to present much smaller markets.

(*d*) *Terminals.* In the freightliner system the terminal is of key importance for it is the transport interface between two modes of transport and a node in the network where goods flows are made up into train lots for high-volume medium- to long-distance rail haul. Effective operation of the terminal is dependent upon quick, low-cost transfer of containers from the collection and delivery road vehicles to the rail flats and vice versa. Structurally the terminal is simple. Road and rail vehicles must be able to be placed parallel with the distance separating them capable of being spanned by a straddle or gantry-type crane. The rail track under the crane or cranes must be sufficient to accommodate the full complement of trains handled in the terminal each day. This combination of factors, which can be generalised as the terminal throughput capacity, determines whether the crane is to be a straddle or more complex gantry type. Generally cranes are provided to cover a minimum of three rail tracks, and one or two roadway tracks. This core of the terminal is backed up by a large paved area for road vehicle movement and administration offices. The terminals are equipped for the International Standards method of handling containers, that is, top-corner lifting. Originally, lifting was to be solely by a bottom-lift system to facilitate the handling of the open-type containers; now both methods are possible.

Above, in section (b), the threshold requirement for a train service was estimated to be 120,000 tons per annum and whether this minimal requirement of a service is sufficient to justify a terminal is a separate consideration. It is essential that a terminal should have traffic equivalent to the thresholds of two complete services, because this would generate sufficient traffic to utilise the cranes, as the calculations below indicate. Hence, the threshold necessary to justify a terminal would be of the order of 240,000 tons annually, and if this is the minimum possible then it should be generated on a maximum of only two services for the services operated to be viable in themselves. This means a movement of 240 10 ft modules through the terminal per day, and on the basis of the present composition of container flows by container size this would be approximately 95 containers per day, based on the data presented in Table 5.8 above. This throughput can be handled by a small-size terminal with simple straddle-crane units, since each container movement from rail to road and vice versa should only take a maximum of three minutes, thus meaning only 10 crane-hours per work day—a low utilisation level for a straddle crane, or pair of cranes. It is expected that, on a viable route, container movement should rise to approximately 80 per cent of capacity, meaning that the throughput of a terminal should be 280,000 tons per year, or approximately 110 containers per day. From an examination of Table 5.9 above a population centre must have approximately half a million persons before it can generate sufficient traffic to justify a terminal.

Above this threshold tonnage required for a terminal, it would seem that the terminal should not impose problems of indivisibility on the system. Crane capacity can be varied to suit the throughput of a terminal, and the supply of collection and delivery vehicles can be varied to suit the demand which is relatively stable over time and not subject to wide fluctuations.

Although it was noted above that the level of utilisation of the cranes is relatively low and therefore results in considerable labour and capital costs being incurred in container handling, the nature of the system appears to preclude a more intensive use of the resources.

The reason for this is the retention of the train of flat wagons on the tracks under the cranes during the day as the holding point for the containers. Note the contrast with the shipping operation. Here the trunk vehicle is unloaded and loaded directly to and from extensive container parks, and not held while collection and delivery units are assembled. Several factors control this method of operation in shipping. Firstly the high capital cost of the ship must be used as effectively as possible, thus making fast ship turnround the most important aspect of the terminal operation. Therefore, containers must be assembled and, if necessary, placed in order, before the ship arrives. Secondly the holding time this operation involves is not a critical factor in a comparatively long-transit operation, or one where competing modes are faced with extensive loading/unloading times. In contrast the rail flat wagons are not a major capital item—in fact they cost little more than a container—and also the rail system is in direct competition with road transport on delivery times and cost. Consequently, despite the relative low use of the terminal resources, holding of containers on trains minimises handling costs and is therefore the more acceptable alternative.

The mode of operation is, therefore, that a train arrives at a terminal in the early morning and is unloaded directly onto delivery vehicles during the morning. It then awaits the return of the loaded containers which starts in the early afternoon and reaches a peak just prior to the closing time of the train in the late afternoon. When services are more fully developed with day-time services, as well as the overnight ones, more efficient operation will be possible, but the basic problem will not be completely solved as fewer day-time services will be offered. This mode of operation is essential to the system, but it does incur relatively heavy costs.

Finally, the location of terminals needs description and explanation. It has been an element of policy to site the terminals as centrally as possible in the city or conurbation being served. British Rail has accepted the broad constraints of avaliable railway land and selected a site as close as possible to the city centre. Gushetfaulds in Glasgow is an example, being located three-quarters of a mile from the city centre and central to the conurbation. It is clear that the determining factor of location is different to that of the I.C.D. rail terminal which is dealing with overseas trade. Since the freightliner terminal is drawing the bulk of its traffic from a relatively short distance for a relatively short trunk haul, it is considered by British Rail that it should be sited centrally to this potential market for its services. The I.C.D. terminal for overseas trade, on the other hand, is serving export and import traffic which, per unit of employment, is generated in smaller volumes. Consequently longer collection and delivery distances must be expected to draw in sufficient traffic to justify a terminal, and provide regular and frequent flows of grouped-up loads to the destinations served. These distances are acceptable in the light of very long 'trunk' hauls. Hence, whereas the Gushetfaulds freightliner terminal is intended to serve the West Central Scotland area, the Gartsherrie I.C.D., to the east of Glasgow, is designed to service central Scotland.

(*e*) *Collection and delivery operation.* An integral part of a freightliner terminal is a collection and delivery lorry fleet which ideally should be equipped with articulated vehicles and skeletal trailers and the standardised twist-lock method of securing the container to the trailer flat. Originally it was intended that commercial hauliers and 'C' licence owners should operate the bulk of collection and delivery trips, but this was opposed by the railway unions who wanted only railway operation of the collection and delivery operation. The result was an agreement to split the operation sixty–forty, with 60 per cent of collection and delivery work being done by the railway vehicle fleet and railway employees. The dimensions of these costs will be evaluated below in Chapter 6, where the operating features of the system which give rise to these costs will be considered.

The key feature of collection and delivery operation is the marked peak of activity before the departure, and to a lesser extent, after the arrival of the trains. The main reason for this problem is the demand by customers for morning delivery and afternoon despatch. This results in queueing and delays and throws the burden of work in the terminal on to a limited number of hours of the day. With some effect the peak is spread by staggering the departure times of trains in the evening.

The organisation of collection and delivery is the most critical single element in the freightliner system, for it creates a set of high fixed costs for the operation. The articulated lorry capable of carrying loaded containers is expensive to operate and, in terms of actual haulage performed, inefficiently used. This, therefore, creates a series of costs which are not dependent upon distance driven, to any significant extent, but are largely dependent upon the efficiency of the consignors and consignees in loading and unloading respectively. Several factors contribute to this: lack of loading bays, loading bays not equipped for efficient unloading of containers, and the peaks in collection and deliveries from factories and warehouses in the mid-to-late morning and mid-to-late afternoon. Even the charging of demurrage cannot overcome the main problem of the utilisation of an expensive heavy-duty road vehicle, namely that, used in collection and delivery work, the greater part of its day is spent standing queueing or loading and unloading.

Furthermore, it is difficult to see how major improvements in utilisation can be achieved, given the present scheduling of vehicles: load early morning; travel to consignee—a distance averaging seven miles and taking a half hour; queue for unloading; unload—for a full 30 ft container this could be up to two hours or as low as 20–30 minutes; then return to the depot at mid-day, or go on to a consignor for afternoon loading. In the afternoon pick up a load for evening consignment with similar time periods and delays. Such a schedule for collection and delivery is a reasonable average and one difficult to make major improvements on, but it means that a vehicle of 22 tons payload capacity is averaging approximately 30 miles a day and is being very poorly utilised. It is an operation essential to the system but one which does not contribute to the actual trunk haulage process; it is, rather, a grouping operation making up train loads which the railways can then operate efficiently on medium- to long-distance hauls.

Note also the implications of the rail container operation for road traffic. It is common to hear the case made for the transference of traffic to rail on the grounds that such a development will ease road congestion. The summary in Chapter 8 will show that the shift to rail will be limited in extent while the effect will not be uniformly spread over the whole road system. It is true that freightliner gains from road haulage do mean reductions in the movement of lorries on trunk routes, although these will be marginal savings of long-distance trunk movements and total road freight traffic will continue to grow. Meanwhile, within the urban areas in which terminals are located it is likely that freight transferred to rail could generate greater road traffic movements for the same volume of freight. This is seen to stem from the movement patterns of collection and delivery lorries outlined above. Consequently it is difficult to see any significant saving possible in road traffic and particularly in urban areas where congestion is greatest. In addition to this is the point that at the present time the most striking improvements in road-ways are taking place outside urban areas and relatively few projects are in the pipeline for urban road improvement on any notable scale.

(*f*) *Groupage depots.* The use of the container, with its minimum capacity of 500 cubic feet, necessitates the integration of groupage depots into the freightliner system, for 90 per cent of consignments travelling over 100 miles are in lot sizes below that which will efficiently utilise the smallest container, let alone the larger 20 ft and 30 ft units. This problem is certain to be a continuing one in the system, for small consignments will continue to be an important proportion of the goods flows and must be catered for, despite the aggregation of firm units and the building up of loads into container lot sizes to take advantage of the economies of container transport by firms. Essentially, two groupage systems are operated at present. The first is a sophisticated operation on the London–Glasgow route by the Tartan Arrow organisation and may be described as a groupage terminal integrated with a special liner-train service hired by the organisation. The service operates between rail siding terminals in London and Glasgow and groups small consignments for direct loading into the rail containers. Large part container loads can be loaded direct into a container delivered by road at the customer's door; small parcel-size consignments are collected and delivered by a van service. The second system utilises existing road and rail groupage terminals. Generally these terminals are separately located from the freightliner terminal and linked to it by lorry collection and delivery runs. In most instances the terminals have been only recently relocated and rebuilt to serve conventional road and rail services but not container services.

Each method has its own advantages and the former system is applicable to the high-volume flow routes where a daily train load between two terminals can be justified. The organisation of less than train-load flows on a series of routes would introduce the problems of train marshalling and the best solution is a separate groupage terminal, using the flexibility of the road vehicle in conjunction with the flexibility of the freightliner terminal for the marshalling of train loads. Note that by 'separate' is meant a separate functional unit. The groupage building itself should be adjacent to the freightliner terminal. Such an operation would preserve the advantages of the specialised operation of groupage and train assembly, and at the same time minimise the need for large and expensive road units to link the two. Special light trailers could be used to convey the containers from the freightliner terminal to the adjacent groupage terminal, preferably on private roadways, and a minimum number of tractor units could be used to operate a shuttle service. Unfortunately this type of operation will take time to develop because of the recent investment in groupage facilities and individual interests.

5. *Conclusion*

The system of inland container transport is made up of six key units which have been defined arbitrarily: the container, the train, the route, the terminal, the collection and delivery operation, and the groupage terminal. An understanding of each, and its operation in the system, is essential to an understanding of the system and the constraints imposed by several of the units have been seen to be critical. The container is important in its role of the unit of movement facilitating cheap and efficient flow through the system. Since it is the unit of movement it defines the split in the market for either direct door-to-door transport over which the customer has control, or for indirect movement routed through groupage terminals where the trunk transport decision is taken by a groupage agency. Consequently a threshold consignment size of 4–5 tons or 500 cubic feet must be broached before direct use of a container by a firm is feasible, and generally this must be on a regular basis. The train and its service impose further constraints on the system—this time in relation to the population size of an area that can efficiently use a service. On the assumption of a break-even capacity of 70 per cent, a service should carry 120,000 tons per annum on a two-way flow. The constraint imposed by a route is, of course, the same as that of a train, and this is the limit which must generally be exceeded before a route and service becomes viable, unless a joint route can be organised, with the train being split at one destination and carrying on to another. The requirement to justify a terminal is the final constraining factor on the supply of freightliner services in an area. If an area can generate sufficient traffic for two full services then a terminal appears feasible. Groupage facilities do not impose any further limitations on the system.

CHAPTER 6

COMPETITION IN INLAND TRANSPORT

In Chapter 5 the inflexible constraints of the freightliner system were evaluated, constraints which are largely set by the technology of the system itself. Here we shall go on to consider the cost and charging patterns of the system and those of its main competitor—road haulage. This competition with road haulage imposes further economic constraints which are of a more flexible and less clearly defined nature, but nevertheless highly significant in their effect on the freightliner system's growth. No definite answer can be given of the exact balance between road and rail, only an estimate of the probable penetration of the various sections of the inland transport market. Furthermore, competitive positions can be altered by changes in costs and taxes and in technology, and consequently the discussion must be expanded beyond a simple static position to consider these changes and their implications. The subsequent discussion must take into account the full pattern of door-to-door costs and not, as is so commonly done in transport studies, a section of the system, such as the costs of the trunk haul from terminal to terminal.

One of the important general conclusions of the *Road Track Costs*[1] report, which has relevance to the present discussion, illustrates the type of interpretive error which can arise if full system costs are not taken into account. The study analysed the cost of road trackway and allocated these costs to the types of vehicle using the road system. It came to the conclusion that heavy road vehicles in the past have not paid the same factor of costs as other vehicles and that if track charging was introduced 'the incidence of the charge (for track costs) will be greatest for large vehicles engaged on local collection and delivery where rail is rarely competitive'.[2] In this the report overlooked the importance of the road collection and delivery

[1] *Road Track Costs*, a report by the Ministry of Transport (HMSO, 1968).
[2] *ibid.*, p. 37.

operation to the freightliner operation with its use of heavy vehicles for short trips. It is true that rail does not compete for the complete haulage operation over short distances, but it has been seen above that rail does use road vehicles to a considerable extent and it will be argued that in the freightliner system, road haulage is a vital and important cost element. Any increase in short-distance costs for road vehicles, and particularly large lorries, will affect rail and will not necessarily favour rail over road, if the total door-to-door haul is considered.

1. *The road and rail transport systems*

Figures 6.1 and 6.2 show the essential operation units of the two competing inland transport systems and illustrate, reading from left to right, the passage of a consignment from the consignor (C'OR) to the consignee (C'EE). The first Figure, 6.1, analyses the movement of a consignment which is compatible with both container and lorry

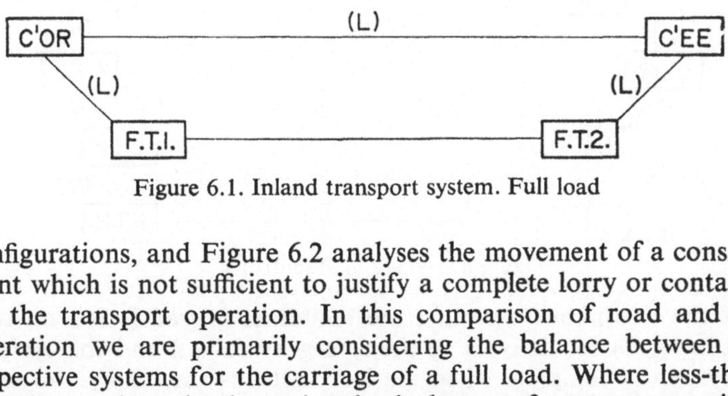

Figure 6.1. Inland transport system. Full load

configurations, and Figure 6.2 analyses the movement of a consignment which is not sufficient to justify a complete lorry or container for the transport operation. In this comparison of road and rail operation we are primarily considering the balance between the respective systems for the carriage of a full load. Where less-than-container or lorry loads are involved, the use of groupage terminals becomes necessary, and the groupage agent is then the consignor of a full load considering the comparative advantages of the two systems. The groupage operation is similar for both road and rail, and though the unit groupage costs of a road system will differ slightly from those of a rail system, for ease of comparison the collection and groupage functions and costs have been assumed equal for the two systems.

By road haulage the pattern of movement of a full load from

consignor to consignee is simple and direct. Before the actual loading of the lorry there is the lorry journey from a depot, or from the last unloading point, to the consignor (C'OR). After loading, with possible delays and queueing, the load is then transported direct to the consignee's (C'EE) door for unloading into the store or factory and, apart from the loading and unloading operations, no further handling of the load is required. This door-to-door single movement of a load has given road its competitive advantage over rail transport in the post-war years, and it is this feature which the rail operation attempts to emulate through the use of containers. In the freightliner system, Figure 6.1, the container is delivered from the freightliner terminal (F.T.1), to the consignor, or routed directly to the consignor after unloading at a local consignee. The lorry (L) then waits with the container, while loading takes place, and returns the loaded container to the local terminal (F.T.1) for transfer to the rail flats for haulage to the terminal nearest the consignee (F.T.2).

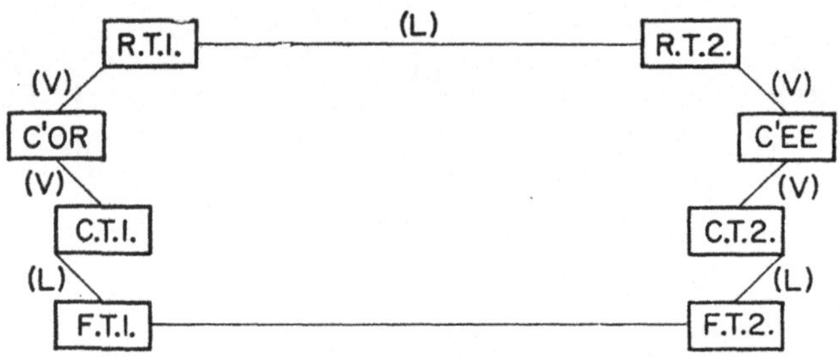

Figure 6.2. Small load (cubic)

At the destination terminal the container is transferred on to a road lorry (L) for delivery to the consignee (C'EE) and the cycle of the system is complete when the lorry returns the empty container to the terminal, or delivers it direct to a new local customer. The incidence of delays at the premises of the consignor and consignee may be assumed to be similar for road and rail vehicles, providing that the premises are favourably equipped for the loading and unloading of a container. This generally requires that a firm has either an elevated loading bay, or a fork-lift capable of stowing palletised goods in the container from ground level. Numerous instances were noted during the surveys carried out by the authors where such was not the case: where delays in excess of those involving an ordinary road vehicle would occur, and hence result in extra costs for the container system. For less-than-container loads two comparable collection and delivery operations are added both to the rail and road systems using vans or small lorries (V) and groupage terminals (R.T.1 and 2) and (C.T.1 and 2): see Figure 6.2.

Compared with the road system the freightliner involves the following operations over and above those of the road haulage of a full load: inter-vehicle transfer of the loaded container at the two terminals, and a collection and delivery operation using heavy articulated lorries. The loading and unloading process of the lorry or container is common to both systems and basically similar, although the container operation may be more expensive in the short run. It is in the trunk haulage operation that the cost savings of containerisation come, for it utilises the rail haul of large volumes of freight over medium to long distances with low running costs per capacity ton-mile. If rail is to compete with road over distance then this saving must offset the extra costs involved in the additional operations incurred in the freightliner system, assuming at this stage that other factors such as service and incidence of damage are equal for both forms of transport.

2. *The pattern of costs*

In this section we will attempt to develop cost estimates for road haulage and rail operations separately, and to assess the break-even point for road and rail general freight services.

(*a*) *Road haulage costs*. The basic elements of the costs of transporting a load as a function of distance can now be broadly formulated, based on the foregoing discussion and published estimates of cost. Road costs are made up of two main elements, vehicle costs—the costs directly attributable to the running of a lorry—and overhead or establishment costs—the costs attributable to the management, administration and depot operations of the firm. The latter costs vary widely with the type of haulage activity a firm is engaged in and its management efficiency. Typical problems of organisation are whether the firm has to manage extensive groupage facilities and whether it can arrange back loading efficiently. These necessary functions create overhead costs which vary widely from firm to firm in an industry which is characterised by small, specialised firms.

The operating costs of a vehicle and the consequent costs of the door-to-door container equivalent movement can be derived from the estimates published in the journal *Commercial Motor*.[3] The *Commercial Motor* tables distinguish five items of vehicle standing costs: namely, licences, wages, rent and rates, insurance, and interest. Running costs are also made up of five items: fuel, lubricants, tyres, maintenance, and depreciation. This is the grouping of costs as presented in the tables and is presumably a view that the industry has of costs. They may not accord with the economist's view of fixed and variable costs unless the period concerned is a very short one of one or two weeks. In the medium and long term, wages and licence fees are capable of being varied to suit demand and should therefore be regarded as variable costs of road haulage, but in the following discussion, the *Commercial Motor* grouping of costs will be used.

For a 22-ton payload articulated lorry of the type used on long-distance road haulage,[4] vehicle costs per mile travelled fall rapidly as weekly mileage increases up to 800 and 1,000 miles. This is mainly a result of the high fixed costs (£50 5s) of the vehicle. As higher weekly mileages are accumulated, fixed costs fall as a proportion of total costs and total costs per mile therefore fall. Fixed costs as an element of total costs decrease from 85 per cent at 200 miles per week to 31 per cent of costs on a schedule of 1,200 miles per week (see Table 6.1). On a 200-mile weekly schedule, fixed costs amount to approximately 3d per capacity ton-mile, while on a 1,200 miles per week schedule they amount to 0·5d per capacity ton-mile. Against this pattern of variation of fixed costs with distance, variable running costs make up a correspondingly greater proportion of total costs as mileage increases. The overall effect is that total costs decline from 71d per mile (3·3d per capacity ton-mile) on a 200 miles weekly schedule to 33d per mile (1·7d per capacity ton-mile) over 1,200 miles. Consequently there is a strong incentive for a haulier to operate his vehicles as intensively as possible, given statutory limitations on working hours, loading/unloading delays and load variability, and in practice 1,000 miles per week or 50,000 miles per year

[3] The series used here are the 'Tables of operating costs for goods and passenger vehicles, 1968', and especially the 22-ton capacity vehicle section in Table 6.

[4] Vehicles of 32 tons are now being used on trunk haulage with the revision of the *Construction and Use Regulations*. Unfortunately the articles, 'Tables of operating costs', in *Commercial Motor*, have not been reviewed recently enough to incorporate the operating experience of these vehicles.

TABLE 6.1: *Variation of costs with distance covered per week for a 22-ton articulated lorry*

Miles per week	Vehicle costs in pence per mile: fixed costs	variable costs	total costs	Fixed costs as percentage of total costs
200	61	10	71	85
400	30	23	53	56
600	20	24	44	47
800	15	23	38	40
1,000	12	23	35	35
1,200	10	23	33	31

Source: *Commercial Motor*, Tables of Operating Costs, Table 6, 22-ton articulated lorry.

is a low average mileage more typical of lorries on 100- to 200-mile routes.[5] It is worth noting that the Tables of Operating Costs do not see major cost savings accruing on running costs for different weekly mileages.

It is necessary then to translate these costs of vehicle operation per week into costs per container equivalent over various length routes. Unfortunately, many factors arise in the allocation of vehicle costs to consignments: to name but a few, the nature of route (whether it is long or short, motorway or conventional road) availability of back loadings, and length of travel in urban areas. There is therefore wide variation in the patterns of allocation by firms, and to estimate the pattern of costs we have made the following assumptions regarding the method of operation of the vehicles: for vehicles operating regularly on routes up to 300 miles, 1,000 miles are totalled per week; on routes of 300 and up to 400 miles, 1,500 miles; and over 400 miles, 2,000 miles. These are a very unsophisticated set of assumptions and they will mean discreet jumps in the pattern of variation of fixed costs with distances at 300 and 400 miles, whereas

[5] In the *True Costs* study it was assumed that the annual mileage of a road vehicle varied between 56,000 and 103,000 miles, so the assumption here of 50,000 miles per year is low on this comparison.

in reality a continuum doubtless exists. Nevertheless, this simplified view is sufficient to demonstrate the point, and in Figure 6.3 a continuous pattern of variation of fixed costs and total costs is indicated linking points plotted for routes of 50, 100, 200 and 300 miles.

Under this assumption a 100-mile haul will be completed ten times a week by a lorry and therefore each consignment will have £5 of fixed costs charged with it. Correspondingly the 200-mile haul will be performed five times a week and therefore £10 of fixed costs will be incurred per operation. On routes of 300 miles and 400 miles,

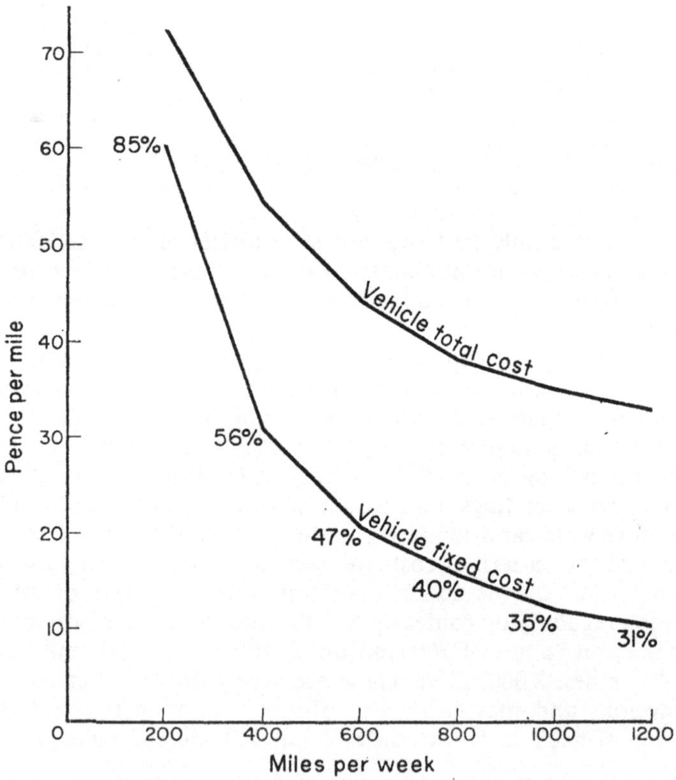

Figure 6.3. Costs per week. 22-ton articulated lorry
Source: *Commercial Motor*, Tables of Operating Costs

fixed costs of £10 will be attributable to the consignment (see Figure 6.3).

Variable costs can be estimated directly from the *Commercial Motor* figures which attribute 22·27d to this source for a vehicle operating over 800 miles a week. To allow for cost increases these have been assessed at 24d per mile. Therefore, a 100-mile haul incurs variable vehicle costs of £10, a 200-mile trip £20 and so forth. The total costs at these mileages are then the sum of the two cost elements and have been plotted in Figure 6.3.

The most important feature of this cost curve of a container load equivalent by road haulage is the relatively low fixed costs over all distances (the broken line), and particularly for the hauls of up to 100 miles where it is £5 or less per consignment. The second feature to note is the curvilinear relationship with distance. This is explained by the assumption concerning the allocation of fixed costs in this simple model. It must also be remembered these costs are being considered in the short run, and therefore the haulage firm is seen as being committed to certain costs which are not fixed in the longer term. If this assumption is relaxed to allow a more realistic situation with the operator having some expertise and a view of the future beyond say a month, then there is considerable flexibility in managing his fixed costs. It is probably this flexibility, coupled with the fact that the Tables give average figures rather than target costs, which makes operators and writers consider the costs established in the Tables 'high'.[6]

(*b*) *Freightliner costs*. The pattern of costs within the freightliner system is more complex, and only details of the aggregate costs of operation of sections of the system are presented here. For this reason only broad cost items will be discussed here. Three transport operations, the rail trunk haul, the road collection and delivery, and the terminal operation make up the three cost components relevant to this discussion.[7] The collection and delivery costs and the terminal costs can be classed here as fixed costs of the system. This is because

[6] See, for example, A. J. Harrison, *Investment in Liner Trains*, p. 206.

[7] Note that within each of these sections fixed and variable cost items exist and can be identified, but because detailed information is not available they will not be dissected. On the rail haul, for example, fixed costs, in any short- or medium-term view, include the capital costs of the vehicles and track, signalling costs and wages; variable costs include fuel, depreciation and maintenance.

they are a necessary function for the operation of the high-capacity trains but do not contribute to the movement of freight from one centre to another, nor do they vary with the length of haul of the freight. Collection and delivery and terminal costs vary mainly with the planned throughput of the terminal.

It is possible to simulate the costs of the road collection and delivery operation from the foregoing discussion of road haulage costs. If the fixed costs of a vehicle are £50 5s per week and ten collections and deliveries are performed a week then the fixed cost of collection and delivery on a through movement is £10. To this must be added the variable costs of vehicle operation which will be £2 10s for an average of 20 miles. Therefore collection and delivery incurs a fixed cost for the system of £12 10s.

To this must be added the terminal operation costs for handling the container.[8] Here data must be drawn from the *True Costs* study dated 1964. In this the British Railways Board estimated capacity ton costs for a 12½-ton container to be 5s. These were only a third the level of the terminal costs of conventional rail operation (excluding marshalling costs) and were clearly the costs of the system operating at full capacity. With terminals operating at below capacity levels, as at present, terminal costs will be running above this level, for costs once incurred are largely inflexible and determined by high fixed-cost elements set by the planned investment. However, since it is difficult to say what the capacity ton cost should be, we must accept the *True Costs* figures. This adds a further £3 at least to the fixed costs of the freightliner, giving a minimum total fixed-cost element of £15 10s. These estimates are greater than those made in the *Reshaping Report*[9] and *True Costs* study, and while they represent a more realistic picture, it is likely that they are below current actual costs, in so far as they assume a system operating at full capacity.

Finally, to attain comparability with the road-haul costs, to these fixed costs the standing costs of the containers and rolling stock must be added. No precise estimate can be made, although an indication

[8] It is assumed here, although not made fully clear in the *True Costs* study and the *Reshaping Report*, that the administrative costs of the system are contained in this terminal costs item. It does not appear, however, that the share of total railway overhead costs incurred by the freightliner system are included in this item.

[9] The *Reshaping Report* assessed collection and delivery and terminal costs at £11 per 16-ton container with £7 being attributable to collection and delivery.

of the scale of these capital costs can be gauged from the cost of a container. A 30 ft unit is valued at approximately £1,000 and life expectation at present is ten years, meaning £100 plus interest charges is the annual capital cost of the container. Then, on an assumption of an average of 150 trips per year,[10] the capital cost would approach £1 per trip. In total these fixed costs of the haulage operation are assumed to be £2 10s per trip making the total fixed costs of the rail haul £18.

As far as variable (ton-mile) costs are concerned, we can accept the *True Costs* study estimates of the capacity ton-mile costs of rail haul. These figures are well established, and the cost of the rail haul, at 0·34d per capacity ton-mile, is significantly lower than those established for road haulage in the same report, 0·65d for a 16-ton lorry on a motorway route and 0·76d on a conventional road. This means that the variable costs of rail haulage of a container over distances up to 200 miles would be approximately £3 10s and over 200 miles approximately £5 10s. Note that these figures are based on

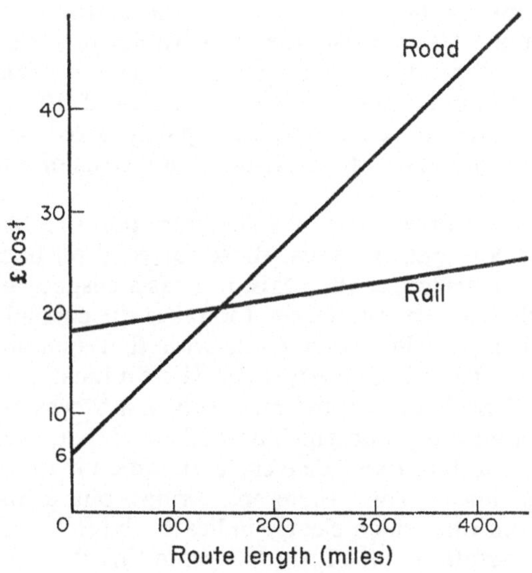

Figure 6.4. Operator cost of a consignment by road and rail over distance

[10] Based on *Reshaping Report* assumption, p. 146.

the capacity of 12½ tons assumed for a 20 ft container in the *True Costs* study.

(*c*) *The competitive balance.* The pattern of these costs is summarised in Figure 6.4. Fixed costs are the same for all lengths of haul on the freightliner system and total approximately £18, or at least three times the level of fixed costs of road haulage on routes of 100 miles. However, the low capacity ton-mile costs of the system resulting from the high-volume movement compensate for this high fixed-cost disadvantage on the longer-distance hauls and give rail an absolute advantage. From these estimates of cost patterns of road and rail container haulage, it appears that the distance beyond which rail costs are lower than road costs is approximately 130 miles. It should be noted, however, that costs as estimated here are biased in favour of rail haulage on two points at least. The first is the general acceptance of the *Commercial Motor* tables of costs, which may be over-estimates, and which use of 22-ton payload as the maximum size of vehicle. The new 32-ton capacity vehicles should have capacity ton-mile costs considerably below those of the 22-ton vehicle. As an indication of the latter point, the 1968 Tables of Operating Costs established the capacity ton-mile costs of a 16-ton vehicle at 1·20d per capacity ton-mile, and a 22-ton vehicle at 1·04d. Second, the above estimates of rail cost have been partly based on 1964 data, and are in any case biased towards minimum costs of a full capacity system.

Taking account of this, we may therefore presume that rail costs per container consignment equal those for road on hauls of about 150 miles. On hauls longer than this, rail has a cost advantage which increases with distance, and below 150 miles the cost advantage lies with road. This conclusion contrasts with that established in the *Reshaping Report* and *True Costs* study where a break point of under 100 miles, and probably approximately 70 miles, was estimated.

Another important point which arises here is that, even on a haul of 400 miles, collection and delivery costs amount to over half the total haulage costs. This, therefore, brings out a rather ironic proposition and one which clearly indicates the fallacy in the *Road Track Costs* quotation in the introduction to this chapter. Since road costs amount to at least half of the total operating costs, a rise in the road costs of container transport would add more to door-to-door rail costs than would an equal cost increase in the rail haul. In other words, the container innovation has therefore made rail operation more susceptible to changes in road haulage costs. Also the inflexible pattern of operation with high fixed costs allows little room for cost saving in any short-to-medium-term period. Under conventional rail operation, road costs amounted to approximately 30 per cent of total rail costs, so that total costs were less sensitive to increases in road transport costs

The discussion to date has assumed a constant technology for both road and rail and is, as a result, a static analysis. For rail, for the next ten to fifteen years at least, the main technological change is the container. It is the new force which will be developed further during the next ten years but will not derive further major cost saving for reasons developed below. Road transport, on the other hand, can look forward to significant changes which could promise cost savings and in turn improve its competitive position. For 32-ton lorries are now operative and 44-ton vehicles have been constructed. The 32-ton lorry means that it can carry one-and-a-half times the load of a 30 ft container. The gas-turbine tractor unit is a foreseeable future improvement. Roads will also improve and by the mid-1970s many current trunk-route bottlenecks should have been eliminated by new motorways—to mention but two, the M6 route between Penrith and Kendal, and the West Midlands links of the M1–M6 and M6–M5. Moving beyond the static cost relationship then, it would appear that changes over time will favour road haulage or at least maintain the present balance.

3. *Charging policy*

The above is a discussion of the nature of the costs which underlie the actual charges made to customers, and the pattern of variation of the charges with distance will vary from that of costs, depending on the pricing policy of the operators.

(*a*) *Road haulage charges*. In the present comparison, road haulage charges are more complex than those for the freightliner operation, partly because of the numerous firms in the industry each with its own operating structure and policy, and partly because pricing is based on the nature of the load. It is common, for example, for a firm to receive widely differing quotations for the transport of a particular consignment, and many examples of this were cited during the course of the surveys. Consequently, even if a pattern of actual charges was established, it would be a broad average subject to wide variation about it. In this analysis of road and rail charges an estimate is established by simply assuming that the 'average' haulier took a 40 per cent mark-up on fixed costs to cover establishment costs and a net profit margin.[11] For many trunk-road haulage movements the vehicle costs plus a smaller mark-up is the rate charged. For example, own account haulage 'charging' is generally reckoned at cost, that is vehicle costs plus establishment costs. Also the commercial haulier who is tendering for a load or contract from a favourable operating position will have low overhead costs and will therefore quote a charge close to vehicle operating costs. Hence the estimated pattern of charge reflects that of costs developed above—actual charges will vary about this 'average' with more below than above, because these estimates are biased on the high side.

(*b*) *Freightliner charges.* The charging policy for freightliner services has brought a major change to railway pricing policy, for instead of widely differentiated commodity rates the new system is based on the three container sizes used, regardless of the commodity despatched. In other words it is a charge based on the cubic transport space supplied and not the value and/or weight characteristics of the consignment. On a trunk haul of 200 miles this meant a charge[12] of approximately £8 for a 10 ft container, £14 for a 20 ft container with twice the cube, and £18 for a 30 ft container with three times the cube. Hence there was, and still is, a major scale economy for a consignor who can use the 30 ft container. While these figures related to the trunk haul only, with the minimum distance collection and delivery at each end of the haul, they rose to £16, £28 and £34 respectively, and the economy from use of size was maintained.

Discounts were also given for the frequency of use of a particular

[11] The *Commercial Motor* recommends a 40 per cent mark-up on total operating costs—20 per cent for establishment costs and 20 per cent for profit margin. This is a very high mark-up since vehicle costs include items such as rent and rates.

[12] The charges discussed here were those operated up to December 1968. Changes were made then both for trunk charges and collection and delivery. While significant changes were made for individual routes the overall pattern discussed here is believed to have been maintained. Rates have been changed on a 'what the traffic will bear' basis with rates on high volume routes being increased and vice-versa.

service. They were classed as the 'A', 'B' and 'C' category rates, and the discounts were given on the frequency of use of a route and not the whole network of routes, though large users of the service were able to negotiate separate discounts for large volumes despatched on the network as a whole. 'A' rates were charged on a flow of one container per week per route, 'B' rates on from two to nine containers per week per route, and 'C' rates on ten or more containers per week per route. On average the 'B' rates meant a 10 per cent discount over the 'A' rate per container movement, and the 'C' rate a 14·5 per cent discount. A further discount was allowed to users who order a return movement of the container, a discount aimed at encouraging balanced flows of traffic. This discount varied between 12 and 13 per cent and was of the order of £8 for a 30 ft container on the London–Glasgow route. Hence for a large user who can despatch containers at a rate of two or more per day on a route and can arrange to backload the container, a saving of approximately 25 per cent can be effected. In the hypothetical instance of his using 10 ft containers the saving would be approximately 50 per cent.

The variation of charges with distance was extremely interesting, particularly in the light of the cost curves developed above. For example, for the trunk haulage of a 30 ft container—that is without collection and delivery—a fixed charge of £10 10s could be inferred at the 'A' category of charge.[13] The mileage charges for the container averaged 7·2d up to 230 miles. Beyond this distance an increased mileage rate was charged—19·2d per mile for the 30 ft container. Comparable data for the three container sizes are given in Table 6.2. This change in the charge per mile is seen in the kink in the graph at 230 miles. (See Figure 6.5 below for the variation of the 30 ft container 'B' rate charges.) It is clear that the mileage charges for haulage less than 230 miles are close to those incremental costs per container-mile developed in the *Reshaping Report*, while those for hauls beyond 230 miles are significantly larger, and comparable to those of road haulage. Hence there is evidence of subsidisation between routes on the basis of length of route, with the 'long' routes either paying the deficit of 'short' routes, or making the larger profit margins.

Collection and delivery charges are also differentiated by container size and distance, but with no discounts for number of

[13] The fixed charge was inferred from the 'a' parameter in the regression equation fitted to the plot of charge against distance.

TABLE 6.2: *Charges for freightliner containers at the 'A' category charge*, 1967–8

Container size	Inferred fixed charge*	Mileage rate per container (pence per mile)		Collection and delivery	
		Up to 230 miles	Over 230 miles	Fixed charge (£)	Mileage rate (pence per mile)
10	£6	2·4	12·0	4	60 (5s)
20	£9	7·2	16·8	6	72 (6s)
30	£10 10s	7·2	19·2	7	84 (7s)

Source: British Rail published rates.

* Calculation of this value is discussed in footnote 13.

containers dispatched. For the minimum distance collection or delivery the charge for a 30 ft container was £7 and the charges for distance were based on a series of five-mile-wide rings centred on the terminal. The mileage charge for a 30 ft container averaged 7s per mile. (The features of the collection and delivery charges are also set out in Table 6.2.) It will be noted that this mileage rate was higher than that of the long-distance road haulage—at 2s per mile—and that the charges noted above for minimum-distance haulage were a fixed charge base for the collection and delivery service. These charges reflect very closely the scale of cost of the collection and delivery operation, and though some hauliers have stated that the operation was run at a loss it appears to cover costs. The charge for the average collection and delivery operation was £16 10s for a 30 ft container and compared with a charge of £14 for a minimum distance collection and delivery operation, or £25 if collection and delivery totalled 40 miles. A company does not face this scale of charge if it collects or delivers the container itself although it does bear the cost of the operation.

4. *The inland freight systems in competition*

In assessing which freight transport form to use, a firm is faced with the consideration of two types of costs: the first, the 'direct' costs of the operation expressed by the charges of the transport operators; the second, the 'indirect' costs of the operation.

The 'direct' costs that the transport user faces have been developed here in this discussion of charges and are shown in Figure 6.5, where the 'charges' for a 30 ft container load and a 22-ton lorry load over distance are set against each other. The graph shows both the trunk haul charge and the total charge for the 30 ft container at the 'B'

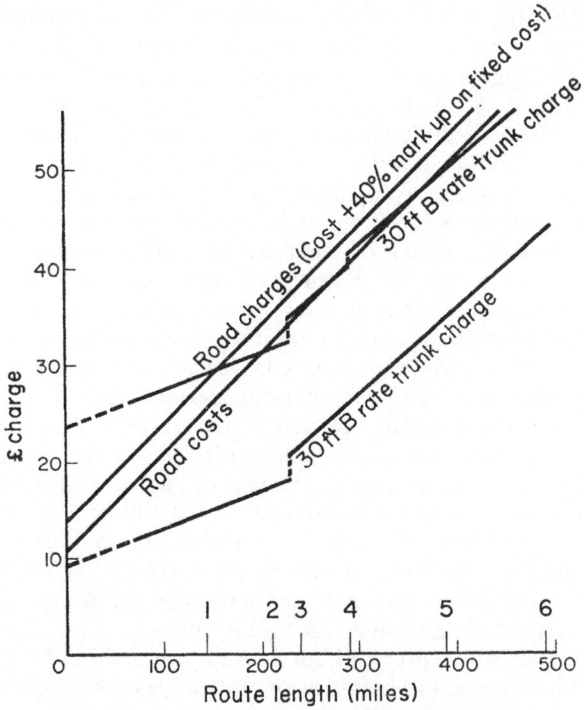

Figure 6.5. Charges for a consignment by rail and road over distance

1 Glasgow–Aberdeen
2 Glasgow–Liverpool
Manchester
Leeds
3 Glasgow–Sheffield
4 Glasgow–Birmingham
5 Glasgow–London
Edinburgh–London
6 Aberdeen–London

Note: The linked services like Aberdeen–Birmingham are not shown. On average a £4 charge is made for the transfer operation.

rate, as this is the most commonly used container size and rate. Collection and delivery of a container is charged for the most commonly used distance—the 0–4 mile ring for both collection and delivery. The kink at 230 miles is clearly evident in the graph of container charges. The magnitude of the fixed charge is a key feature of the container graph—for a 30 ft container it can be inferred to be £23, of which collection and delivery is £14 for the most commonly occurring collection and delivery trips, while the total charge at 200 miles is £30 10s, and at 300 miles £41 10s. For road haulage total costs are shown as well as the simulated charges pattern.

On comparing the costs of the road operator with the charges of the freightliner, it can be seen that road competes with rail up to 200 miles. However, allowing for the constant 40 per cent mark-up on fixed costs discussed above, it would seem that a haulier was able to compete effectively up to 150 miles. For reasons discussed above, such as assured back loadings, it is evident that some hauliers can compete effectively on 'direct' customer costs on trunk routes beyond 150 miles because special features of their operation mean lower costs of operation. What is most interesting in the relationship between the freightliner charges and the simulated haulier charges is that if the haulier and freightliner charges are even at approximately 150 miles, on the freightliner charging pattern of 1967–8, then the increased mileage rates for the freightliner on routes over 230 miles mean that the two charges are close on routes over 150 miles, and not widely divergent as one might expect. These relationships can only be inferred at a very general level, but it will be seen below that they do explain many of the features of present traffic movements.

Therefore, on the basis of the direct costs of the door-to-door transport operation as the customer sees them, road haulage has an absolute advantage on hauls up to 150 miles at least. This means that the haulier will capture all but a small proportion of this market. Beyond this distance rail assumes an advantage on charges, although this is not as clear as the cost patterns of rail would lead one to expect. It is also reasonable to expect to find rail competing very closely with road on hauls of over 150 miles but probably increasing its domination of the market with distance.

CHAPTER 7

THE USE MADE BY FIRMS OF INLAND CONTAINER TRANSPORT

1. *Introduction*

This chapter will consider the importance of the factors controlling the use of inland container transport by firms and how this will affect the demand for containers in inland transport. It will examine the importance of the various factors which firms take into account in selecting a transport medium, and then go on to examine the extent to which the features of container transport considered in the above chapters fit the present pattern of operation of firms as well as the extent to which alterations in these patterns of operation will be necessary to make efficient use of container transport. From this discussion can then be drawn some concept of the potential demand of firms for inland container transport.

Chapter 6 has already dealt with the competitive price relationship between conventional and container transport. But the price is by no means the only, and perhaps not even the most significant, factor in the transport decision; the various aspects of quality of service must also be considered. Even more, it is not even the objective comparison of the components of quality which is important; because quality is in many instances so intangible, it is the subjective evaluation of the decision-maker which is the critical factor.

Each decision will have a different balance of price and service considerations, and measurement difficulties preclude any direct comparison. Nevertheless an interesting illustration of their relative importance has been given by Deakin and Seward who compared price per ton-mile by rail and road haulage in 1966.[1] They took twenty-nine different commodity groups and found that, in all except five, the rate for rail was lower than that for road haulage. They admitted, of course, that factors such as size of load, long-term

[1] B. M. Deakin and T. Seward, *Productivity in Transport*, Cambridge University Press, 1969, Chapter 4.

contracts, and length of haul could crucially affect the rates charged, and therefore tried to allow for these by taking those commodities for which the average length of haul was similar for both road and rail and by taking the total cost of transporting a single ton. The result can be seen in Table 7.1.

TABLE 7.1: *Comparative transport costs in selected commodities, 1966*

	Total cost of transporting one ton				
	Rail		Road		Average length of haul (miles)
	s	d	s	d	
Flour	29	1	45	9	87
Coal, coke, patent fuels	16	4	25	4	54
Petroleum and petroleum products	13	2	38	11	92
Crude and manufactured fertilisers	19	5	35	10	92
All other chemicals and plastic materials	40	8	52	10	124
Tars from coal and natural gas	24	2	33	6	62

Source: Deakin and Seward, *Productivity in Transport*, page 62.

These prices naturally cannot be regarded as precise, but merely as reflecting orders of magnitude. Moreover, it might be argued that these are commodities where rail would expect to have a comparative advantage, although only with heavier unit consignments. Nevertheless, the differences reflected in Table 7.1, together with rail's price advantage over the wider range of commodities, were so marked that Deakin and Seward could only explain road transport's supremacy in terms of quality of service.

Differences in quality of service naturally mean different costs for the user, albeit indirect rather than direct. We must now examine the composition and relative significance of these various components of quality. These indirect cost factors which arise from the operating characteristics of the transport modes and the demand characteristics of the particular consignments include such items as service frequency, flexibility of service, perishability of product, urgency of the consignment, and personal attention of transport operators. The direct costs of the transport operation can usually be clearly assessed by the transport customer simply by his asking for quotations on the particular contract; the indirect costs are more difficult to quantify.

Estimates of cost placed on each item for the respective transport modes are subject to wide variation from one user to another, indeed these costs are rarely assessed in monetary terms; generally the user weights the rate quoted by his idea of the importance of the various indirect cost features. Even in a well-informed atmosphere, biases of previous experience and the problems of assessing unquantifiable items will make the decisions open to wide variation. In fact, there is much evidence that the supply of relevant information is poor and the ability of most firms to use such information, were it available, is doubtful. Therefore decisions concerning any transport mode are certain to be very complex and to be heavily weighted by non-economic factors, particularly if these vary widely from one mode of transport to another. In many instances it is to be expected that these supplementary features and their indirect costs will be the main deciding factors in any transport decision. For example, a consignor with an urgent delivery date to meet will place a high indirect cost on a slow and unreliable service and conversely a low cost on a fast reliable one. Furthermore, these indirect costs could alter the balance in favour of a particular transport mode, even if the balance on direct costs pointed strongly in the other direction. Note, however, that the more directly comparable the transport modes are in the features contributing to indirect costs, the more likely it is that the direct cost differential would be the deciding factor in any transport decision.

It is therefore impossible to make a definitive and precise statement as to the balance of the indirect cost features when comparing rail container and road transport, since indirect costs are subject to the variation of the characteristics of consignments despatched by firms, and the even wider variations from firm to firm in their demands for transport. Nevertheless, in view of their obvious importance, we must take these qualitative indirect cost factors into account by considering representative series of key features and asking whether the future balance will move in favour of rail container transport, and if so how far this might go.

To do this, the information currently available on the factors which control the allocation of demand between modes of transport must first be considered. Then current features of use of container transport and how these affect the balance of competition with road transport will be considered to determine first, whether these will mean any alteration or continuation in the method of operation of firms, and particularly in the operation of the distribution systems; and second the implications for the demand for container transport given this understanding of the balance between features and the secondary effect of possible alteration in the internal operation of firms.

2. *Transport for industry*

The report, *Transport for Industry*,[2] provides the most valuable insight into how various factors influence the choice of a particular mode of transport by manufacturing industry. The study analyses the importance of twenty-five factors in the allocation of traffic between modes of transport—defined as own account, public road haulier, railways, and GPO—and finds, perhaps somewhat surprisingly, that there is a limited number of factors of importance. For the present discussion this study has several limitations which arise from points of incompatibility between the Ministry study and the present discussion. Firstly, *Transport for Industry* examines manufacturing industry and includes in this definition the distribution activity of manufacturers, whereas the present study is primarily concerned with distribution activity as such. Also, to narrow the field of survey to allow intensive analysis and to fit with existing work on a transport cost model the study examined consignments on only two routes: London–Newcastle and Liverpool–Glasgow, and is, therefore, only directly applicable to these routes.[3] Secondly, the study is dated September 1966 and was therefore carried out in the very early stages of freightliner operation when the system was just developing. Consequently, it does not throw any definite light on how the system competes in inland transport and how transport users view its supplementary indirect cost features, although it does indicate some interesting trends which were then developing. In technique the Ministry report makes a major contribution to the understanding of transport allocation between modes. It allows the

[2] *Transport for Industry*, HMSO, 1968.

[3] Both of these routes are now served by freightliner.

analyst to study the influence of a factor in the choice of a mode of transport in the environment of all other factors, without these being assumed away or artificially held constant. Previous studies have not had these capabilities and have resorted to a simple ranking of the factors.[4]

The most important finding of the survey was that concerning the relative importance of the direct and indirect costs as determining factors in the allocation of demand among transport modes. Analysis showed that the freight rate *per se* was an unimportant factor in the decision, and that features categorised here as indirect costs were of much greater importance. This accords with the findings of Deakin and Seward. Furthermore, within the direct costs group the features of the consignment, i.e. the features dictated by the operations of the firm, were more important than the attributes of the transport modes themselves. It is therefore worth while considering the findings in more detail.

In the allocation of demand between transport modes, the survey found that:

> 'Most firms used more than one mode of transport, and comparatively few, including those operating their own vehicles, were heavily committed to a single mode. For nearly half of the establishments the expenditure on the main mode was two-thirds or less of total expenditure on transport' (page ii).

On long-distance transport this pattern was particularly well developed. It must be recalled that road transport was classified into several modes and this accounts, in part, for the observed 'even' spread. On short-distance transport own-account haulage did serve a major part of the transport demand.

In relation to the effect of freight charges the report, as a result of the multi-factor analysis, considered that:

> '. . . on an average view, taken over consignments of all descriptions for which data were available, the effect of relative price on the mode of transport selected was small' (page iii).

The role of transport charges was examined in greater detail in a supplementary survey. On a third to a half of consignments alter-

[4] See, for example, J. R. Cook, 'Transport Decisions of Firms in the Black Country', *Journal of Transport Economics and Policy*, Vol. I, No. 3, September 1967.

native costs were known, and in this group more than a quarter were sent by modes of transport that were more expensive than the cheapest alternative. Of those sent by the dearest alternative, a third were sent by a mode that was at least 25 per cent more expensive than the cheapest alternative. Furthermore, industries producing high-value items appear more prepared to meet higher charges to obtain better service than were other industries, presumably because delays in the transportation and sale of high-value goods involve the firms concerned in relatively greater stockholding costs.

Similarly, distance, a factor which might be expected to have an important influence on the selection of transport mode, was considered a minor factor in the field of long-distance transport. The economic analysis based on direct costs, as in Chapter 6, would suggest that as distance increases the price advantage which rail has would be a deciding factor. This does not happen, simply because relative price differences are outweighed by other indirect cost elements.

One group of factors which *Transport for Industry* found dominated the pattern of allocation of demand between modes, were those grouped as 'special features of the consignments' or, as categorised here, indirect cost features which are internal to the firm. Sixty per cent of consignments had one or more of the eight special features as key factors in the decision of allocation of demand. The factors defined in the study were:

a. the need for the vehicle or wagon to have a specialised body, for example, refrigerated, insulated, or otherwise specially equipped;
b. the transit occurred between two establishments which were situated in fairly close proximity to one another so that a 'production line' type of movement was occurring;
c. the movement was a purely local delivery;
d. the commodity involved was perishable;
e. the consignment was urgently required;
f. the name of the consignor was prominently displayed on the vehicle carrying the consignments;
g. an activity other than transport was coupled to the consignment's delivery, for example, servicing, installation, collection of orders, etc.;
h. the load was an indivisible one which could not go by rail.

Table 7.2 summarises the data.

TABLE 7.2: *Number of consignments with special features as a percentage of all consignments carried by each mode**

Feature	Own vehicle	Customer collection	Road haulier	Rail	GPO	All modes
Special body	6	1	3	2	—	3
Inter-establishment move	15	4	8	2	2	8
Local delivery	52	52	13	1	9	25
Perishable	14	2	1	—	—	5
Urgent	33	22	13	13	15	20
Advert	82	42	14	2	4	34
Extra service	9	1	6	2	1	5
Indivisible load	3	1	3	—	—	3
Average number of features per consignment with a special feature	2·3	1·5	1·4	1·0	1·1	1·8

Source: General Survey, *Transport for Industry*, page 47.

* The figures in this table do not add to 100 per cent because more than one feature was often listed per consignment.

On average the number of special features per consignment was 1·8 and only own account transport exceeded this with 2·3 features per consignment despatched by this mode, while rail and GPO were lowest with 1·0 and 1·1 respectively. Road hauliers were lower than average with 1·4. This indicates the favourable nature of road transport towards special requirements of a consignment, particularly when a closer examination shows that 13 per cent of consignments despatched by rail for urgent reasons were small consignments sent by scheduled passenger services and thus not a major source of traffic in a conventional freight service. The feature which was most commonly stressed and which favoured road transport, the display of producer's name or product name, is one which is very difficult to assess and impossible to assign a value. The second most important feature, use of the mode for local delivery, is of course not an issue in long-distance transport. Urgency, the third feature, is critical for long-distance transport and one which does favour road freight over rail freight for medium- to large-size consignments. Other features such as the need for a special body, perishable nature of the commodity, extra service, and an indivisible load all favour road transport.

Consequently, the total balance of these indirect cost factors internal to the firm tips the scales in favour of road transport, both by own account and public haulage. Conventional rail freight services, in comparison, had few consignments with these special features in its favour. The features of the transport modes themselves were considered to have an important and direct effect on the transport decision, although secondary importance was attached to them. The flexibility of the mode in being able to meet the routing and timing requirements of a consignment, speed and reliability of the transport service, the record of the transport mode for incidence of damage to consignments, and the security of loads in transit are all features which are each individually important over the total range of consignments, though they may assume varying levels of importance for various consignments.

Two examples can usefully be considered. A survey of consignment transit times showed that rail had an inferior record to that of public road hauliers and particularly own-account haulage. The latter can be discounted here because of its concentration on short-distance haulage but the pattern of use of public hauliers is not very dissimilar from that of rail. Over half the consignments took three days to complete transit by rail, compared with a figure of one-third for road, and the total experience significantly favours road haulage (see Table 7.3). Experience also indicates that the record of incidence of damage and loss told against railways to a similar extent. For road haulage, for example, 0·7 per cent of consignments were damaged and 0·6 per cent lost, compared with the figures for rail, 2 per cent and 0·8 per cent respectively.

In total these factors favoured road haulage. The difference in performance, while not being radically different, does appear to have been significant enough to justify the more moderate complaints one hears of the railways, and certainly sufficient to cause firms to alter demand patterns. To strengthen this effect is the point that the occurrence of one of these features in a road transport consignment can be dealt with by a direct approach to the haulage company and personal attention to the matter by a senior person.

TABLE 7.3: *Transit time and mode of transport*

Delivery	Own road vehicle* (%)	Road (%)	Rail (%)	GPO (%)	All modes (%)
Same day	59	33	9	47†	31
Next day	16	16	14		18
Second day after despatch	13	11	12	27	17
Third day	6	9	10	14	10
Subsequently	6	31	55	12	24
	100	100	100	100	100

Source: General Survey: *Transport for Industry*, page 43.

* Includes some deliveries on the same day.

† Predominantly short haul traffic.

This is much less likely to happen and less likely to be effective in the case of the railways.

Stress was laid in the report on the importance of change which was taking place in the choice of mode, and whereas, prior to the survey date, change was predominantly to rail from road, at about the time of the survey there was evidence of a favourable net change towards rail, and this was also true of the forward planning of firms. This, it was considered, was largely in response to the development of the freightliner system, and whereas the changes in the past away from rail were mainly based on slow services, delays and losses, the freightliner appeared to be competing favourably with road on these criteria over the short period of its operation.

The finding of approximately 12 per cent of shippers changing transport modes for a significant range of consignments in the two years prior to the survey and a further 5 per cent planning changes indicates the constant change going on in transport use. The analysis, however, showed the proportionate penetration of these changes by consignments to be more limited—the prime reason being that short-haul work dominates the pattern of consignment movement and that this type of movement is still best served by road transport, and own account transport in particular. In the special field of long-distance transport the change is therefore probably more substantial and is almost certainly based on special features of the consignments and the modes of transport. Whether this trend will continue must be considered below.

The survey also indicated that the use of containers extended to 6 per cent of consignments in 1966. This figure may seem high and also appear to contradict later discussion, but it must be recalled that the survey examined two trunk routes, both of which were served by the freightliner service. It is unrealistic to base a national estimate of container use upon statistics collected from these two exceptional routes.

The *Transport for Industry* survey of the use that manufacturing industry makes of transport indicates, therefore, that the price of transport was of little importance in the allocation of demand amongst the modes of transport considered, and this even over long-distance hauls. Instead other indirect cost factors were the deciding ones. Whether this pattern will continue in the new competitive situation with container transport and larger road vehicles is open to question. Evidence in the survey shows the balance of these indirect cost features of transport as factors in the transport decision swinging in favour of rail container services; just how far this will go is the pertinent question.

3. *Some features of use of containers by firms*

Before examining the factors highlighted by the *Transport for Industry* survey in the light of container technology, it is possible to examine the patterns of use of container transport which have already developed. Apart from aggregate movements on the system published by The Freightliner Company, only one other source of data is available, namely, a small but detailed survey of traffic through the Glasgow (Gushetfaulds) terminal in 1968.[5] Although these data deal only with the specific routes operated from Glasgow and naturally have this disadvantage, they nevertheless give some very useful indications of the pattern of utilisation of the freightliner service, such as the economic activities using the service, the importance of various weekly use patterns by firms to the flow through the system, and commodities carried on the service.

Instead of classifying container movement by the broad industrial

[5] This survey was carried out over a three-week period in September 1968, for all traffic moving through the Gushetfaulds terminal.

groupings, each container movement was allocated into one of four classes of economic activity which the movement served, based on a knowledge of the firm consigning the container and other data on the consignment. Just under half (45 per cent) of the containers were consigned by *transport agencies*, both British Rail itself, and hauliers, either direct from customers with full container loads, or from groupage terminals. *Distribution* activity was the next most important generator of traffic and was defined as movement to the final user of the product and not to further stages of production. This activity was estimated to generate 35 per cent of container consignments and was approximately twice the proportion of movement destined for further *manufacture*—15 per cent. Consequently in the field of direct transport demand, where the activity generating the movement can be identified, distribution appears to be twice as important as manufacturing.

From a contemporary survey of wholesale distribution agencies in the Clydeside area,[6] it was evident that the change towards container services noted in *Transport for Industry* was being maintained and was a feature of the distribution policy of many firms, although the change was by no means a universal phenomenon. About one-third of the wholesalers visited in 1968 had never received container loads, while less than one-tenth sent goods out in containers (which is not as surprising as it might seem, for a major wholesale function is to break bulk). It was found that firms were, on the whole, interested in studying the potential of containers, and indeed some were actually in the process of evaluating the position.

The pattern of use of freightliners by number of containers despatched per week per firm indicated the importance of the large user in the system. Container flow was grouped into three sets corresponding to the three charging rates discussed above, in Chapter 5. As one might expect, there was an inverse relationship across the three groups between number of firms and number of containers despatched or received. What is striking, however, is the high relative importance of the 20 largest users sending containers in and 19 largest sending containers out. They accounted for nearly two-thirds of container units carried, yet comprised only one-tenth of the customers. Large users held a similar, and even marginally stronger, position in outbound traffic.

[6] A detailed sample survey of wholesale distribution activity was carried out in 1967–8 in the Clydeside area by the authors.

A detailed classification of commodities carried in containers was impossible because firms are not required to disclose the contents of the container, although most do record the nature of the consignment. Consequently any classification must be very general and subject to possible inaccuracy. Nevertheless, examination does give some indication of the type of commodities being containerised and it shows the concentration of high-value goods in freightliner traffic. Foodstuffs, other manufactured goods and grouped loads of sundries all comprised approximately 20 per cent of the number of container movements, followed by a miscellaneous group of approximately 13 per cent, and whisky and steel with approximately 5 per cent each. Crude materials were rarely containerised.

4. *The indirect cost factors*

Having considered the types of firm using the system and the economic activity generating the movement, and having briefly indicated the commodities being despatched, we must now consider the operation of the indirect cost factors and their impact on distributive systems. In the subsequent discussion leading towards the balance of competition between the several modes of road transport: road and rail transport will simply be compared. First, the factors which are internal to the firm or the features of a consignment will be discussed and then the external factors, or those set by the transport systems, will be introduced.

(*a*) *Features internal to the firms.* The *Transport for Industry* survey highlighted the importance of the vehicle being able to carry the producer's name, or the product brand as a livery because it was claimed to be a very valuable form of advertising. This must continue to be a field of advantage for road transport and particularly for long-distance own-account or public haulier long-term-hire transport. Container transport can partially meet this problem if the customer is willing to purchase or rent containers with the livery of the firm or product on the container. This may not have the same advertising capacity, as a major part of the working life of the container is spent on rail tracks away from potential viewers.

Urgency, the next most important special feature of consignments which is relevant, can be very adequately met by rail containers.

Container loads despatched in the evening are delivered by noon the next day, and next-day delivery is available over any freightliner route in the country. Road finds it difficult to emulate this performance on routes over 300 miles, although it is feasible on shorter routes. Furthermore, despite the inflexibility of the scheduling of trains, a container despatched in the morning takes little more than 24 hours for delivery. The same patterns cannot be expected for less than container loads and here the delivery performance is dependent upon the efficiency of the groupage agencies, though 24-hour delivery services can be attained, as the Tartan Arrow London–Glasgow service shows. Road transport still has advantages for urgent consignments. For example, if a firm wishes to despatch a consignment in the morning for delivery to a consignee in the afternoon on a 100- to 200-mile route it is possible with road. The overall balance is, however, more nearly equal and in favour of rail container services over long distances.

Other factors, it will be recalled, were commonly quoted but were not of widespread importance. A firm requiring a transport service which can be integrated with production line operation will find the scheduled freightliner services ideal, particularly if backloading between two production units can be arranged. Perishability of the consignment should also be a factor in favour of rail containers. Refrigerated units are available and the rapid transit of a container load is a further positive factor meeting the requirements of these consignments.

The need for a special body and the indivisibility of a consignment are in some ways allied factors. Special container configurations can be built for customer ownership as well as many being available from leasing organisations and the Freightliner Company. Consequently this should not be a hindering factor, although intensive use of the units by the firm concerned is necessary to utilise efficiently the more specialised configurations. Indivisibility of the consignment only applies if the dimensions exceed the internal ones of the container and some very large products might still be containerisable if designed sectionally for assembly after transport. In summary, both of these factors, while not completely negating the possibility of use of containers, do place it in a more unfavourable position than those previously discussed.

Containers do not necessarily remove the potential for the features categorised in *Transport for Industry* as 'extra service'. If a firm operates its own collection and delivery or engages a haulage contractor for the purpose, then it can operate detailed collection and delivery patterns, or service equipment as well as deliver items or loads. This could be limited, however, by the loading/unloading periods allowed by the freightliner organisation. Retention of the container away from the terminal longer than a certain period incurs demurrage charges, but this should not be the final consideration of a firm if these costs can be offset against the saving of stockholding depots. All of these factors can be subsumed under the broader heading of the 'organisation of distribution or production', and under this heading there are also a series of other factors. Some are interrelated with those discussed above, as well as with one another and all are part of what is, or should be, an ordered production and distribution system. A firm may not find that any one of these factors or the cost of it is sufficient to preclude the adoption of a particular transport system, although it may well find that a total distribution cost analysis of the situation will, by considering all the factors together, result in an unfavourable decision for one of the transport modes. To take an example, a firm may wish to use containerisation and on examination find that it could derive saving from use of a large container, but find also that this would incur costs in building up this larger consignment unit by necessitating a special stockholding operation, possibly reorganising production, and that it would also introduce problems at the receiving plant or warehouse where such loads might not be able to be accepted without incurring further significant costs. On the other hand, the total reorganisation of production, stockholding and customer ties which would be necessary to utilise containers efficiently might yield significant savings in total cost and effective service.

Many pre-war, and sometimes post-war, premises are not able to accept the modern 22- or 32-ton lorry with a full load, be it container or conventional lorry load. In some instances this is caused by the limited access through roads or alleyways and in others by the size of the loading bay. Where large unit loads are delivered to such premises, costs, internal and external to the firms concerned, may accrue in the form of long and expensive loading/unloading times and traffic congestion. It is not uncommon, for example, for a firm to have to employ a team of men with handbarrows up to two to three hours to unload a vehicle onto which the palletised goods were loaded in 20 minutes by fork-lift truck from an elevated loading bay.[7] In such a case the savings derived by the despatch organisation are passed on as costs to the receiving one and total costs over the distribution system are probably not reduced.

Other factors also need to be taken into account. Containers demand a change in materials handling methods to facilitate efficient loading/unloading procedures. Many depots were constructed in the fifties and early sixties for the loading/unloading of open-back lorry flat trailers from ground level. To change this is, in some instances, very difficult and expensive to effect and can easily negate other savings from containers. This will be particularly true if a firm is receiving only 10 to 20 per cent of loads by container and would have to adapt for these, probably with a low subsequent utilisation of the investment.

These are not, however, technically insurmountable problems. Given time, obsolete systems will be reassessed and old investment cleared, followed by investment in new systems compatible with containerisation. In a similar manner the location of factories and warehouses in green field sites at some distance from freightliner terminals was partly a decision to utilise the advantage of road transport in the congestion-free areas with motorway access. Many of these sites are beyond the effective range of freightliner collection and delivery and are, therefore, another example of a distribution decision taken before the development of container systems operating against the possible use of freightliners by firms, whereas road transport will be favoured.

The conclusion of this discussion is that many specifically developed systems are not capable of adaptation to alternate serving elements and this can preclude the development of the full potential of a new service, at least for the period of the investment. Although an innovating firm may sell buildings or equipment which preclude its use of the new technique, these will still remain in the capital stock of the economy and will probably preclude the use of the innovating service by the purchasing firm. In such a setting, progress towards an optimum structure of distribution keyed to, in this instance, the freightliner development can be measured by the expansion by new warehouse premises or handling equipment in the total stock of these facilities.

[7] A survey of distribution firms in Glasgow by the authors showed that one-third of the firms had elevated loading bays capable of allowing direct access to a container by fork-lift trucks.

(*b*) *Features external to the firm.* The features of container transport impose more clear-cut limitations on potential use than do those which are internal to the firm. As seen in Chapter 5 the size of the container, for example, limits the number of firms that can use the transport mode directly. The availability of a route to serve the particular consignment is even more critical. Only large population centres are served, and then only 10 to 15 per cent of the possible links between these centres have freightliner services. Road transport is, on the other hand, capable of any routing pattern. All of these features can be broadly termed as inflexibility and their aggregate implications for potential freight tonnage have been assessed in Chapter 5.

The location of the freightliner terminals in relation to the customer is more flexible in its control of potential use, but it also affects the probability of a consignment being despatched by freightliner. Clearly, a consignor 40–50 miles from a terminal will rarely consider using the service, while another at 20 miles from the terminal will have strong reservations. Two main reasons can be identified to explain this relationship. Firstly, the high cost of the collection and delivery operation, particularly on the shorter trunk hauls, adds considerably to the total freight cost, and thus makes the operation uncompetitive on cost grounds. Secondly the further a customer is from a terminal the higher his probability of being served or contacted by local hauliers and the less likely his contact with freightliner services and marketing.

If, however, the route pattern and terminal location do not preclude the use of the container system, other features are positive advantages. Some, such as speed and efficient scheduling, have been discussed above in relation to the demands of the consignment; others also require consideration. The sealing of a container and the complete enclosure of a load in the closed type of container is very important for the security of the consignment. A full container load moves as a unit with no individual handling of items in the load, outside that at the premises of the consignor and the consignee. Consequently opportunity for pilferage is minimised. Furthermore, the direct through movement of the load with the elimination of standing in open lorry parks is an added advantage. When the load does stand in terminals awaiting loading/unloading, it has some check or guard on it. Even when stationary, while through door-to-door movement is being effected, sealing of the container considerably reduces the opportunity for pilferage.

Damage incidence might be improved over that of road by the rail container system, but the advantage is really relative to conventional rail and marginal in relation to haulage. For the full container load, savings in packaging similar to those possible with road haulage can be derived. They are not as large as those possible on overseas trade since packaging for internal trade is necessarily lighter, but there is significant saving over the packaging costs necessary for conventional rail freight. This improvement derives from the minimised handling, weatherproof container and direct routing of the freightliner system.

Table 7.4 summarises the discussion of this chapter so far. Considering the features of the system external to the firm, the first three listed absolutely limit the ability of the freightliner to serve firms directly. Then if these factors do not come into play, the remaining

TABLE 7.4: *Summary of indirect factors in the competition between rail container and road transport*

	Favour rail containers	Similar	Favour road
a. Internal to the firm			
1. product/firm name on vehicle			✓
2. urgency	on > 350–400 miles	✓	
3. integration with production line	✓		
4. perishability		✓	
5. special body		in medium term	at present
6. indivisibility of load			✓
7. extra service features (i) vehicle			✓
for service			✓
(ii) organisation of production and distribution		✓	

	Limit rail	Favour rail
b. External to the firm		
1. size of container	✓	
2. routes available	✓	
3. terminal location	✓	
4. speed and schedules		✓
5. sealing of load and security		✓
6. damage incidence		✓

three factors favour rail containers in competition with road haulage. For features in the demand for transport services which are internal to the firm, the balance is, in total, probably against the rail service. In two instances, urgency and the requirement of a special body for a consignment, the direction of the advantage is dependent upon the time period being considered. While the overall balance is against rail, several of the more important factors are considered to be of similar significance and it is this which gives rise to the conclusion that the balance in favour of road may, for containerisable services over routes served by freightliners, be relatively minor.

5. *The implications of containers for the overall distribution policy of firms*

The main trend in distribution activity and the systems that serve it has been the progressive development of large integrated units, with many factories, retailers and wholesalers, integrating vertically along the channels of distribution. This has demanded that more complex and extensive systems can be managed and physically operated, and communication and transport developments have been facilitating factors in this evolution. Firms at the forefront of these changes have utilised the new developments to the maximum with periodic revision and redesign of their distribution systems, to be followed by others learning from their experience and using fully developed and tested practices. In this pattern containerisation fits as another technique which large-scale organisation can effectively utilise. The very need to be able to organise minimum flows of 10 tons per week per route to use efficiently the service indicates the advantages accruing to large-scale users of this transport system. Smaller users with part-container loads reap only a fraction of the possible time and cost savings—the main part goes to a groupage agency.

Furthermore, the development of container transport will not be able to be immediately utilised by all large firms if they have recently completed investment programmes orientated to road haulage, so that the effect of containerisation will not be an immediate but rather a phased development. In addition very few firms can completely containerise their large goods flows. 'Local' movement of up to at least 100 and generally 150 miles, is largely excluded, and in addition most firms will serve some areas without freightliner links.

Consequently a firm will rarely approach high levels of containerisation.

In relation to the actual patterns of movement of goods, containerisation also plays the role of an agent facilitating current developments. The sixties have seen distribution firms examining their policy of depot location in terms of the trade-off possible between service provided and the costs of that service. There is evidence that American firms are tending to reduce the number of depots through which they distribute.[8] An excessive number of depots results in high stockholding levels and high operating expenses, particularly in relation to the contribution to customer service levels that a smaller number of depots could attain (see Chapter 2). Consequently the reduction in number of depots has meant an increase in depot size, larger stockholding at each depot (but not in total) and therefore larger goods movement to serve these depots. Container transport can efficiently serve this type of organisation, as can road transport with the despatch of full loads. Hence containers do not operate against such a development but instead facilitate it.

Inland containerisation is, therefore, for distribution a development in line with other contemporary innovations. It can, with proper management, be effectively used by deriving cost savings to promote current trends in the industry; it is not, however, likely to alter, either radically or otherwise, the current trends in the industry.

6. *The competitive balance between road and rail container transport*

It remains, therefore, to assess the total balance of competition between road and rail container transport. If the Deakin and Seward analysis of competition between conventional road and rail transport applies with less force to containerised long-haul traffic and the indirect cost factors in the transport operation favour road only to a minor degree, where it is in competition with rail container services, this brings the direct cost features of the two modes into the position of greater importance. In Chapter 6 charges for haulage were considered to favour rail on hauls over 150 miles although the scale of this advantage does not increase appreciably with distance because of the pricing policy used by British Rail. Consequently, one might expect on the combined direct and indirect cost factors

[8] See Issue 28, November 1966, by Industrial and Commercial Techniques Ltd., prepared by A. T. Kearney and Co. Inc. and summarised in the NEDO publication, *Planning Warehouse Locations*.

that rail has some advantage on hauls over 150 miles; that for distances up to 200 or 250 miles the advantage is a limited one; and that rail's advantage should thereafter improve progressively with distance both on direct and indirect cost factors. However an important qualification is necessary. In Chapter 6 it was noted that estimates of road costs and charges were probably rather high relative to those of rail. Our assessment of the balance of competition may therefore similarly favour rail, and a considered judgment would be that our statement of the competitive break between road and rail favours the latter by up to fifty miles.

CHAPTER 8

THE PRESENT AND FUTURE ROLE OF INLAND CONTAINER TRANSPORT

Now that a concept of the present and future competitive position of the freightliner system in relation to road haulage has been established, it remains to compare this with the actual performance of the system, and also to compare the performance of the system with that expected in the *Reshaping Report*. After some consideration of the impact of the Transport Act, 1968, and the importance of future technical developments in transport, it will then be possible to go on to a final assessment of the potential of the freightliner and its future role.

1. *Operating experience*

The *Reshaping Report* envisaged that the freightliner system would develop rapidly and by four years attain a complete penetration of its potential market—estimated to be approximately 30 million tons—and then continue to grow at the same rate as total freight. Break-even with costs was expected to be achieved in the second full year of operation when 12 million tons were expected to be carried on the system. What then has been the reality?

Table 8.1 briefly summarises the predicted and actual pattern of growth and it is clear from this that expectations have been far from realised with tonnages running at approximately one-tenth of estimated levels. This appears a clear failure to meet a stated goal, although there are two considerations which go some way to account for the scale of the short fall. The first is the point that although the *Reshaping Report* considered estimates 'to be conservative',[1] they were almost certainly optimistic both in terms of growth rates and total tonnages, but particularly in relation to growth rates. Second, there is the point that little more than a third (in numerical terms) of the facilities and services have been developed, with Stage II of

[1] *The Reshaping of British Railways*, p. 142.

TABLE 8.1: *Predicted and actual performance of the freightliner system*

Year of operation		Performance predicted in *Reshaping Report* Million tons	Receipts (£m.)	Actual performance	Million tons	Receipts (£m.)
Year 1	1965	4	7	1966	0·25	—
Year 2	1966	12	21	1967	1·00	2·5
Year 3	—	—	—	1968	3·00	6·4
Year 4	1968	30	51	1969	6·00 (est.)	—

the programme, involving 18 terminals and approximately 50 services having been completed at the end of 1969. In contrast the *Reshaping Report* envisaged investment being completed by the fourth year—which is in practice 1969. This would appear to justify the conclusion that the Beeching estimates should be reduced by a third, but there is the consideration of the policy followed in the development of routes. To test and ensure the viability of the service as early in its life as possible the routes with the largest potential tonnages and the longer hauls were established, with the result that those already operating were estimated[2] to carry 640,000 tons per route by 1984, compared with 150,000 tons on those routes planned but not developed by the completion of Stage II of the plan. Consequently the individual routes already established have approximately four times the potential of those planned, i.e. although approximately 30 per cent of routes by number they should carry approximately 60 per cent of the total traffic in the network envisaged in the *Reshaping* and *Trunk Routes* reports.

Hence the failure to meet the goal is, even in the light of these considerations, very real and it could be that rates of growth will fall again in 1969 with a probable doubling of traffic to approximately 6 million tons.[3] Unless future expansion of the network is undertaken, and this seems unlikely at the time of writing as many concerned with the planning of the system consider consolidation of the existing position is essential, growth rates will slow further in the early seventies. By then the first initial high growth rate of traffic on

[2] See *Trunk Routes Report*, Appendix, Table C.

[3] Indications in the first half of 1969 point to a growth in traffic of less than a doubling.

routes will drop to a rate possibly double that of total traffic growth, i.e. approximately 5 to 6 per cent per annum. Note, however, that the goal of traffic growth is not being taken as an argument for network expansion. A smaller network than planned may be a more viable proposition, as the cost of serving and attracting this additional traffic might exceed the revenue from it. If considered apart from the projected figures of the *Reshaping Report* the growth of 3 million tons over three years and to possibly 6 million tons in four years is a very sound performance, although not one of revolutionary proportions.

Penetration by the freightliner system of the total freight market on the routes that it currently serves is the critical test of the conclusions reached above, in Chapter 7. Market penetration by route length groups allows an examination of the actual competitive position of the system and also an evaluation of the reality of the competitive process and position discussed above. It will be recalled that the competitive position of the freightliner was considered to be dependent upon distance, primarily because competition is expected to be mainly controlled by freight rates. Therefore, one should expect the market penetration of the freightliner to vary with length of route.

To test this hypothesis information was drawn from the 1964 freight traffic data which were used above in Chapter 5 on all road and rail movements, as well as data of traffic on freightliner routes in February 1969. The 1964 data, which were used in the compilation of the *Trunk Routes Report*, were available in a 78×78 matrix showing traffic flows between all pairs of the 78 zones. The traffic origins and destinations largely within a 15-mile radius of terminals were included in the appropriate route totals. Estimates of the present level of traffic (1969) were made by expanding the 1964 data by the growth rate of total traffic tonnage over the period, approximately 3 per cent per annum. The assumption inherent in this, namely that the overall growth rate was the same for all routes, is a simplification but one difficult to improve upon unless detailed information is collected on economic activity levels in the various areas concerned, as well as on the presence of any changes or developments in trading patterns. For example, a new steel mill in a centre may generate major new flows on a particular route or set of routes. Tonnage movement by the freightliner is also estimated, in this instance from the number of 10 ft modules carried on the route, and this figure

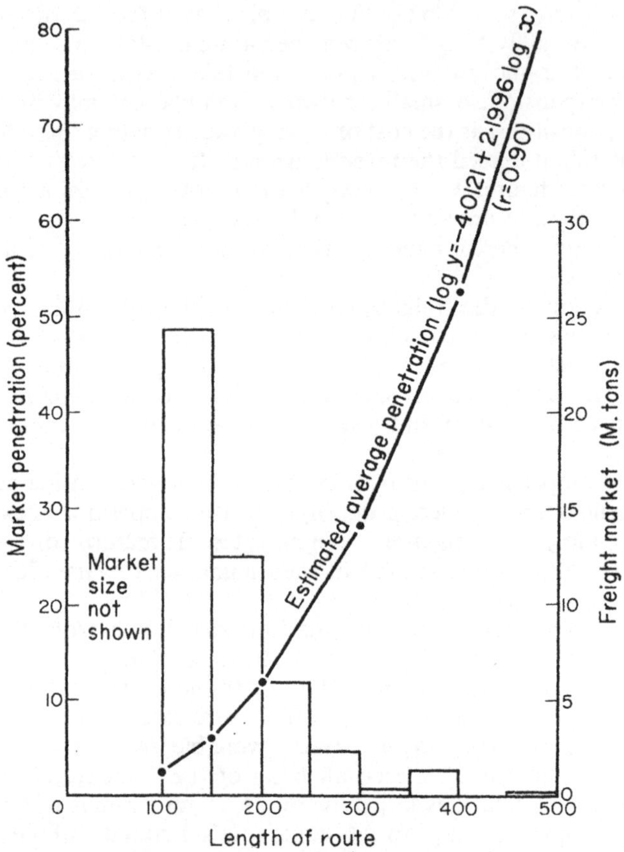

Figure 8.1. Penetration of the freight market* by the freightliner (on routes served by the freightliner only), and the total market system open to the freightliner
* As defined in Table 5.3

then expanded to a tonnage estimate by a factor of 4 tons per 10 ft container length.

The pattern of market penetration is summarised in Figure 8.1 where the regression average of the relationship between market penetration and route length is shown.[4] The superimposed bar chart

[4] Actual points have not been indicated on the graph so as not to disclose data on individual routes.

with scale on the right-hand axis of the graph indicates the estimates of size of the market in 1969 by 50-mile mileage groups for routes operated by freightliner.[5] The coefficient of determination (r^2) of 76 per cent indicates the extent to which distance explains market penetration using a simple linear regression line. The presence of a clear curvilinear trend in the data, particularly in the mileage range 100 to 300 miles, is demonstrated by the increase in the value of r^2 to 81 per cent with a double logarithmic transformation of the data. This transformation is used in the regression estimate and shown in the figure primarily because it yields an important increase in accuracy in the fit of the line in the 100 to 200 mile range, and a consequent improvement in the r^2 coefficient.

TABLE 8.2: *Predicted and actual market penetration by the freightliner system on the routes it serves* (*February* 1969)

Route length groups (miles)	Predicted market penetration* (%)	Actual market penetration† (average range for mileage groups) (%)
100–149	45	2·5–5
150–199	60	5–11
200–299	65	11–28
over 300	90	28–60

* As derived above in Chapter 5, Table 5.7.
† On routes served only.

Table 8.2 summarises the actual market penetration on routes served and compares this with that predicted in the *Reshaping Report*. Figures such as 5 to 11 per cent market penetration in routes of 150 to 199 miles compared with an expected figure of 60 per cent indicate that performance is well short of expectations, even if allowance is made for slower development. It is this comparison of actual and expected market penetration which is the most critical point for examination of the system.

Also the very low market penetration figures on routes of less than 200 miles, and even 250 miles, together with the rapid improve-

[5] The market estimates are those developed in Chapter 5.

ment of market penetration with distance on longer routes indicates that the competitive position of rail container transport is not as favourable as the discussion of the previous chapters indicated. In Chapters 6 and 7 it was considered that, on routes over 150 miles in length, rail containers had some freight rate and cost advantages and that these would not be dominant until hauls of 200 to 250 miles were reached. It will be recalled, however, that in the estimates of costs those of rail were considered to be low and those of road high. In addition rail costs were those of the system operating efficiently near capacity—something the freightliner in early 1969 was not doing. This empirical evidence, while limited, does throw considerable light on the foregoing discussion and conclusions. It shows that rail only competes on the margin on the 150 to 250 mile routes and only approaches dominance in the markets that it serves on routes over 300 miles.

In relation to the distribution of the market over the 50-mile groupings the most disappointing market penetration results are those in the under 200 miles range where only two out of fourteen routes captured more than an estimated 10 per cent of potential markets. Routes of up to 150 miles fail to exceed 5 per cent penetration of the market, whereas on routes of 300 to 500 miles, market penetration is very favourable and indicates containerisation levels, in line with, or above, those attained on short-sea shipping services, e.g. a level of 55 per cent on the Irish Sea traffic. Even given possible pleas from the freightliner organisation of limited marketing effort and a limited network, the competitive position of the system all too clearly shows the presence of highly competitive road haulage on routes up to 200 and 250 miles long. For the inland container system itself the message is ominous, for unless the position on routes of less than 200 miles alters radically the capture of even 50 per cent of this market seems highly unlikely, and it is on these routes that the major part of the traffic potential of the system anticipated in the *Reshaping* and *Trunk Routes* reports lies. Clearly, on this empirical evidence the freightliner system is a weak competitor on routes of less than 150 miles, favoured in certain sections of the market from 150 to 200 miles, and then approaching the position of a dominant force on routes up to 300 miles and more.

A point made above, in Chapter 7, concerns the importance of the competitive position of the system in its service of an area around a terminal. In the conception of the rail container system it was anticipated that depots would be located to serve the major population centres and areas surrounding these, and that the network would effectively serve the greater part of the country by attaining effective service radii around terminals of at least 30 miles. The *Reshaping Report* gave no indication of expectations but other writings indicate belief in an effective radius of 30 to 40 miles.[6] Failure to attain the effective penetration of the market within and on the fringe of conurbations will mean loss of access to major sections of the potential market.

As in other spheres of the freightliner operation, comprehensive data are scarce and recourse must be made to the Glasgow freightliner traffic survey. In this the origins and destinations of containers in West Central Scotland were studied as well as the destination of containers around the terminals of the six routes to Southern centres. The comparison of the West Central Scottish pattern with that about the Southern terminals shows no evidence to suggest that the Glasgow pattern is at all dissimilar from the others, although there still remains a remote possibility that the section of the system studied is significantly different from the total pattern.

By the 5-mile wide collection and delivery charging rings used by

TABLE 8.3: *Distribution of trips for the C & D of containers for Gushetfaulds and for traffic to southern terminals from Gushetfaulds at their destinations*

	Total C & D in Glasgow (%)	Out-movement from Glasgow delivering at destination (%)
0–4	55	85*
5–9	33	
10–19	5	7
20–29	5	4
36	2	4
TOTAL	100	100

* *Note:* These rings have been combined in the table because the two inner charging rings are combined in London and West Midlands.

[6] See, for example, *Modern Railways*, August 1964, pp. 76–7.

British Rail at the time of the survey, the pattern of origin and destination of containers in West Central Scotland was the same as that in Southern areas.[7] Table 8.3 summarises the results. Eighty-eight per cent of origins and destinations in West Central Scotland were within 10 miles of the Gushetfaulds terminal, located three-quarters of a mile south of the Glasgow city centre: in the six southern areas the proportion was 85 per cent. In West Central Scotland it was possible to disaggregate the total into two rings: 0–4 miles and 5–9 miles. The concentration of traffic originating from and destined for locations close to the terminal was emphasised, with over half (55 per cent) being to and from locations up to 5 miles away, a distance which approximates to the boundary of the City of Glasgow, the centre of the conurbation.

Analysis of the origins and destinations in West Central Scotland in greater detail illustrates the concentration of traffic around the central area. Table 8.4 presents the results of allocation of origins

TABLE 8.4: *The distribution of origins and destinations of containers compared with employment distribution about the Gushetfaulds terminal*

	A Container (%)	B Employment (%)	Index (A/B)	Average distance from Gushetfaulds (miles)
Central area	9·2	12·1	0·76	0·5
Ring 1	41·4	14·1	2·95	1·75
2	14·7	8·5	1·73	3·75
3	18·0	14·2	1·27	6·5
4	8·7	14·6	0·60	9
5	7·2	23·7	0·30	25
6	0·8	12·8	0·04	40

and destinations into the concentric rings of the Greater Glasgow Transportation Study (GGTS). The Central Area is a box in the city centre approximately 1 mile square and is demarcated by the proposed and developing Inner Ring Road. The subsequent rings around this area increased in width with distance from the Central Area, and

[7] These areas are London and the South-East, West Midlands, Merseyside, south-east Lancashire, and the Leeds and Sheffield areas of Yorkshire.

their average distance from Gushetfaulds is indicated in the final column of the table. A similar pattern to that of the charging rings analysis is seen, with a decrease in origins and destinations from inner to outer rings. However, the feature of a low percentage of traffic from the Central Area is brought out by the finer spatial divisions used and it indicates the unsuitability of activities and premises for the use of container transport in this area. Within this pattern, allowance must be made for the contribution to the 41 per cent of origins and destinations in ring 1 which results from the location there of two main groupage terminals, namely, the (then) BR Sundries Depot at Sighthill north of the city centre and the BRS Parcels Depot at Dixon's Blazes south of the city centre near the Gushetfaulds terminal.

It is necessary to judge this pattern of decline of traffic against a measure of traffic generation potential. Such a measure was developed by taking the total employment in these rings in 1964, less that in agriculture and office employment, and then expressing this as a percentage distribution across the seven rings.[8] Where the service area of the Gushetfaulds terminal overlapped that of the Edinburgh one, allowance was made in the employment total for the 50 per cent of potential traffic which would be London traffic and would use the Edinburgh terminal because of its proximity.[9] It will be observed that employment distribution does not follow a regular pattern of decline with distance, as does that of container origins and destinations, and the comparison of the two percentages for each ring gives an interesting index. This compares actual container origins and destinations with those expected on the assumption that employment numbers, as defined here, are the main explanation of container traffic movements to and from an area. After the low value below 1·00 in the Central Area the index rises to nearly 3 in ring 1, then falls progressively through rings 2 and 3 (though higher than 'expected' at 1·73 and 1·27 respectively) to 0·3 in 5 and 0·04 in 6. These latter two rings are respectively at 25 and 40 miles on average from the container terminal. Clearly, seen against an

[8] The GGTS survey of employment used ten categories and was carried out in 1964.

[9] Traffic through the Glasgow terminal approximately divided 50 per cent London, 50 per cent other centres, and this proportion was applied to employment totals from the Edinburgh area. Note also that the London service is the only one operated from the Edinburgh (Portobello) terminal.

expected pattern of traffic generation, and apart from the unique features of the Central Area, the pattern of container traffic origins and destinations around a terminal is inversely associated with distance from the terminal. This can be alternatively stated as the proposition that the probability of an employment group using the system is reduced significantly as distance from the terminal increases.

Ring 4 is worth closer examination. Here, at an average distance of only 9 miles from the terminal, the index is half that of the next inner ring yet only 9 per cent of traffic is derived from ring 4, compared with 15 per cent of employment.[10] The location of this ring and the types of activities that it houses are very important. It is the outer ring of the Clydeside conurbation, as defined in the GGTS study, and it is the site of much of the urban growth and new town development as, for example, at Cumbernauld. It is the type of area in which many of the large-scale modern distribution depots and light manufacturing units are being sited, activities which could be producing and using the type of commodity and traffic ideally suited both to road and rail container transport.

The explanation of the rapid decline of traffic with distance from the terminals must be sought on grounds other than charges, because between the Central Area and ring 4 charges were only differentiated by a maximum of £2 for a 30 ft container.

The importance of other alternatives meeting the transport demands of 'remote' customers was hypothesised in Chapter 7 and present evidence emphasises this factor. The customer's conception of the utility of alternative transport facilities increases with distance from the freightliner terminal. There is, for example, the 'local' haulage contractor with an established position who quotes door-to-door rates and does not include an explicit charge for haulage to a 'distant' terminal. In the mind of the customer these types of considerations, while not consistent with a rational total costing of the transport operation, will carry considerable weight.

It was also hypothesised, on the basis of cost, that the collection and delivery distance would be greater the longer the trunk haul, because the greater cost advantage of the rail system would allow it to absorb higher collection and delivery costs and remain competitive. No substantiation for this was found, although movement

[10] Note also that no attempt has been made to adjust the employment totals for growth and the outer rings, such as 4, are the location of employment growth in conurbations.

volumes at the level of disaggregation of data necessary were small and could contribute to the lack of a definite finding. Inspection and correlation analysis of the data indicates weak grounds for believing that this happens on the few routes over 300 miles long. However, the pricing policy of the rail system with its 'high' charges (in relation to costs) for long-distance freight movement could be important in accounting for this feature not being clearly apparent, even given the limited data sources available.

Therefore, in the total market of a conurbation and its tributary region, the competitive strength of the freightliner system decreases with distance from the terminal, and the probability of a firm or employment node at 10 miles using the service is much lower than that of one at 3 miles. Furthermore, beyond 10 miles the amount of traffic generated per employment unit is very small.

2. *Government intervention*

The background for the current phase of Government intervention in the allocation of demand in the freight market, was set in the White Paper, *Transport of Freight*,[11] and implemented in the controversial Transport Act, 1968.[12] It is not intended to review the Act and its implications in detail but rather to consider the main sections and comment on the impact on various aspects of competition between road and rail transport.

Essentially the changes brought in by the Government are an attempt to further the use of appropriate cost procedures in the selection of a transport mode and to intervene in the allocation of transport demand by costs through a licensing procedure. Also several of the provisions are intended to improve operating practices. To take the latter first, the Act creates a new legally recognised manager: The Transport Manager. He is required to hold a certificate of training and is responsible for the operation of the transport fleet, and particularly two aspects of this. The first is the safety of the vehicles and their mechanical condition. The second is less easy to define, but is more important for the purpose of the Act in that it aims at the efficient utilisation of the vehicle fleet, with efficiency

[11] *Transport of Freight*, HMSO, Cmnd. 3470.

[12] For a detailed review of the provisions of the Act, see D. C. Munby, 'Mrs Castle's Transport Policy', *Journal of Transport Economics and Policy*, Vol. II, No. 2, May 1968, pp. 135–73, especially pp. 146–54.

based on cost of use. In this category the Act also makes special provision for reductions in the hours a driver shall work within various specified time periods.

Both of these provisions, and particularly the latter, are seen by hauliers and transport operators as increasing their costs of operation and therefore altering their competitive position. It must be noted, however, that many hauliers are, or have been, bound by strict speed scheduling, some even at rates as low as 30 miles per hour. Such agreements with drivers are capable of increase particularly on motorway routes and no doubt the force of competition both on hauliers and unions will result in upward revisions. The 'A', 'B' and 'C' licence categories were dropped and own-account operators are now allowed to operate for reward as well as for their own use. This could mean more active competition for the freightliner from the own-account operators, but in general the effects of own operators on the road/rail competition position can probably be expected to be small.

In the provisions for quantity licensing, the Act enters directly into the field of competition between road and rail transport. Using the estimated 100 mile break-point between road transport and rail containers, the Act provides for the implementation of licensing of all loads carried over 100 miles on vehicles of 16 tons and more. Unlike the other provisions these are to be enacted in the future at a time when the Minister judges that the freightliner system is developed to a reasonable level of efficiency and ready to cope with additional traffic. The licence to carry particular traffics will be granted to road haulage if it can prove that it is a more efficient mode of transport both on indirect and direct costs. As such, the Act should bring more rational costing of the transport operation into the allocation of demand. The effectiveness, of course, depends, upon, first, the scale of the present misallocation of demand and, second, the efficiency of the new licensing system.

Uncontested licences will be granted automatically and the Freightliner Company will contest in the Licensing Court for the loads it expects it can carry as efficiently. This introduction of public accountability of the rail operation for container transport could have a positive effect on the operation of the system and finally banish the old rail maxim of traffic at all costs. In this the Act is a two-edged sword. The feeling in the freightliner section of British Railways before the vesting of the Transport Act on January 1, 1969 was that they would be very sure of their grounds before contesting a case, as a series of losses in the Licensing Courts could only be harmful to their marketing effort. A survey carried out by the authors showed that hauliers, while being apprehensive of this new control over their operation, have also realised this opportunity, and those with wide experience consider the provisions will result in little alteration of their position. Opinions of hauliers actually using the freightliner vary. Some think they could lose all traffic over 200 miles, others consider themselves safe from freightliner competition up to 300 miles.

The change in the organisation of the nationalised transport industries is seen as being a step in the right direction, particularly with the separation of activities into interest groups and the broadening of attitudes within the controlling authorities of these groups. The removal of the freightliner organisation from direct British Railways Board control to that of the newly created National Freight Corporation with its combined road/rail interests should broaden considerably the internal attitudes and understanding of the competitive position of the container system. In this it could be very constructive. Much of the thinking in the railway freight field has been orientated towards the maximum rail system and the maximum tonnage, and not to the most efficient possible system in terms of profitability. Rarely did the railways accept the presence of an alternative system which, in many instances, could do the job more efficiently. Under the new structure the Freightliner Company as a unit of the National Freight Corporation will market the service, operate the terminals, and decide the service provision, while the railways will provide the trains to meet the demand transmitted from the National Freight Corporation. Furthermore, with the separation of the freightliner organisation from rail and the publication of individual statements, the accountability of this service should be further improved.

In the future, further Government intervention may include some system of road pricing in urban areas as a method of easing the build-up of traffic and congestion. Technically this is now feasible and if introduced it could have impact on competition between road and rail container transport. It was noted in the introduction to Chapter 6 that concepts of the incidence of road track charges, and particularly charges for road track in congested city areas, were poorly formulated and were expected to operate in favour of urban road pricing. On the 100- to 200-mile freightliner routes collection and delivery road costs outweigh all others and an increment in these, such as a special charge for road track use in congested areas where collection and delivery occurs, would add significantly to total costs and move the competitive balance in favour of road transport which has lower total costs in this field. The flexibility of road transport is its key advantage if road pricing is introduced. Firstly, it will be recalled from the discussion in Chapters 5 and 6 that the freightliner system uses heavy lorries more on urban roads than long-distance hauliers with the common pattern being an in and out routing from the terminal for a collection or delivery. Road haulage generally avoids this double movement. Secondly, road haulage is free to use whatever urban roads are suitable, whereas the collection and delivery fleet of the freightliner system has two fixed points, the terminal and the customer's premises between which it must operate in the urban region. Finally, the migration of warehouses and manufacturing plants to peripheral locations on main ring and arterial roads means that urban area transit can be minimised if flexible renting is feasible. On these grounds it appears likely that the freightliner system will be more susceptible to the costs of a road pricing system. To sum up: road pricing will have desirable effects in the allocation of urban road space but it will not reallocate freight traffic from road to rail, if that is its intention.

3. *Future technological change*

Any consideration of the impact of technological change on the competitive position of road and rail container transport can be only in very broad terms. The importance of developments now pending can be considered with some hope of future realisation and comments will be limited to these types of change which should occur by the mid-1970s. More basic and important changes might take place like hover trains, linear engines, etc., but the roles of these are even more difficult to assess and will be disregarded here.

For the rail system it is difficult to see major changes which will benefit its competitive position. The container operation is the new system of general merchandise transport and must continue in its present form and with its present cost structures. Savings in traction costs may be achieved but this can be only a minor contribution to total cost savings since unit costs on the trunk haul are, as noted in

Chapter 6, extremely low. Within the terminal, improved cranage technology is unlikely with the current investment requiring at least ten years' operation to earn a satisfactory return on the investment. Local collection and delivery is also a field with little change possible in the immediate future, as road vehicles currently used are entirely adequate and new developments will not yield major savings on short haul. There is, however, considerable opportunity for cost savings in cities with urban motorway development programmes and in areas with modern industrial estates and shopping centres where loading/unloading will be expedited. The system itself, therefore, is largely the same now as the one that should be operating in 1975, and one would hope that by this time economic load factors for the scale of the development will have been attained. It seems very unlikely that technological change will significantly alter the operating and cost structure of the system.

In the field of road transport, however, technological progress will continue at something approaching the rate of the last ten years. Road has not experienced the same technical jumps that characterise the railways with their large-scale investment in the container system. Instead, technological change has been a continuous process necessitating investment year by year and a continuing programme of adaptation, rather than development for a unique system. Also there is the point that lorries have a shorter working life than trains. This does create problems as, for example, with incompatibility between transport units, but this does not prevent operation of the road vehicles and it does not require a complete, unified, door-to-door system for reasonable operating efficiency. This is another example of the flexibility which characterises road transport. To take one example of past changes, there has been a constant improvement in the efficiency of traction units and this has led to increases in lorry size and lower unit costs. Also trackway improvements, in the form of inter-urban motorways, have favourably affected both the running costs and transit times of road operation.

Further improvements in traction units, particularly suited to long-distance haulage, appear to be nearing commercial use in the form of the gas-turbine unit. These should give road a further advantage in competition with rail, for trunk haulage costs are a major portion of total costs and savings here are therefore more significant. Trackway improvements are, of course, constantly being made and the completion of such motorways routes as the 'Midland

Links' between the M6, M1 and M5 will make a significant difference to haulage in England, while the northern extension of the M6 will complete a near motorway-standard road from London to Glasgow. The freightliner market penetration data used in the plotting of Figure 8.1 indicated a pattern of negative residuals for routes of 100 to 200 miles which parallel motorway routes; that is, poorer market penetration than predicted by the regression model on these routes; and positive residuals for routes which were in direct competition with road haulage on conventional roads or on partial motorway routes. This can be no more than an indication because of the series of assumptions involved in the use made of the data, but it does reinforce what one might expect and the pattern was clearly evident. Consequently, further improvement in the road networks can only help to maintain, or advance in favour of road, the break-point on freight rates.

In summary, the balance of foreseeable forces of technological change would appear to be in favour of road transport. It is indeed a paradox that the increase in rail haul efficiency of the freightliner makes the rail system more susceptible to road transport cost increases. Beyond 1975, of course, there is a possibility of completely new systems of transport, such as hover trains, which could radically alter the competitive position developed above, whereas the changes seen here at least fit within the basic competitive structures.

4. *The division of inland freight market in the* 1970*s*

The revision of the concepts of the competitive position of the freightliner necessitates an estimate of the probable tonnage that the service might carry in the 1970s and from this the division of the inland freight market.

Firstly, to set the scene for these estimates, the freightliner market anticipated by the *Reshaping Report* must be seen in its perspective and then an estimate made in relation to this. The 39 million tons predicted to be carried by the container system by 1973 would be a small part of a total freight market of approximately 2,000 million tons—something approximating to 2 per cent of total freight movement. When, however, account is taken of the pattern movement through the system discussed in Chapter 6, the rail haul plus the two separate road hauls must be considered and the freight tonnage carried by the container system is trebled to approximately 120 million tons or 6 per cent of total freight movement in Great Britain. In the total pattern this is a relatively small movement.

Estimates of the future market and the freightliner share are particularly hazardous and must be subject to wide variation in reality. Broad aggregates are prone to wide errors and in estimates of supply and demand in limited sectors such as this errors are even more likely and more significant. A prediction is a function of its underlying assumptions and its limitations must be stated so that shortcomings are realized. To take the example of demand: the change in demand for freightliner services will depend upon urban growth, as well as that in manufacturing and distribution and the changes in the use of long-distance transport by these activities. For example, a move towards centralised distribution depots and more long-distance haulage of stocks could increase demand for long-distance transport between major centres, without a growth in total traffic.

Several approaches can be suggested for estimating the future freightliner tonnage. The first is a simple aggregate one based on present and past volumes carried on the system and an extrapolation of this, having regard to implementation of new routes and possible growth rates on established ones. The second method is more detailed and relates the market penetration performance established above in Figure 8.1 to the market assumed to be open to freightliner competition. The third is impossible to apply here with the limited data sources open to the authors, but the method will be discussed and possible results suggested. This uses the detailed considerations of each terminal hinterland and route and then combines these for total freightliner traffic. This is the most comprehensive predictive tool developed here and the one most capable of meeting changes in basic parameters and relationships. Each will give a different estimate, but together they will frame the scale of the system of the future.

In these estimates total freight transport will be assumed to grow at a rate equal to the average annual growth of the last ten years with an increase allowing for some improvement in economic performance and, more important, higher growth rates in long-distance traffic. The performance of the freightliner will be based on the experience and anticipations discussed above. A 'low' and 'high' limit will be set in the estimates presented and it is anticipated that the actual volumes will lie somewhere between those limits.

The figures for the first method of estimation have already been presented in Table 8.1 of this chapter. In 1966 a quarter of a million tons were carried and, with a fourfold increase in the second year of operation and a threefold increase in the third year and possibly a doubling over the last year, the 1969 tonnage could total 6 million tons. In this there is a clear and expected slowing in the rate of growth common to all growth rates in new enterprises. Over this period new routes were progressively opened and these were established in markets with large tonnages, averaging 640,000 tons per route according to British Rail estimates of 1984 potential, and approximately half a million tons now. Therefore the rate of growth of the system, based on a simple extrapolation of past routes, must continue to fall, even assuming further new routes are established. On the assumption of new routes being progressively opened, a pattern of growth rates ranging from 50 per cent in 1970 to 10 per cent in 1975 would seem realistic. On these assumptions 22 to 25 million tons per annum could be the volume of the freightliner traffic in 1975.

The current outlook within the freightliner company is for the present set of routes to be maintained and the profitability of the system proved before further expansion is undertaken, particularly since future developments on average offer smaller markets—recall the average of 150,000 tons per route drawn from the forecast for 1984 in the *Trunk Routes Report*. On this assumption, assuming

50 per cent growth in 1970
30 per cent growth in 1971
25 per cent growth in 1972
20 per cent growth in 1973
15 per cent growth in 1974
10 per cent growth in 1975

the pattern of future growth must be curtailed severely and the growth rate of the system relegated to something like the current average rate of growth for established routes. With well-directed marketing effort it seems possible to maintain a rate of growth between extremes of 5 and 10 per cent per annum. Assuming the former growth rate a tonnage of approximately 8 million tons would be attained by 1975, and the latter, approximately 11 million tons.

To sum up the conclusions of this method: the system could handle something in excess of 20 million tons in 1975 with the continued expansion of the network to the full system planned in 1964, but, with the existing network only being maintained, then 8 to 11 million tons appears a realistic estimate. It is believed that the estimate for full development of the system is an over-optimistic one and is more realistic at a level below 20 million tons, because the network as developed serves the routes with 60 to 70 per cent of the total estimated potential of the system in the *Trunk Routes Report*. The projection of future growth rates depends to a considerable extent on the performance of the system in 1969 because the greater part of the network operating now is well established and beyond the early growth phase. At the time of writing the prospect for a doubling of the tonnage carried was not bright and, if not attained, then the estimated annual growth rates for the complete system of the *Reshaping* and *Trunk Routes* reports would certainly be too high and approximately 18 million tons a more realistic estimate.

In the second method of estimation, using aggregate market penetration or route-length groupings, two assumptions are also made to give 'high' and 'low' estimates. The average market penetration pattern from Figure 8.1 is applied to the total market estimate of all traffic on routes longer than 100 miles between centres of over 400,000 persons grouped as shown in Table 8.3. For a 'high' estimate, the average penetration for a route length group is expanded by a factor of 3, and for a low estimate by a factor of 2. In both cases the 'average' penetration is taken as a point 75 per cent above the lower class limit—for example, approximately 138 miles in 100 to 149 miles. Also it should be recalled that a double logarithmic transformation appears to overestimate penetration percentages in the 100- to 200-mile groups. Both of these factors therefore create an upward bias on this estimating method and this bias is greatest in the two largest market groups. Note that to accept the pattern of market penetration in Figure 8.1 is to adopt a pattern of low market penetration on the shorter routes and high penetration on the longer routes.

The two estimates indicate a narrow range from a 'low' limit of 13 million tons to a 'high' limit of 18 million tons. This emphasises the importance of high levels of market penetration on the shorter routes under 200 miles which are expected to contain 48 out of 63 million tons of freight in 1975. The attainment of this order of performance is, however, based on the system serving all routes over 100 miles between major population centres. If the system is expanded then the greater part of this market would be served, but with routes existing at the end of 1969 only 60 to 70 per cent of the market is capable of service by freightliner routes. Therefore if the 1969 network is maintained until 1975 on the 'high' estimate of market penetration 11–12 million tons will be carried and on the 'low' estimate 8–9 million tons.

The third method of estimation is only suggested here in outline as the working is long and complex and the key pieces of data are not available to the authors. Its use is greater at the detailed planning and investigation stage when individual routes are considered and these then aggregated for market estimates. It too should give different results to the other two methods and the working would give a deeper understanding of the system, as well as allowing evaluation of the concepts of the system developed here. This method utilises the understanding of the system derived from the detailed analysis of the above chapters and is discussed here both as a method of estimation of future potential of the system and as a summary view of the key elements and constraints in the rail container system in its relationship with road transport. A flow chart of the operation of the system is presented in the Appendix to this chapter.

The model develops in three stages. The first stage examines the size of the population node either in population terms or, better, in terms of employment characteristics. Ideally employment numbers by broad types should be mapped in areas defined by the sector and ring method used in transport studies. Then the total employment numbers in these areas should be weighted by two factors:

(i) the distance from the terminal;
(ii) the employment mix in an area.

In the first weighting one would be given to employment modes within one mile of the terminal and their various proportions standardised by the distance decay pattern of traffic generation around a terminal for other distances. The second weighting is based on the observations of types of industry using the service. Transport and distribution might be assigned a value of 1 and then heavy industry, say 0·7, steel manufacture 0·6 and then heavy industry 0·1. This then gives a measure of the importance of the employment mass as a container traffic generation centre. Each centre under consideration should be defined in this manner.

Potential tonnage routes can then be determined by a standard gravity formula.

$Tp = A(E_1E_2)^{\alpha}d^{\beta}$

when T_p = potential tonnage
E_1 = employment (adjusted) in centre 1
E_2 = employment (adjusted) in centre 2
d = distance separating the centres
α, β = some power determined by calibration of the model.
A is a constant.

These tonnage estimates by routes could be compared with estimates of container traffic based on the population of centres by generating total freight traffic between centres using a gravity equation, and then allocating this to road or rail container transport by an adjustment the market penetration factor of Figure 8.1.

The estimate of tonnage on a container route should be tested against the threshold tonnage for a viable route—that is 120,000 tons—and converted to a percentage of this threshold. Repetition of this for all routes from a centre should then allow the assessment of the potential of the centre as the site of a terminal. If two complete routes appear feasible from the foregoing analysis then a small terminal can be justified. In this it is generally best to commence the examination of feasibility with the route to London. If two complete routes are not feasible but one complete one and several part ones, then the location of these part routes should be examined to determine whether a joint service is feasible. If at least two routes cannot be justified then that centre should be omitted from consideration for a terminal. Such a centre could only be included in the network on a company train/terminal basis.

With the rejection of terminals from the network the model should be recycled to test the viability of terminals already accepted by the model, by examining their continuing viability given that some of their potential routes might have to be dropped.

This method would require detailed study and calibration and when operating would allow a comprehensive analysis of the network on the basis of individual routes and terminals. It takes account of the distribution of traffic generation centres around the terminals and the possibility of these generating traffic suitable for rail container operation. Traffic is predicted either directly from the equation which is constructed to yield only potential container tonnages, or by estimating total traffic on a route and then allocating traffic to the freightliner by an estimate of modal split. Taking the two approaches would give a range of estimates for the route. The former has the advantage of being able to cope more adequately with employment changes in the area under consideration. Such a model recognises the importance of economic thresholds and treats the network as an interdependent system and not a system within which individual *centres* can be justified in isolation.

5. *Summary*

TABLE 8.5: *Estimates of market penetration by the freightliner system by 1969 (m. tons)*

		By aggregate growth patterns	By market penetration patterns
High estimates	with full system	25	18
	with 1969 system	11	12
Low estimates	with full system	22	13
	with 1969 system	8	9

With the progressive development of routes to make up the network envisaged in the British Rail reports, the system could carry between 13 and 25 million tons, with the most likely figure being around 18 million tons. If however no further routes are developed, then estimates range between 8 and 12 million tons.

Compared with the *Reshaping* and *Trunk Routes* estimates, these estimates are about equal to or less than half those of the *Reshaping* and *Trunk Routes* reports, assuming full development of the system and maintenance of the present network respectively. Trebling the present estimate of tonnage in 1975 to arrive at the total transport effort of the freightliner system, either 54 or 33 million tons are set against the 2,000 million tons anticipated in 1975—that is either 2½ or 1½ per cent of total traffic. Another comparison relates the estimated potential traffic on the system to its field of specialisation—the freight market over 100 miles. In Chapter 5, the present traffic over 100 miles was estimated to be 150 millon tons and this should increase to approximately 180 million tons by 1975. In this particular market rail containers are estimated to capture approximately 10 per cent with further development of the system, or 6 per cent with existing rates. (In this instance only the actual rail haul can be compared.) In the very narrow market of routes over 100 miles between major population centres the total rail market should be approximately a third that of the total freight market over 100 miles. Here the freightliner is estimated to capture either 30 or 20 per cent of the market, depending on the development of the system in 1975.

The above estimates are based on simple tonnage and a more realistic measure of economic 'effort' expected from (or value added by) the container system can be made using ton-mileage estimates. Total freight ton-mileage was 73,200 million ton-miles in 1967 and this should increase to approximately 90,000 million ton-miles by 1975. If it is assumed the average length of haul of a container is the same as the average length of route, that is 230 miles (see Chapter 5), the estimated freight ton-mileage by freightliner in 1975 will be approximately 4,200 million ton-miles with a complete network, or 2,500 million ton-miles if the existing network is maintained. That is, the freightliner will carry either 5 or 3 per cent of freight on a ton-mileage basis. One further point can be considered in this comparison. In freight ton-mileage figures, coastal shipping carrying bulk commodities is an important factor and accounts for 21 per cent of traffic. Therefore a more realistic comparison takes only the total of road and rail freight. On this basis either 7 or 4 per cent of rail and road ton-mile freight is estimated to be carried on rail containers in 1975.

Seen in the perspective of these estimates, the potential of the freightliner system in the mid-seventies is considerable and the system will be a notable development in the field of long-distance transport in Great Britain. It will not, however, be a complete revolution, even within this specialist field of long-distance transport, mainly because of the scale economies inherent in the system and because the market is one of limited spatial extent and therefore only partially favourable to the transport system, with its competitive advantage upward of 200 miles.

APPENDIX TO CHAPTER 8*

The model suggested in section 4 of this chapter is briefly outlined in the accompanying flow chart, Figure 8.2. It facilitates study of concepts of the system and its various parts as well as providing estimates of the aggregate size of the system and viability of routes and terminals. The estimating equations require calibration to determine the parameters.

Freight movement is estimated either from employment or population in a centre. Starting with employment, the better of the two, this is distributed by a ring and sector division of space in the urban region, and then weighted both by distance from the terminal and composition of employment by occupation type. These data are then used in an estimating equation of container traffic generation, after the selection of a centre and a route from the centre. This is then repeated for every possible route from that centre, or, if limitation of size of the programme is considered necessary, routes considered extremely unlikely to generate sufficient traffic volume can be omitted. If the model is entered with population data, total traffic is estimated from a traffic generation equation and then a proportion of this estimated flow allocated to container haulage by an arbitrary definition of modal split based on Figure 8.1.

The tonnage estimated on a route should then be tested against the assessment of a viable threshold established in Chapter 5, that is 120,000 tons and the percentage of this threshold recorded for each route out of a centre. When all routes under consideration from a centre have been assessed, then the viability of a terminal is tested by the requirement of at least two routes exceeding the threshold tonnage for a route. If the centre fails this test it is worth considering the possibility of one route with greater than the threshold tonnage and one or more pairs of routes being operated as a joint service to attain a service threshold. In the interpretation of these results the

* This type of analysis using a time sharing system a computer is discussed by Sonia Stairs, 'Selecting a traffic network', *Journal of Transport Economics and Policy*, Vol. II, No. 2, pages 218–31.

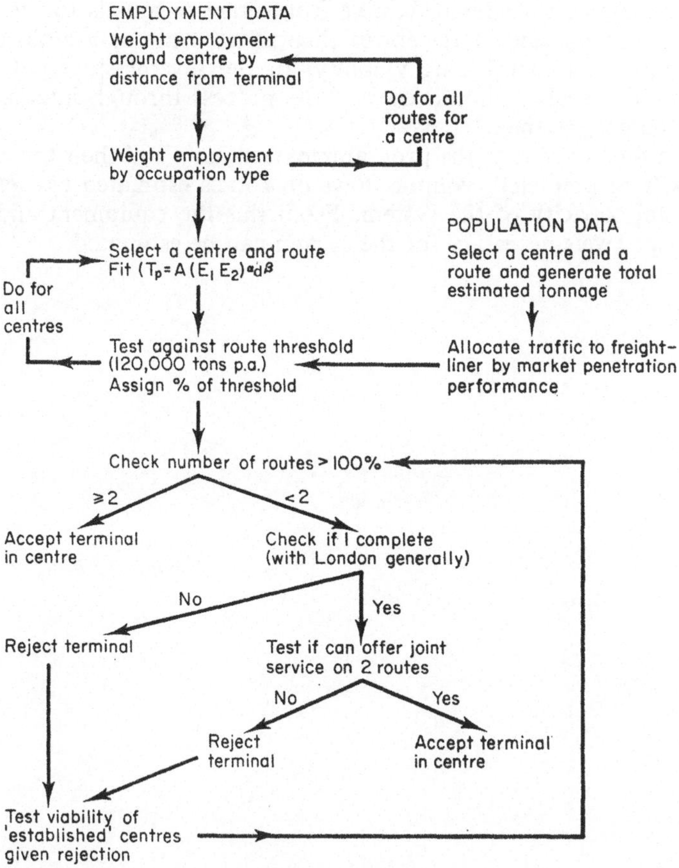

Figure 8.2. Flow chart of suggested programme for analysis of freightliner network

use of an interactive programme in which the analyst assesses the results of calculations, such as the number of routes over threshold size and the operational feasibility of joint routes, is extremely valuable.

If a terminal is accepted as being viable in a centre then the tonnages for route and terminal are recorded and the next centre selected. If a terminal is rejected then the model must be recycled and the routes considered feasible from other terminals to the one in question rejected. The centres thus affected are re-examined to determine their continuing viability. In the several stages of this process the analyst should oversee the process through interaction with the programme.

As a final output of the programme, terminals and their throughput will be predicted, volume flows on routes estimated as well as the total capacity of the system. From this the equipment and investment levels necessary for the system can be estimated.

CHAPTER 9
CONTAINER TRANSPORT AND PLANNING

Previous chapters have outlined the meaning of containerisation for overseas and inland distribution. Its likely impact has been evaluated, as well as the short- and long-term problems it poses for transport operators and their customers. This chapter draws together these threads and assesses the implications of container transport for those concerned with port, inland clearance, groupage and freightliner depot planning, as well as its effect on the locational decisions of manufacturing and wholesaling firms. In the section dealing with port planning, the changing criteria for port location will be discussed, followed by the Rochdale Committee's reaction to this in recommending more central control. Still more positive direction from the centre has been proposed by the recent White Paper on 'The Reorganisation of Ports'. After an analysis of the validity and likely practicability of some of the White Paper's proposals, the technical problems of port investment appraisal will be outlined. This section will conclude with an analysis of the role of ports in national and regional planning. In the section on inland container transport, the previous chapters' discussion of the future role of freightliners will be discussed as well as the role of central government in controlling the freight transportation environment. Finally, the role of container transport in regional policy and in economic activity in general will be evaluated, with examples drawn from Scotland, the region studied in greatest detail by the authors.

1. *Containers and port planning*

There are some 300 harbour authorities in Great Britain, although the ten largest plus the British Transport Docks Board's ports control 90 per cent of overseas trade and 75 per cent of coastal trade. This implies that ports have been developed mainly to satisfy local (not even regional) needs; a locality requires or required a port to ensure its economic viability, the only noteworthy exception being Birmingham. In fact many of the trust ports such as London, Liverpool and the Clyde are bodies dominated by local users. The 1966 Martech study for the Port of London Authority[1] found port hinterlands to be relatively small: 66 per cent of exports and 86 per cent of imports originated from or were destined for locations within 75 miles of the port through which they passed. In their justification for the rejection of the Port of Bristol's Portbury development,[2] the Ministry of Transport constructed a gravity model of traffic flows between inland origins and destinations and ports. A high degree of negative correlation was found between distance from a port and the trade flows to that port. All this evidence seems to imply that a dispersed pattern of port development is required by the community.

There is little doubt that this was so in the past, partly because of the high cost of inland transport and partly because of its unpredictability. Even today inland transport costs can form a large proportion of door-to-door overseas distribution costs (about 28 per cent of North-West Europe–North American total transport costs[3]). The Rochdale Committee recognised that delays were more likely to occur in the inland than in the sea journey and in that sense inland distribution had an importance in excess of its contribution to the freight rate.[4] Even now, the case for locally based ports is strongly argued. The history of the development of containerisation shows the determination of each region, and even each coastal urban area, to have its container berth, although of course the case was often couched in terms of the national interest.

However, the situation has changed in some notable respects since Britain's harbours were originally constructed. Inland transport is cheaper and more efficient. In the case of container transport, shipping lines have concerned themselves with the complete door-to-door movement of consignments, which has removed some of the uncertainty from the process. Ports are also technically more efficient: in bulk and general cargo much larger quantities can be

[1] *Britain's Foreign Trade*, a report by Martech Consultants Ltd. for the Port of London Authority, 1966.

[2] *Portbury: Reasons for the Minister's Decision not to Authorise the Construction of a New Dock at Portbury*, Bristol, HMSO, 1966.

[3] OECD, *Ocean Freight Rates as Part of Total Transport Costs*, 1968.

[4] *Report of the committee of enquiry into the major ports of Great Britain* Cmnd. 1824, HMSO, 1962.

handled per annum than previously. Ships are much bigger, partly as a result of technological advances in marine engineering and partly because of these very improvements in port efficiency. Because of the higher capital costs involved, both ships and ports are required more than ever before to do the job for which they are designed, carrying and transhipping goods respectively, for as much of the time as possible. This implies short in-port times for ships plus as few ports of call as possible, and high annual throughputs for ports, which can only be achieved by having fewer ports. In the past this would have caused an undue increase in inland distribution costs, but recent technical developments there have largely eliminated this potential problem.

The Rochdale Committee was appointed in 1961 partly because of the lack of new investment by British ports. The apparent inability of locally orientated ports to react to technical changes in shipping encouraged the Committee to recommend that some national body be set up to act as a catalyst. The Harbours Act of 1964 established the National Ports Council to formulate and keep under review a national plan for the development of harbours in Great Britain. Its role was to be that of adviser to the Ministry of Transport and of consultant to the port industry. Port authority development plans costing over £500,000 had to be submitted to the Ministry which was to be advised by the National Ports Council. In fact the National Ports Council has supported a large proportion of the proposals. It has also acted as a consultant to individual ports in, for example, the design of container berths.

The Rochdale proposals certainly succeeded in stimulating port investment for in 1964 about £20 million was invested in British ports and by 1968 the figure had risen to almost £60 million annually. The National Ports Council has an obligation to see the national view but this is very difficult to achieve. Each port has correctly tried to estimate the likely demand for its new facilities, but unfortunately for the National Ports Council, there has often been an overlap in these estimates leading to an accumulated estimate which is greater than total traffic. For example, Greenock and Liverpool justified their claims for container berths partly on the assumption that each would capture the North of England trade. The best and most controversial example of this over-optimism is the £27 million Portbury development proposal. The Port of Bristol Authority estimated that 2 million tons would be exported through the port by 1980; the

1963–4 figure was under 200,000 tons. This ten-fold growth in the port's exports was to be achieved through an expansion of trade coming from London and the Midlands, facilitated by the new M4 and M5 motorways linking Portbury to those areas. It was also thought that such a development could be justified on the grounds that a new port away from the London–Liverpool axis would serve the overall national interest.[5] The project was recommended by the National Ports Council, and included in its Interim Ports Plan issued in July 1965, but rejected by the Ministry of Transport:

> '. . . the case for allocating a substantial part of the resources available for port investment to the creation of a new major liner terminal, whether at Portbury or elsewhere, has not yet been made out'.[6]

The Ministry thought that Portbury was unlikely to attract as high a volume of cargo as it expected and it questioned the validity of forcing cargo there by diverting investment away from other ports.

This current national planning procedure is essentially negative. Although the National Ports Council and the Ministry have must an overall view as to how they wish British ports to be developed, they are relying for the fulfilment of that plan upon the proposals of individual ports working independently. The underlying assumption is that the optimum plan emerges through a competitive process. In fact the National Ports Council has an obligation to foster competition while avoiding excessive overprovision, but it is hard to see how these objectives can be reconciled. It is even more difficult to see how competition is efficient when the economics of containerisation are such that, for example, only one port is required for the Australian trade. The National Ports Council and the Ministry have given their approval to this port monopoly, but on the other hand allowed a large number of ports to construct berths for transatlantic trade.

The Labour Government decided that more positive control from the centre was required although the Ports Bill failed through lack of time before the election and the Conservative Government is opposed to nationalisation. The introduction to the White Paper on 'The Reorganisation of Ports' claimed that experience had shown that the Rochdale Committee was right to conclude that 'a Council

[5] See W. F. Tanner and A. F. Williams in the *Journal of Transport Economics and Policy*, September 1967, Vol. 1, No. 3.

[6] *Transport Policy*, para. 108, Cmnd. 3057, 1966.

with purely advisory functions would not be sufficiently effective or influential to ensure that essential changes are brought about'.[7] The Rochdale Committee did not, of course, advise nationalisation but the kind of Ministry of Transport control established by Section 9 of the Harbours Act of 1964: the right to veto projects costing more than £500,000. The White Paper went further and proposed a National Ports Authority 'to plan the future development and rationalisation of physical facilities, whilst at the same time adapting the organisation of work in the ports to modern needs'.[8] It recognised that the technological changes in shipping and overseas distribution in general would mainly affect the larger ports and therefore advocated the nationalisation only of the ten largest harbours plus the already nationalised British Transport Docks Board ports. Annex 1 to the White Paper showed a natural break at 5 million tons handled per annum: the smallest of the ten, the Forth, handled 7·3 million tons in 1967; while the next port, Blyth, handled only 2·9 million tons.

In the case of container trade, this division is of doubtful validity for the total annual throughput of a port handling a high proportion of trade on any of the more lucrative routes will be much less than 5 million tons. For example, the total containerisable cargo estimated by the Lancaster study for the 1965 UK–Australian trade was less than 1·5 million tons and the UK–North Atlantic volume was similar. Therefore a port specialising in container (i.e. general cargo) trade may fall outside the direct control of the National Ports Authority. The best example of such a port is Felixstowe: it is expected that Felixstowe will handle almost 50,000 containers in 1969 and in 1968 it was the third largest container port in Europe.[9] Given the stated purpose of nationalisation, it seems illogical to distinguish between large and small ports on tonnage alone. The White Paper was in effect proposing the nationalisation of ports handling bulk cargoes

[7] *The Reorganisation of Ports*, para. 1, Cmnd. 3903, HMSO, 1969. It is worth noting that in a speech during the House of Lords debate on this White Paper (see *Hansard*, No. 726, April 28 to May 1, 1969, page 347 onwards), Lord Rochdale spoke against the amount of direct power proposed for the National Ports Authority. His committee recommended a National Ports *Authority*, but only with the powers of the current National Ports *Council*. It was therefore unfair for the White Paper to imply his support for an *Authority*.

[8] *ibid.*, para. 3.

[9] *Ports and Terminals*, October 1969.

and yet major technical changes have taken place in the carriage of general as well as bulk cargo. Although the volume of general cargo is much less than bulk, the shipping value added is similar and therefore general cargo is in no sense less important than bulk.

The National Ports Authority was to have responsibility for planning, investment, pricing policies, and the promotion of research and development. It was to delegate to the ports day-to-day managerial authority over all the services offered (that control is over *all* services aroused considerable opposition). The subsidiary authorities were also to have an obligation to prepare and submit to the National Ports Authority proposals for the development and improvement of the harbours under their jurisdiction. The White Paper expected subsidiary authorities to be organised on an estuarial basis, although it was to be the National Ports Authority's initial obligation to prepare a scheme of organisation. The estuarial idea has provoked some opposition in, for example, Scotland where some authorities feel that Scottish ports as a whole would prosper better if they acted together instead of in competition.[10] In this particular case, containerisation provides a basis for competition between the two main Scottish ports authorities, Clyde Port Authority and Forth Ports Authority. Each has specialist container terminals, although Sea–Land's berth at Grangemouth has been in operation longer than the Greenock terminal. Even if all Scotland's containerisable trade passed through a single Scottish port, frequent direct services with large ships could hardly be supported. It has been estimated[11] that the total potential container flow based on 1965 data between Scotland and North America would have been 23,000 outwards and 15,000 inwards. The export figure implies about 450 containers per week, which would only fill a fortnightly 1,000-container vessel. The 1975 export figure is unlikely to be in excess of 35,000 containers, which still leaves a weekly 1,000-container ship with spare capacity. In fact a high proportion of the Scotland–North America trade (the trade route Scottish ports are best placed to serve) passes through Liverpool and London.[12] Therefore, if there is to be competition

[10] The Scottish ports would not necessarily have been organised on an estuarial basis. Paragraph 19 of the White Paper suggests that a Scottish ports authority might be set up.

[11] This estimate was made by Mr R. Alpine of the University of Strathclyde in course of the investigation mentioned in the Preface.

[12] See Martech report referred to in footnote 1.

between ports for the North American container trade, it would be better for Scottish ports if they acted as one not two units.

It is of some relevance to the short-sea container trade that the White Paper omitted British Rail-owned harbours from the proposals, although it was stated that a subsequent transfer of its harbour undertakings (and those of the British Waterways Board) was possible. Even if the Authority does not specifically consider British Rail developments, it will have to take account of their existence and viability in appraising proposals from the many other short-sea ports. In addition, there will be a point of contact between the two nationalised organisations in the Freight Integration Council, which was set up by the 1968 Transport Act.

Although the emphasis was to be on co-ordination of investment and planning and of operations within ports, the National Ports Authority had to ensure competition on service and price between individual ports in the public sector. Yet one of the justifications of nationalisation would appear to be that ports cannot meaningfully compete with each other, for two main reasons:

a. With container ships economies of scale are such that the optimum size of port tends to have capacity to handle all trade on a given route. This is true of the Australian container trade, which is planned to pass through Tilbury alone.

b. With conventional ships, port hinterlands are so restricted (see Martech Survey[13] and Ministry of Transport Portbury analysis[14]) that each would appear to have an element of local monopoly. The rapid decline of traffic with distance from port even applies to relatively high-value manufactured goods, the inland distribution cost of which forms a very small proportion of final selling price. Therefore the use of local ports would seem to be more than merely a function of inland costs. It may be related to inadequate distributive decision-making or the lack of concern over door-to-door distribution on the part of exporters.

Competition between ports, even with smaller and less efficient conventional general cargo vessels, would appear to be marginal. It only happens for the trade offered by conurbations such as Birmingham, which is roughly equidistant between Liverpool and London, and in areas such as the south-east where there are a number of ports offering container services. There is also marginal competition

[13] *ibid*. [14] *op. cit*.

in that some consignments travel to a port other than the nearest. The Ministry of Transport calculated from the Martech data that about 10 per cent of exports and 2 per cent of imports travelled over 150 miles in Britain.[15] These small percentages must include much of the trade coming from or going to ports which might be expected to be competing with the one nearest to the importer or exporter. But some of this trade is travelling to or from the more distant port because of the timing of sailings. A shipper does not want to hold back an export consignment for a month waiting for a direct sailing from his local port when one is currently available from another.

If the lack of competition has been partly a function of high inland costs and unit trains lower these costs, then we may conclude that a higher degree of competition is possible with containerisation. The success of container ports in the east and south-east of England in attracting trade away from London is evidence that such competition works. However, the effect of lower inland costs in extending port hinterlands and therefore the competitive scope of ports may be eventually to substitute one kind of monopoly for another, national for local. Whether competition produces the long-term least-cost solution is another matter. The success of ports such as Felixstowe and Grangemouth must be partly a function of timing; in other words, the success of Felixstowe against London and Grangemouth against Greenock must be partly due to the earlier completion of their container terminals. If, at a particular point in time, a new shipping technology is sufficiently understood to enable the rational planning of a system of ports to provide the best allocation of shipping, terminal and other distributive resources, then it seems reasonable to adopt a planned solution. National planning and free competition are not ends in themselves, but means to achieve the same end, an optimum allocation of resources. In the case of ports, the former provides a better opportunity to assess social as well as private costs, as will be discussed below, and positive national control is all the more necessary if the characteristics of the technology are such that national port monopolies will tend to (or, given the cost characteristics, should) develop. In the past there was an element of local monopoly and the community (the shippers and others) responded to this threat by obtaining representation on the port authorities. Now the threat comes from national port monopolies

[15] *ibid.*, Table 2.

and the community representation and control should correspondingly be of a national character.

To take a specific case, there is in fact competition between container berths serving the North Atlantic trade, but it is doubtful whether the gain in competition is worth the cost involved in achieving it, or whether the competition itself is effective in achieving the economic ends defined above. The large ACL multi-purpose unitised vessels will call at a number of British, European and American ports, which is more costly than operation through one or two ports at each end, although they doubtless increase their revenue by doing so. Many of the British ports themselves have the capacity to handle relatively large container ships and therefore their equipment is likely to be idle much of the time. A shipper in the Midlands, the north of England, or central Scotland certainly has a choice of container ports, but the cost of that choice is unnecessarily high freight rates.

In the recent past the clearest examples of competition have been for investment, or the government approval of investment proposals, rather than between services. The whole competitive process is unique. First, the ports try to persuade the National Ports Council and the Ministry of Transport that a sufficient number of importers and exporters will use the port to justify investment there. Once the capital has been committed, the port authority has to induce shipping lines to use the port. Only when this has been achieved can direct, specific appeals be made by shipping lines and port authorities to the shippers themselves. Confirmation of these changing salesman/customer roles is obtained from port and shipping line advertisements. Before the completion of their container berths, port authorities advertised the fact that they were, for example, sheltered, without locks, the shortest distance to country *X*, and fog-free; an appeal to shipping lines. Once shipping lines had become committed to the use of their berth, the port authorities joined the shipping lines in appealing to shippers. The most direct sales contact at this stage is between shipping lines and importers or exporters. Therefore the shipper–port competitive interaction is an indirect one and this is likely to continue under nationalisation, as is the inter-port rivalry for investment.

As a basic justification for the nationalisation is the empirically observed lack of competition between ports in the past and the inefficiency of competition in the future, it seems strange that the White Paper should stress the importance of competition. It is obviously desirable where competition does not inevitably result in the overprovision of capacity, but on-going technical changes in all kinds of shipping are such that this is unlikely in the future. The White Paper recognised that the weakness in the past was a lack of co-ordinated planning and investment, and the nationalisation would have been best justified in terms of that alone.

The case for national planning or positive national control over an industry rests partly on the technical ability to control large industrial units. Exactly how to appraise a particular investment proposal, and then decide which is the best among many put forward, is the main technical problem that a National Ports Authority would face. Government policy in this respect is set out in the White Paper, 'Nationalised Industries: A Review of Economic and Financial Objectives', which recommends a discounted cash flow approach with a discount rate of 8 per cent (this has recently been increased to 10 per cent). As R. O. Goss has pointed out,[16] a discounted cash flow type of analysis has to be rejected because ports' charging systems bear no necessary relationship to long- or short-run average or marginal costs. Moreover a discounted cash flow analysis only gives socially optimum results if the pricing system used for inputs and outputs, as well as competing inputs and outputs, fully reflects the social costs involved. Were the ports' pricing systems rational, private and social costs would be essentially synonymous: general-cargo berths do cause a certain amount of traffic congestion in the vicinity of docks, but they do not generate the kind of public concern expressed when, for example, it was proposed that oil and ore terminals be sited in the Clyde. Goss suggests the adoption of the overall social cost–benefit approach. The particular difficulty in the case of port investment lies in measuring the benefits. In normal circumstances they could be obtained by comparing the price of sea freight before and after the investment. However, sea freight rates are very complex varying for different kinds of cargo, routes, types and sizes of ships, and even from one day to the next. In some cases the cost–benefit analysis can be based on operating cost savings, assuming revenue to be as before, but in this case the whole purpose of the investment is to make the port more attractive than before.

Goss proposes that this problem can be overcome by the following procedure (see Appendix to this chapter). For given types and sizes

[16] R. O. Goss, in *Journal of Transport Economics and Policy*, September 1967.

of ships, carrying given cargoes on stated routes, initial and operating costs are estimated and projected over the life of the vessel. A discounted cash flow calculation is made at the opportunity cost of capital for various assumed average freight rates per ton of cargo. Each will produce a different net present value, but one will make net present value equal to zero (i.e. the internal rate of return equals the opportunity cost of capital). This particular freight rate, which is known as the 'shadow price', can be regarded as the long-term equilibrium rate. At a freight rate higher than this the net present value would be greater than the opportunity cost of capital and therefore shipping would attract investors, increasing the supply of ships and forcing the freight rate down. At a lower freight rate, the supply of ships would fall and the freight rate rise. The difference between the shadow prices with and without the investment indicates the change in social costs per ton of cargo and is used to estimate the change in consumers' surplus each year. Any change in port dues resulting from the project is added to the consumers' surplus and any associated change in social costs is subtracted. All items are discounted to their present value in the same base year, and the net present value calculated. The project producing the greatest net social benefit for any port can therefore be chosen.

A national authority is not solely concerned with the most profitable operation of particular ports. A number of ports might produce calculations to show that their project will give a rate of return in excess of the opportunity cost of capital, but each might assume that it would attract traffic from the others (as appears to be the case with the North Atlantic container trade). If all projects were approved, over-investment would result. In such a case the national authority should consider the net present value of improving each port in turn with diversions of cargo, and of improving each combination of ports with such diversions as seem likely, but without overlaps. The improvement or improvements giving the greatest net present value should be accepted.

Goss's investment appraisal scheme was formulated mainly to overcome the practical realities of port charging systems, but, as he admits, the shadow price technique has its own disadvantages and there are practical difficulties in applying such a scheme. Shipping is subject to a higher degree of uncertainty than industry in general, for its booms and slumps are sometimes independent of fluctuations in world trade. In this particular case, increased uncertainty must be allowed for by increasing the discount rate. In cost–benefit analysis it is better to allow the uncertainty to affect the input variables with varying assumptions producing different estimates of net present value. However, in this case it is an output variable, the freight rate, which is subject to greatest uncertainty and therefore the discount rate itself must be varied. Another problem lies in evaluating the benefits to consumers of reductions in time; this is very important in the case of container ships (see Chapter 4). Very little is known on this subject. Estimating the traffic likely to be generated by an investment proposal presents market research difficulties. The Port of Bristol Authority found no lack of customers for its Portbury development, but in fact the plan required a diversion of cargo greatly outside the realms of probability, in the view of the Ministry of Transport. Firms will invariably express a desire to have another facility available if only to increase their choice and bargaining power; whether or not they will use it is another matter. This is a problem faced by any form of market research, but transport facilities seem particularly prone to over-optimistic estimates (see Chapter 8).

The main problem with the overall social cost–benefit approach[17] is derived from the fact that ports are engaged in international trade and that some of the consumers' surplus flows to other countries. It is therefore conceivable that the project showing the greatest surplus may not be that which benefits this country most, although, of course, it can be argued that, under certain circumstances and in the long run, any move favouring more international trade of any kind is in everyone's interests. However, it seems unreasonable to place upon ports an obligation to supply overseas aid; this can be better carried out by more direct means. Of course, were Britain to become part of a larger economic community, then port investment appraisal could be carried out taking account of benefits flowing to other members of the community. If it were possible to calculate the benefits flowing overseas, account could be taken of them in the above analysis but this would be very difficult to do over a long future period. The outward flow of benefits is directly proportionate to the elasticity of demand for exports and imports. To take an extreme case, if the demand for imports and exports were completely

[17] The problem outlined in this paragraph was first mentioned to one of the authors by R. O. Goss.

inelastic the whole of the consumers' surplus would remain overseas because a reduction in shipping (port) costs in no way increases the volume of cargo flowing through the port concerned. It would be extremely difficult to predict future elasticities in international trade. Unless this can be done, the overall social cost–benefit approach is effectively invalidated and perhaps the best practical procedure is discounted cash flow accompanied by a more realistic pricing and costing policy, in economic terms.

Given the need for more positive central control of port planning and the technical ability to achieve this (or, at least improve upon existing investment appraisal procedures), a remaining question concerns the role of port investment and reorganisation in regional planning. Do ports have an active or permissive role? As far as cargo systems are concerned, the ports are an essentially passive element. The ports could not alone have brought about the container revolution. Only when the shipping lines had made the initial commitment could the ports go ahead and construct container berths. In such a case their role is not completely passive; they must foresee future changes in cargo-handling methods and the extent to which, for example, containerisation will penetrate overseas distribution.

In another sense the role of the port may appear to be more active. Some regard ports as essential for the development of a region; others go further and elevate them to the role of regional economic-growth generators in their own right. This is certainly one of the ideas behind the National Ports Council's MIDAS (Maritime Industrial Development Area Schemes) concept, first described in its 1966 Annual Report. MIDAS are mainly of relevance to bulk cargoes. There is a shortage of locations where deep water (required for large oil and iron carriers) and suitable industrial land coincide, for a considerable industrial complex can be expected to develop around oil refineries or steel works. Many such schemes have been put forward and some have been approved.

The problem of deep-water access is of less significance in the case of general cargo, even though large container ships require deeper berths than the conventional ships they replace. There are no container ships with a draught much in excess of 35 ft, whereas some oil tankers have a maximum draught of 70 ft. However, some seem to believe that the industrial development side of MIDAS is applicable to container berths. In November 1967 the *Glasgow Herald* reported the Glasgow Chamber of Commerce's attempts to allay the doubts of those who were pessimistic concerning the prospects of the Greenock container terminal:

> 'The chamber's standpoint . . . was that it was unthinkable that Scotland should not have a first class container port. . . . [It] is important that all those who have the commercial and industrial welfare of Scotland at heart should make every effort to ensure the prosperity and profitability of the port. . . .'

The Greenock development, like those in other parts of the country, has therefore been justified on grounds of regional as well as national need. There is, however, no evidence of firms siting themselves in a locality mainly because of the proximity of a container terminal. There are very few examples of manufacturing firms (those not using bulk raw materials) choosing coastal sites on the grounds of access for sea transport, a possible exception being the General Motors plant at Antwerp. It is difficult to see how a Scottish industrialist would suffer in the absence of container terminals in Scotland. As long as an Inland Clearance Depot is reasonably near (there are two in Scotland) he can be sure of goods arriving at, for example, Tilbury the same day as they are despatched. Even the cost need not be any higher: in the Australian trade container freight rates are the same from any part of Britain. As far as the manufacturer is concerned the I.C.D. has effectively become the port. The I.C.D. is a much more valuable and flexible tool for regional development than the port, for it has much more easily satisfied site requirements. Whereas in the past some firms had to locate in response to the distribution of ports, the I.C.D. can be sited to the requirements of firms. In addition, the I.C.D. provides almost as much direct employment as the docks, even if at a different location.

The main costs of a large number of regionally sited container berths for the North Atlantic trade will be under-utilised terminals and an excessive number of ports-of-call. The throughputs achieved by container berths are such that, in a country the size of Britain, national rather than regional criteria should decide the location of container berths. The McKinsey report even contemplated international criteria: if British container trade with a particular country were less than 20 per cent of the West European total it would be best to feed a European port such as Rotterdam. As the National Ports Council has calculated,[18] this is never the case. In the short

[18] National Ports Council, *Port Progress Report 1969*, Table 19.

run the many ports with berths for the American trade will undoubtedly find customers. Competition on the North Atlantic is such that shipowners are, and will continue to be, prepared to go out of their way to call at a port which can offer a package of local customers. However, as rationalisation proceeds, the bargaining power of ports will diminish and the Australian trade route type of solution, one British port, will tend to prevail.

2. *Containers and inland transport*

(*a*) *The inland transport system.* In some contrast to the port and shipping situation inland container transport should now be moving into a period of steady progress and adjustment to the new competitive and legislative environment. The freightliner system must consolidate its position and establish the commercial viability of the existing investment before any further development is undertaken. Even given further investment arising from satisfactory performance over the next two to three years, possible developments should be incremental to the system, rather than being a reshaping of structure or major addition. In road transport, developments will continue as innovations are made but these should not radically alter the nature of road transport in the foreseeable future.

The *Reshaping Report* saw the freightliner as an answer to the problems of the costly general merchandise services which created a deficit of £29 million for BR in 1966.[19] It was believed that a system with the intensive network of terminals and routes proposed would allow the conversion of the wagon-load traffic, moving slowly between origins and destinations on roundabout, low-volume routes through marshalling yards, into scheduled unit trains moving rapidly between two or three terminals.

This wagon-load is the most common unit of traffic available from terminals and it is generally made up from consignments smaller in size than a wagon-load (see Table 5.6). The origins and destinations of this traffic are as numerous as the railway freight terminals (1,176 in 1967). While some flows between major centres can be directly grouped into train loads a large proportion of these traffics necessitate the loading of multi-destination trains at one centre and then breaking and remaking new trains at marshalling yards until the

[19] D. L. Munby, 'Mrs Castle's Transport Policy', *Journal of Transport Economics and Policy*, Vol. II, No. 2, pp. 154–5.

wagon or set of wagons reach the destination. The *Reshaping Report*, although not clear on this point, appeared to envisage this traffic being assembled from wide areas around terminals into daily train loads and then being directly routed to the destination. In other words, the grouping up of train loads was to be carried out by road transport. With a relatively intensive coverage of terminals and routes an adequate service was to be provided. The failure of this concept and the continuing presence of a large proportion of wagon-load traffic arises from the inability of the rail container system to serve a wide area around its terminal and the importance of economies of scale to the system. These economies necessitate large volume flows that only major population centres can generate. British Rail reconsidered the need for wagon-load traffic in the proposals of the *Freight Plan* 1968, and in so doing admitted the failure of the freightliners to take the greater part of wagon-load traffic. If it is not to make a major contribution in this direction, what role in inland transport does the container system fulfil and what is its future?

The 100-mile break-point with road transport is certainly an over-optimistic one and few now give it credence. Instead an absolute minimum break-point of 150 miles appears realistic, with the rail container system capturing only those traffics between 150 and 200 miles which it is particularly suited to carry. Consequently there is only a very doubtful future for the routes of less than 200 miles which have been planned, but not yet developed, with container traffic volumes estimated to be between 100,000 and 200,000 tons per annum. This leaves only about 50 viable routes of the approximately 250 considered in the *Trunk Routes Report*. Then there is the question of viability of terminals. Centres like Bristol, Exeter and Oxford with predominantly short-distance traffics, were expected in the *Reshaping Report* to handle in total up to 1 million tons, but the future of these terminals must be in doubt as they tend to generate short distance traffic which is open to direct road competition.

This reassessment of the original plans means that with the completion of Stage II at the end of 1969 few further developments should be carried out. Further justification for the reduction in number of planned routes and terminals can be seen in the figure of the 1984 predicted average tonnage of the routes so far developed which is only 150,000 tons per route. On the basis of the analysis presented in Chapter 8, it would appear that very favourable circumstances would be necessary to attain 60 per cent of this average; that is approximately 90,000 tons. In terms of the route tonnage thresholds of 120,000 tons derived in Chapter 5, this is little more than half the traffic flow required to support a service.

While the collection and delivery operation is the major cost component of the service, and one from which major savings would have to be derived, it is difficult to see how improvements could be made. Tachographs, if introduced, present the possibility of accurately timing the collection and delivery operation and thus allow a charge for collection and delivery to be made on this basis. This would encourage more efficient loading and unloading practices at customers' premises. Transit from terminal to customer is, even in conditions of average urban traffic congestion, relatively short and the larger part of the time is spent at the customers' premises in an operation the costs of which are completely time-dependent. It could be, however, that any improvements in operating procedures and competitive charging might be overcome by increases in the administrative costs of this more complicated system.

Groupage should certainly be reorganised. Terminals have been developed to serve conventional road and rail transport and not the freightliner system. If these were located beside the freightliner terminal, with direct access to it, then the expensive collection and delivery of loaded containers on public roads could be significantly reduced. Unfortunately, many depots were specially designed and constructed in the late 1950s and early 1960s by British Rail and hauliers, and currently have a high book value.

(*b*) *Government intervention in freight transport*. There is a very strong case for a minimum of Government legislation in the reorganisation of freight transportation in the seventies. For example, the organisational structure of the nationalised freight concerns should remain unchanged. It should be allowed to operate for some time to permit close observation of its advantages and disadvantages. In the past, changes in policy have been too swift and have allowed little time for the system to establish a clear operating pattern. It is possible that a Conservative administration would repeal quantity licensing, on the grounds that it involves an unreasonable bias in the favour of the railways. However, it has been noted above that some of the road hauliers visited by the authors even regarded quantity licensing as an ally, for it will force all concerned to make detailed *quantitative* estimates of all the costs and benefits involved.

Many of the bodies concerned with rail transport, and the freightliner operation in particular, appear to accept the revised and limited role for the system and few think in terms of the 55-terminals system. The more even balance of rail and road interests in the National Freight Corporation, the parent company of the Freightliner Company, should ensure this. Minor changes in the system may be necessary if, for example, a new terminal is justified by the guaranteed high demand of one or two firms in an area, or if new cranage would improve the efficiency of a terminal. In some instances the coverage of a market area could be more effective with the relocation of a terminal to a more accessible position in terms of the effective radii discussed above. However, given the weight of invested capital such moves would require close evaluation before implementation as considerable relocation costs would be involved. Detailed market surveys should be carried out to determine the nature of the existing market and future location patterns of the market estimated. Also, the effects of alternative collection and delivery policies on the costs of the system and the traffic this might bring, should be closely studied. The policy in the past of accepting available railway land has resulted in some poor locations being established with serious loss in trade. Such adjustments could result in improved market penetration in the local areas and significantly add to the total throughput of the system, without new routes being developed.

Somewhat paradoxically, road developments are the one aspect of transport policy which require close examination to facilitate and improve the operation of the freightliner system. The inter-city trunk road network, while being far from complete, does at least afford fast direct routing between the main conurbations. However, it is in urban areas where roads are least satisfactory and congestion is increasing. Here long-distance road and rail transport use the road system alongside local freight traffic. Many cities and conurbations have no programme for modern road systems, and many of those which do have opted for highly unsatisfactory radial systems orientated to the city centres. It is often said that redirection of traffic to the railways would solve, completely or partially, urban road congestion. This is clearly unlikely. Indeed the reverse is more to be expected, for collection and delivery to centrally located terminals will increase movements of long-distance consignments within urban areas because of the need to use large lorries for these operations (see Chapter 5). In addition, the freightliner, with its large 20 ft and 30 ft unit loads, is increasing the demand for roads which will allow easier and more efficient movement of heavy vehicles.

This means that a much accelerated road programme is needed in urban areas, for it is here that transport costs in real terms will continue to increase rapidly if nothing is done. Also it is here that the greatest marginal improvements can be made both in the freightliner and national transport systems. To date, however, very few urban areas have developed comprehensive plans adapted to the evolving urban structure to cope with the problem. The traditional five-year planning period before implementation, plus the time to complete a road system, means that the solution will not be found quickly and these costs will be with us for some time yet. With free urban motorway access across the conurbation, the need for terminal location near the city centre would be reduced and hence a contributing factor to traffic congestion could be alleviated, to the benefit of the community and the transport agency. The congestion problem is aggravated by the scheduling of freightliner arrival and departure times just outside peak traffic hours in order to meet the demands of customers. This therefore forces traffic to and from the freight trains into the peak traffic flows. More effective service of the outer areas of the city region should be possible with terminals located in suburbs served by urban motorways.

Finally, the development of a road pricing system could achieve a more efficient allocation of road space, but its possible practical impact on freight transport modes should be noted, particularly its impact on the rail container system with its intensive use of urban roads to generate large trunk-haul tonnages. The introduction of road pricing could alter the balance of competition significantly in favour of road transport, and with the freightliner market potential already reduced to a third of the level of operation initially forecast in the *Reshaping Report*, this could challenge the viability of the whole inland container concept.

3. *The location of container transport terminals in a region*

For national distribution patterns change can be expected to follow existing trends. The container system, if used by distributors, will allow further efficient concentration of depot activity in regional centres by the large groups, and this should have the effect of reducing the number of depots necessary. The regular scheduling of services and the necessary high-volume movement is the key factor contributing to this trend. Within the region the development of container transport and associated changes in distribution activity should mean limited but significant alterations in activity patterns. In the average region only a maximum potential of 5 per cent of goods flows is containerisable, and at this scale the total impact on goods movement and location patterns should be limited. For certain activities, however, the development will mean radical change. Rail transport and road hauliers, for example, should be most affected but the importance of this change should decrease rapidly with the extent to which an activity is associated with long-distance transport.

Containerisation will affect the inland movement of export and import consignments as many of the flows on particular routes will be redirected. Instead of the greater part of traffic on routes linking major sub-continental markets moving through the local region port, traffic will be routed through the national port or ports serving that particular route. Only on the North Atlantic and short-sea routes does this trend appear unlikely to develop completely, whereas on other deep-sea routes one or at the most two ports will serve the route. This therefore means the rerouting of flows with longer inland haulage by road or freightliner trains and transhipment through the specialised container berths located at deeper water sites. In terms of Bird's generalisation of port structure on an estuary in his 'Anyport' concept,[20] the general cargo berth moves downstream to deep-water sites as, for example, at Tilbury (London), Seaforth (Liverpool) or Greenock (Clyde). This will therefore lead to the redirection of general-cargo-trade flows within the port area from congested upstream sites to more open downstream ones.

A new focus for these international trade patterns is the Inland Clearance Depot, generally located on the outskirts of the conurbation and serving a wider region than the freightliner terminals. The I.C.D.s essentially relocate one of the major functions of the port, namely, the grouping up of loads, away from the waterside to inland locations, and act as the inland port for the traffic on a particular route diverted from the regional port which has been closed because of the rationalisation of services. Container trains are used for the longer-distance haulage to ports. Where volumes of trade are small

[20] See J. Bird, *The Major Seaports of the UK*, particularly pp. 21–36.

and/or distance is short road transport is used. Feeding into the I.C.D.s is the collection and delivery fleet for container loads and less-than-container loads.

The freightliner terminals for inland trade should be located outside the congested central city core but with direct urban motorway access. Groupage depots to consolidate less than container loads should be in close proximity to the terminals. Both have to be peripherally sited to minimise the time spent by the large vehicles in congested city centres: it has already been noted that urban freight transport costs are time- rather than distance-dependent.

The example of the ideal location for these facilities in central Scotland will serve to illustrate some of the features discussed here. The area is characterised by two population poles 45 miles apart, with growth being concentrated in the intervening belt and, to a lesser extent, to the north in Fife and west in North Ayrshire. To serve effectively the area as a whole and maintain regular daily services to southern centres, the freightliner terminals should be sited in the two conurbations concerned, preferably close to the intervening future growth zone. Therefore, one terminal should be in the east of the Clydeside conurbation and one west of Edinburgh. With the present development of a motorway between the two population centres and the cross-urban motorway in Clydeside this should allow effective service of the urban poles and the important towns of Cumbernauld, Falkirk, Grangemouth and Stirling, none of which is large enough to support a terminal of its own. Located beside these terminals should be the groupage terminals. One I.C.D. should effectively serve the central belt and would be best located between Glasgow and Edinburgh, preferably biased towards the Glasgow population mass. This could cater for traffic through southern ports as well as that through any Scottish container port. For local Glasgow traffic via the Clyde a second terminal near the container port would facilitate movement but would not be essential, especially if there are significant economies of scale in operating I.C.D.s. In fact the freightliner terminals are located near the centres of the two cities, in very restricted and congested sites. One I.C.D. is located in the very location supported by this analysis, while another is sited between Glasgow and the container terminal of Greenock.

With transport terminals sited as proposed here, distribution and manufacturing activities should be able to locate anywhere within the central belt without suffering any particular disadvantage with regard to access to transport services. Their location can therefore respond to the market and supply forces unique to the firms. For example, those firms which make intensive use of transport facilities, for example, wholesale distributors, and serve the Scottish market would find the area between Glasgow and Edinburgh with close access to a terminal particularly advantageous.

Three views are sometimes expressed concerning the role of containerisation in regional development:

(i) Although the overall national effect is small, containerisation will benefit the more remote regions, with high costs of transport 'exports', at the expense of others.
(ii) Container terminals generate employment, directly and indirectly.
(iii) Regions will grow less rapidly if they lack container ports.

The first is not necessarily true, for a reduction in transport costs from, for example, Scotland to London, is also a reduction in transport costs in the other direction. In addition, if manufacturers in the London area already sell to larger markets and, by reaping economies of scale, operate at lower costs, then they, not their Scottish competitors, will gain from lower transport costs. This view is only correct if the more remote and less populous region can now more cheaply 'export' goods for which it has a 'natural' advantage; for example Scotland's whisky-distillers will undoubtedly gain from containerisation. Even where the natural advantage is lacking in the less-developed region, the reduction in transport costs will increase real income in both regions, unless monopolies develop, although employment in some industries may fall.

To deal with the second point, container terminals themselves provide very little direct employment and are unlikely to generate secondary developments. The economies involved in siting at the coast plants which use large quantities of imported basic raw materials do not apply to the users of 'general cargo' imports. In fact, the main problem with containerisation is its capital intensity, i.e. the extent to which it replaces labour with capital and *reduces* employment.

The view is often aired that firms will not come to development areas which lack a container port. Similarly, some feel that exporting firms already located in development areas without a container port are bound to be less competitive than those elsewhere. These views assume that the cost of transporting the export from the region to the port outside the region forms a high proportion of its total selling price. This is rarely true and, in any case, most of the transport value added remains in the region concerned: the transport of consignments to the regional I.C.D. and the stuffing and unstuffing of containers there are the most costly parts of the inland transport component, and they are also the most labour-intensive, so maintaining employment levels, even if employment is moved from the docks to inland sites.

APPENDIX TO CHAPTER 9

The Overall Social Cost-Benefit Approach to Port Investment Appraisal

$$NPV = \sum_{i=1}^{i=n} [(R_i - C_i)(1+r)^{-i}] - C_k$$

where NPV = net present value
n = the life of the project
r = rate of discount
R_i = revenue in year i
C_i = operating cost in year i
C_k = capital cost of project

$$R_i = P_i Q_i$$

where P_i = freight rate in year i
Q_i = quantity of cargo in year i

therefore,

$$NPV = \sum_{i=1}^{i=n} [(P_i Q_i - C_i)(1+r)^{-i}] - C_k$$

The shadow price is the freight rate making the net present value equal to zero. In such a case the internal rate of return, the stream of benefits minus costs, equals the opportunity cost of capital **r**. For simplicity assume $P_i Q_i - C_i$ constant throughout the life of the vessel. The net cash flow stream is now flat.

When $NPV = 0$

$$P = \frac{1}{Q}\left(\frac{C_k}{\left[\frac{1-(1+r)^{-n}}{r}\right]} + C_0\right)$$

where C_0 = operating costs per annum
and P is the shadow price or freight rate.

APPENDIX

The present value of the consumers surplus (*CS*) for any year can be shown to be equal to:

$$CS_i = [(P_1 - P_2)Q_{1i} + \tfrac{1}{2}(P_1 - P_2)(Q_{2i} - Q_{1i})](1+r)^{-i}$$

where P_1 = shadow price without the investment
Q_{1i} = quantity of cargo in year *i* without the investment
P_2 = shadow price with the investment
Q_{2i} = quantity of cargo with the investment

If account is taken of the change in the port's cargo dues and costs, the consumers' surplus for a given year becomes:

$$CS_i = [(P_i - P_2)Q_{1i} + \tfrac{1}{2}(P_1 - P_2)(Q_{2i} - Q_{1i}) + \Delta D_i - \Delta C_{pi}] (1+r)^{-i}$$

where ΔD_i = change in port dues in year *i*
ΔC_{pi} = change in port operating and capital costs in year *i*.

If these are summed, the net present value of the investment is obtained. For more detail see R. O. Goss, *Studies in Maritime Economics*, Chapter 6 and the Appendix to Chapter 7.

INDEX

INDEX